Zero Distance

"When Danah Zohar first published the early ideas of her Quantum Management Theory in the late 1990's, she articulated a new paradigm, inspired by quantum physics, and began a major contribution to our search for a new management theory that can replace outdated Taylorism. Now, in ZERO DISTANCE, the most comprehensive account of her project, she outlines how the theory has been implemented through the revolutionary RenDanHeyi business model of China's Haier Group, and subsequently several other large companies. Zohar's suggestion that the Haier model also offers a new social and political model is thought provoking. This book is a significant addition to our continuing conversation about the best way to manage companies and other human social systems. I recommend it highly."

—Gary Hamel, *London Business School, Author of* Humanocracy

"We live in times when healing is required. In business, we must heal the distance between management and employees. In our globalised world, we need to heal the distance between East and West. And for the sake of both our leadership and our souls, we must find a way for science and spirituality to work together. With *Zero Distance*, Danah Zohar has produced a book that demonstrates how we can rid ourselves of corrosive fragmentation and misunderstanding. She shows that an inclusive, enlightened business can flourish while bringing benefit to all, and that quantum physics and the Tao offer a path for common understanding between East and West."

—Lord Andrew Stone, *Former Global Managing Director, Marks & Spencer Plc*

"I have benefited greatly from the quantum management theory developed by Professor Danah Zohar, which has accelerated our departure from classical linear management models and creation of the non-linear business model that is known as Rendanheyi. In her newest book, *Zero Distance*, Professor Zohar explains with both theoretical depth and practical breadth how to cope with a VUCA world in this networked era."

—Zhang Ruimin, *Chairman of the Board and CEO, Haier Group*

"*Zero Distance* brilliantly describes the revolutionary scope and depth of the management transformation process in which I took part at Roche India. I will be an ambassador for Quantum Leadership for the rest of my life, as I have tried it and there is no single doubt that it works!!! Quantum physics explains the universe, including us, so why should it not work in companies? I thank Danah

Zohar for changing my professional and private life, and for giving me things to get better at in both."

—Daniel Pluss, *Finance Department Head Africa and Global Market Development & Operations Lead, Roche Pharmaceutical*

"This is a terrific book. It leaps from quantum physics to management to some of the most profound issues of our day including COVID-19. It is a stark reminder that connectivity and uncertainty go hand-in-hand, and that the best managers will nurture small self-organized teams and challenge them to produce extraordinary results rather than commanding top-down. The exemplars of quantum management are extraordinary, from the U.S. military to Roche India to the China-based Haier Group. I found the text very stimulating. It made me think."

—Marshall Meyer, *Tsai Wan-Tsai Professor Emeritus of Management and Sociology, Wharton Business School, University of Pennsylvania*

"Danah Zohar' *Zero Distance* is a *tour de force* exposition of the 21st century quantum organization as a complex adaptive system—an inevitable evolution of the rigid, non-adaptive bureaucratic structures of the 20th century. These new organizations, including Haier Corporation and GEA, Roche India and the U.S. Army, resemble not so much a single ship but a fleet with many ships, each with its own captain and crew and its own local mission to accomplish. The overall leader is the "admiral of the fleet" who provides strategic vision, guiding spirit, a central operational system, services and resources for the many ships in the fleet, working not *on* people but, rather, *through* people."

—Stephen Denning, *Author of* The Age of Agile

Danah Zohar

Zero Distance

Management in the Quantum Age

Danah Zohar
The Chinese Academy of Art
Hangzhou, Zhejiang, China

ISBN 978-981-16-7848-6   ISBN 978-981-16-7849-3   (eBook)
https://doi.org/10.1007/978-981-16-7849-3

Cover design by Mind Times Press

This Palgrave Macmillan imprint is published by the registered company Springer Nature Singapore Pte Ltd.
The registered company address is: 152 Beach Road, #21-01/04 Gateway East, Singapore 189721, Singapore

For Zhang Ruimin, my personal "Yinxi" -

Here is your book. Now I must pass through the gate, and leave Zhou.

On Management Model Innovation in the Internet of Things Era: Foreword by CEO Zhang Ruimin

One important topic in the large body of economic research concerns wealth creation and sharing. Organizations today are not yet capable of achieving both goals together, but Haier's Rendanheyi model is breaking ground toward these two goals. In Rendanheyi, "ren" refers to employees; "dan" refers not to orders, but users; and "heyi" means to connect employees and users and to link the value created by employees to the value experienced by users, aligning value creation and value sharing for the employees.

Rendanheyi is a leading management model in the Internet of Things (IoT) era. In the industrial age, Chinese companies learned from Western management models. In today's IoT era, as companies experiment with new management models, Haier is looking to blaze a new trail.

Many examples testify to the importance of blazing a new trail. American high jumper Dick Fosbury invented his trademark flop which he first unveiled at the highly competitive 1968 Mexico Olympics. At that time, the competing athletes all used the straddle technique, so his unconventional method attracted laughs of ridicule from the crowd, until he won the gold medal and set a new Olympic height record of 2.24 meters. He then received a long standing ovation. Fosbury made history and completely revolutionized the sport of the high jump.

Professor Danah Zohar is a thinker who dares to chart new paths. Her fusion of quantum theory with management study has opened up new ways of looking at the world and at management. Her new book *Zero*

Distance: Management for the Quantum Age offers a novel and practical organizational model for individuals, businesses, and society at large. The twenty-first century is the era of quantum management. Grounded in Haier's own practice, the Rendanheyi model draws inspiration from traditional culture, adapts to the changing times, and provides a system for implementing quantum management principles. Professor Zohar has stressed the point many a time that the Rendanheyi model has confirmed for the first time the feasibility of quantum management in an actual business model.

Chinese companies used to be followers and imitators of Western companies and Western management models. Why must Chinese companies always follow in the footsteps of Western companies and management models? Why can't Chinese companies create a new model and lead, as Karl Marx wrote in the preface to *Das Kapital*, "Go on your own way and let people talk."

At Haier, there is a saying, "There is no such thing as a successful company. There are only companies that move with the times." Many companies like to talk about how successful they are, but no company should proclaim victory because perceived success depends on relevance to the current time and such relevance may not last. Even the average life span of Fortune 500 companies is diminishing. Therefore, what matters is to feel the pulse of the times and adapt to future trends.

A very compelling example of this concept is Kodak. Kodak had outperformed its competition to become the dominant film company but lost out to the digital age. This loss was not because Kodak didn't work on digital technology. As early as 1975, Kodak made the first digital camera prototype (although with only 10 megapixels). However, Kodak failed to keep up with the times and, despite research and development spending, it lost relevance in the digital age. During bankruptcy reorganization, Kodak's digital patent portfolio sold for a meager USD1.175 billion. One can say that Kodak did not lose to competition, but to the changing times.

Andy Grove, former president of Intel, says organizations need Cassandra. Cassandra was a priestess in ancient Greek mythology who foretold, among other things, the fall of Troy. However, organizations can't pin their hope on prophets. Instead, organizations must rely on people who truly have zero distance from their users.

The Golden Circle theory, proposed by American management scientist Simon Sinek, consists of three concentric circles. The innermost circle is "why" (direction), the middle circle is "how" (pathway), and the outer circle is "what" (goal). One goes from asking "why" to achieving "what" and then asks "why" again. The cycle repeats itself. Today, my talk is built upon the Golden Circle framework.

Why is Haier disrupting the traditional management paradigm? Because it is doomed. How does Haier achieve disruption? It depends on the "RDHY scorecard, win–win value-added statement, and ecosystem brand" which we are experimenting with at Haier. Our ultimate goal is to become a leader in the IoT era.

WHY DISRUPT THE TRADITIONAL MANAGEMENT PARADIGM?

The traditional management paradigm has failed in the following four aspects: First, classical management theories are not adapted to the current era; Second, classical management models informed by the classical management theories are not adapted to the current era; Third, the organizational purpose under classical management theories is wrong; Fourth, the traditional management paradigm leads to traditional brands, yet traditional brands are no longer suited to the current era.

1. Disrupting classical management theories

    Three great pioneers laid the foundation of classical management theories that are still followed by organizations today. The first pioneer was Frederick Taylor, the "father of scientific management." Taylor's publication *The Principles of Scientific Management* upended the small workshop model. Even before this, Adam Smith had spoken of the "division of labor" in the first chapter of *The Wealth of Nations*. He believed that it was thousands of times more efficient to divide production rather than to leave it entirely to one entity. The second pioneer was Max Weber, "father of organizational theory." He developed the idea of a "hierarchical organization," also known as a bureaucracy. The third pioneer was Henri Fayol, "father of modern management theory." He developed the modern operational management theory, which is used to examine how the various departments of an organization operate.

Efficient mass production was made possible through the application of Taylor's theory. Now, user needs are highly personalized, and therefore, the scientifically managed mass production model will have to be retooled for mass customization in order to meet individualized needs.

Similarly, the bureaucratic organization should be transformed into a decentralized, distributed matrix organization. In the past, C-suite executives had more information than others because of information asymmetry in the business world. Now that information sharing tools are more widely available, C-suite executives may only receive information marginally faster than others.

Fayol's general management theory primarily addresses the linear management of one-sided markets. But Jean Tirole, winner of the 2014 Nobel Prize in Economics, proposed the idea of a "two-sided market" (or even "multi-sided markets"). He argues that there is no need for so many departments in an organization. Haier, for example, removed approximately 12,000 middle-management positions. These managers either moved on or became autonomous entrepreneurs.

2. Disrupting classical management models
   Since the industrial revolution, two classical management models have been widely studied by companies around the world, the Ford model and the Toyota model. The Ford model is centered around efficient mass production, while the Toyota model is centered on continuous improvement with zero defects. Ford reduced production costs through the assembly line, bringing the price of a car from a high of more than USD2,300 to USD360. This innovation made cars affordable for every American household. Toyota, on the other hand, adopted a just-in-time (JIT) model, which enabled faster production and higher-quality products.

   Neither model is a good fit for the IoT era today. William Malek, an American strategy scholar, proposed a management idea akin to Haier's Rendanheyi model. However, the model received harsh criticism at Stanford University where professors found the idea unfathomable. Malek was thrilled to see what Haier had done in the management space, as Haier's work has proved his theory. Malek sees Haier as the benchmark for organizational revolution.

Traditional organizations regard employees as tools, but Haier sees them as value creators. Traditional organizations have no users, only customers, and when a product is sold, the deal is done. Haier's customers are users. The sale of a product is not the end, but a beginning. Haier continues to engage with users throughout product iterations.

According to Liz Wiseman, a Thinker50-ranked thinker, Toyota stands for zero defect, while Haier stands for zero distance. Toyota's zero defect works in the realm of products, but when a product becomes a networked appliance, it is merely a node in a network. The physical attributes of the product are no longer of greatest importance because users need the product, and more importantly, the whole network behind it.

3. Disrupting classical organizational purposes

The guiding ideology of organizational purpose in Western capitalist societies can be found in a 1970 New York Times essay by Nobel laureate Milton Friedman titled, "The Social Responsibility of Business Is to Increase Its Profits." Friedman argued that the responsibility of business is to make profits, and its purpose is to put shareholders first, maximizing shareholder value. To this end, companies are seeking long-term profit maximization. This is no longer the case today. In 2018, a CEO roundtable in the United States joined by CEOs of some 200 large companies issued a joint statement to pursue the maximization of interests for all stakeholders. This is still not enough. What's more important is to unlock the value of employees and users.

Gary Hamel, a leader in the strategic management field, published the bestselling book, *Humanocracy: Creating Organizations as Amazing as the People Inside Them*, which devoted a considerable section to a Haier case study. Hamel opposes bureaucracy, arguing that many of the models to address the problems of bureaucracy only treat the symptoms, not the root cause (as they fail to change the DNA of an organization). This is likened to a poorly built building. Remaking the rooms can only do so much when the entire structure must be rebuilt.

Since its inception in 1984, Haier has lived through new strategy phases every seven years. Now, it has entered the sixth strategy phase. Throughout its journey, Haier has always adhered to the purpose of "maximizing human value."

In 1985, Haier was known for "smashing defective refrigerators," but underneath this symbolic gesture was our effort to change the employees' beliefs that "we can't make good products" and to ensure that all employees were in alignment with the Total Quality Management (TQM) system. TQM was invented by Deming, an American thinker. Unfortunately, TQM did not catch on in the US, but rather, in Japan. This is because American culture promotes individualism, while Japanese culture is collectivist. The beauty of TQM is that users are the next step. The system may not have caught on in America because there, workers like to focus on their own jobs and rarely look elsewhere.

In 1999, Haier began to build its brand through exports. Haier was among the first Chinese companies to set up factories in the US. There was some skepticism in the media about Haier, saying that our facilities in the US would surely fail. Haier's approach was unlike others; while other companies sought export revenues in foreign currencies, Haier set its mind to building its brand through exports and its connections with local cultures and users.

In 2012, Haier bought Sanyo Electric's white goods business. At the time, Sanyo's business had been on a loss-making streak for eight years in Japan. Ruth Benedict, an American who wrote a bestseller about Japanese culture, *The Chrysanthemum and the Sword*, pointed out that the Japanese are characterized by polarized behaviors. Japanese companies used the seniority-based wage system to create an economic miracle, but in the IoT era, the same system had become fatal for business, making the organization extremely immobile. After acquiring Sanyo, Haier implemented the Rendanheyi model. Though the trade union initially rejected the model, they came to accept it.

The story of frontline salesperson Michiko Hayakawa is a case in point. She bid for an ambitious target that won her the directorship of the logistics department when her predecessor was still in the position—this was unthinkable in Japan. Even more unthinkable was for a woman to become head of a department. In Japanese culture, one can only succeed when the former director retires. As a general rule, people under 50 years of age are unlikely to become directors.

The failure rate of cross-border M&A is 70%, and 70% of these failures are caused by culture. Haier has acquired many companies, such as GEA in the US, Fisher & Paykel in New Zealand, Sanyo in

Japan, and Candy in Italy. These acquisitions have been successful thanks to Haier's "salad culture." There are different vegetables in a salad. Each represents a country, a company, and a culture, but the salad dressing is the same, that is Rendanheyi. All countries and nationalities can embrace the Rendanheyi model because it values dignity for all. The Americans take pride in the "everyone is created equal" statement in the Declaration of Independence, but American companies have not truly achieved this. The Rendanheyi model, however, truly allows everyone to shine with value.

4. Disrupting traditional product brands

Traditional brands focus on products. Economist Robert Gordon referenced a great deal of data in his book *The Rise and Fall of American Growth* where he concluded that "the average growth rate of total factor productivity in the third industrial revolution was only 1/3rd of that of the second." The electrification process of the second industrial revolution produced many inventions, such as household appliances, airplanes, and highways, each leading to sustained and widespread growth throughout the world. Conversely, the third revolution based on information technology did not bring forth as many inventions.

George Gilder, one of the three great thinkers of the digital age, once said, "All the changes converge in one epochal event: the overthrow of matter." The so-called "overthrow of matter" refers to the Internet of Things enabled by microprocessors, sensors, and the like. We are no longer in a time of product brands. Brands must adapt to the IoT era. Haier's observation is that "products will be replaced by scenarios, and industries will be enveloped by ecosystems."

Now, all influencers/promoters like to claim that they offer "the lowest price across all channels" in their live streaming sessions, but users need more than just products—they need scenarios. For example, for the smart home, users don't need singular products; rather, they need scenarios made up of a portfolio of products. Similar to shopping for a designer jacket, shirt, tie, and shoes. You won't pull off the look if your outfit doesn't match. To mix and match clothes for a look that aligns with the character of the wearer is an apt analogy to the statement that "products will be replaced by scenarios."

Joseph Pine, author of *The Experience Economy*, once said, "Goods are tangible, services intangible, and experiences memorable." Product brands that focus on the product economy face fierce competition and operate in what is now a red ocean. Platform brands (e.g., internet platforms) can still focus on the service economy while the blue waters last. Ecosystem brands focus on the experience economy and play in "uncharted waters." "Uncharted waters" are ecosystems that are difficult—if not impossible—to imitate.

In 1993, American economist James Moore put forward the idea of the business ecosystem and described its three main characteristics, light, inimitable, and scalable. "Light" means you don't need to plant trees. Plants thrive on their own, as in the Amazon rainforest. "Inimitable" means it is possible to build a similar garden, but impossible to copy an ecosystem. "Scalable" means that an ecosystem thrives sustainably and may produce new species, whereas a garden does not.

The most important idea in Hegel's philosophy is reflection, the movement of "negation of nothing" back to "reflection in itself". Self-reflection is the study of one's own problems. The last thing organizations want is complacency. In Haier's 30-plus-year journey, we have made three "smashes," each a self-disruption in its own right.

The first was "smashing defective refrigerators," the result of deep self-reflection on "high-quality products are made by high-quality people." Why can't we make high-quality products? Because we don't have high-quality people. Why don't we have high-quality people? Because we don't want to improve. Because of the first smash, in 1988, Haier received China's first quality gold medal in the history of the refrigerator industry.

The second was "smashing the organization," when we came up with the world's first management model for the IoT era. Haier grew by learning from overseas classical management models. Since the implementation of the Rendanheyi model in 2005, Haier has transformed itself into a networked organization with more than 4000 micro enterprises (MEs).

The third was "smashing the label." Haier has remained the world's top white goods brand for 11 consecutive years. The next step is not to play defense, but to upgrade. Like "smashing defective refrigerators," the idea is to make better refrigerators rather than giving up refrigerators. "Smashing the label" is Hair's effort to upgrade from a home appliances brand to an ecosystem brand.

How to Disrupt: The Workable and Replicable System of the Rendanheyi Model

How can Haier disrupt? It depends on the "RDHY scorecard, win–win value added statement, and ecosystem brand." These three tools make up the workable and replicable system of the Rendanheyi model.

The goal of Rendanheyi is to transform a company into an ecosystem brand. Brands normally come in two categories: traditional product brands (such as Adidas and Nike) and e-commerce brands (such as Taobao). Haier is the only ecosystem brand on the BrandZ Top 100 Most Valuable Global Brands list and the only one to make the list for two consecutive years.

The financial tool for ecosystem brand valuation is the win–win value-added statement, whereas traditional organizations generally use the balance sheet, cash flow statement, and income statement. The American Institute of Management Accountants regards Haier's win–win value-added statement as a financial tool for the IoT era and a "fourth statement" that all start-ups and listed companies need. Most investors and consumers would love to read this statement because it contains both financial and non-financial metrics.

Management guru Peter Drucker attended a conference of business leaders in his 90s. There he first asked, "Who knows the least about the business in an enterprise?" His answer was the CFO. The audience was confused. He explained, corporate finance must be based on the future, while CFOs only look at past performance. Corporate finance is a dynamic picture, but CFOs only take a screenshot. So, in a sense, what they see is the past.

The strategy tool in the Rendanheyi model is the Rendanheyi scorecard. The European Foundation for Management Development has developed a Rendanheyi scorecard certification system. Unlike other certification systems that are led by foreign companies, this is the first global certification system led by a Chinese company.

1. The goal of Rendanheyi: Ecosystem brand

An ecosystem brand differs from traditional brands in three ways: offering a seamless experience, a boundaryless ecosystem, and contactless payment.

Neither the traditional economy nor e-commerce has achieved a seamless experience because they are based on transactions, not interactions. A seamless experience is about understanding user needs, delivering scenarios instead of mere products, and being able to iterate. In the past, companies organized their own sales. Now, they need to collaborate with many other companies to create value and share in the value-added returns. Today, mobile payment still requires manual confirmation, but the IoT era will no longer need that. For example, our washing machine can dispense detergent automatically according to the laundry size, material, water quality, and types of stains. When the detergent is running low, a refill will be purchased automatically and delivered to your doorstep as per the user agreement. This is true contactless payment.

2. The financial tool for ecosystem brand valuation: Win–win value-added statement

In the past, companies followed the value chain theory proposed by Michael Porter in 1985. Haier's win–win value-added statement however, takes a very different approach.

First, the win–win value-added statement reflects value streams rather than a value chain. Porter believes that in the value chain, only a few key strategic sections can create value and the others do not. Therefore, there are profit centers and cost centers. However, in the win–win value-added statement, all nodes are centers of value creation, and everyone must create value or risk becoming a liability to others.

Second, traditional statements only show product revenue, and revenue minus cost is profit. Conversely, the win–win value-added statement shows the ecosystem revenue as well. The guiding indicators of the value chain are key performance indicators (KPIs), while the guiding indicators of the win–win value-added statement are user performance indicators (UPIs). The traditional statement shows how much value users create for the enterprise, while the win–win value-added statement reflects how much value the enterprise creates for users. Therefore, these are two distinct ideas.

The win–win value-added statement is comprised of six core elements, the first of which is user resources. The win–win value-added statement highlights the importance of users, while traditional statements leave users out of the picture. Therefore, the traditional statement has a static balance, while the win–win value-added statement has a dynamic balance. The common accounting method used by most organizations is double entry bookkeeping invented by the Italians whereby a debit entry corresponds to a credit entry, and the two must match down to the penny. User resources are dynamic. We create when users have needs. We recreate when users have new needs. It is an iterative cycle in dynamic balance, just as American scholar James Carse said in his book *Finite and Infinite Games*, infinite games have no ending and cannot be reproduced.

Third, diminishing marginal returns is an ironclad law of economics, but thanks to ecosystems, Haier can achieve incremental marginal returns. If Haier only manufactures washing machines, it can only have diminishing marginal returns. But when Haier upgrades to an ecosystem and becomes an Internet of Clothing brand that encompasses the clothing industry, it now has incremental marginal returns.

3. The strategy tool of Rendanheyi: Rendanheyi scorecard
The Rendanheyi scorecard embodies the system theory in traditional Chinese philosophy. The root of traditional Chinese philosophy comes from *The Book of Changes*, the core of which speaks of overall connection and dynamic balance.

The *Book of Changes* deals with the relationships among the five elements: metal, wood, water, fire, and earth. The adjacent elements generate one another while distant elements restrict each other. Among them, water, wood, and fire are adjacent, therefore, water generates wood and wood generates fire. Water and fire are distant, so water restricts fire. Similarly, an organization should not claim to be the industry champion, because it is but a node in the entire system. The organization must complement, check, and coordinate with other organizations.

The *Tao Te Ching* says, "the deepest cut doesn't sever." It speaks to the indivisibility of a system. In her new book, *Zero Distance: Management for the Quantum Age*, Professor Zohar also says, "There are no causes, only relationships." We can draw a parallel between these two ideas. They both emphasize integrity and systematicity. As the founder of quantum management theory, Professor Zohar integrates quantum theory with management science. Quantum theory has disrupted Newtonian mechanics. The idea of "quantum entanglement" says that two particles, no matter how far apart, exert influence on each other. Einstein described it as "spooky action at a distance." In Rendanheyi, the relationship between employees and users is also like quantum entanglement.

On the horizontal axis of the Rendanheyi scorecard are leading targets and from left to right are premium brand, scenario brand, and ecosystem brand. On the vertical axis is the ecosystem microcommunity (EMC) contract. MEs spontaneously organize themselves around user needs to form clusters (EMCs) on the value chain. EMCs cooperate with one another to accomplish goals and realize the "four self's," namely, self-organized, self-driven, self-value-added, and self-evolved. Where the two axes intersect is value-added sharing. Haier has no compensation department. The self-organized EMCs create and share value autonomously. They are responsible for identifying value targets and sharing the value-added returns, but they will automatically disband if the targets are not reached within three months.

For example, Haier Biomedical entrepreneurs identified a pain point while supplying hospitals with blood-storage equipment. It is difficult to collect blood, but there is still a serious waste of blood in hospitals. A blood bag that leaves the blood bank cannot be returned, even when the blood is not used in the operating room. Recognizing this problem, the entrepreneurs engaged blood banks, hospitals, and other partners to establish the U-Blood platform and became an entrepreneurial ME. Haier didn't invest in U-Blood, but VC firms and the start-up team co-invested. Later, Haier Biomedical went public with a high PE ratio of 140x (around 100 × now). At the same time, the entrepreneurs' shares were converted into public shares of the listed company. No one asked these employees to start a business; it was purely self-organized.

A LEADER IN THE IoT ERA

Haier has an ecosystem brand, COSMOPlat, and a scenario brand, Three-Winged Bird. COSMOPlat was inspired by Chaos, the ancient deity of beginning in Greek mythology, also known as the Cosmic Egg. Chaos predated all gods, even Zeus. The Three-Winged Bird is a self-portrait of Chaos, representing a strange attractor. Chaos refers to the phenomenon that a small change in a dynamic system can lead to a long and momentous chain reaction throughout the whole system. The Chaos system starts with only a small change and experiences a massive shift. The purpose of the reference is that one can seize user pain points produce a huge market through constant iterations via the "butterfly effect." A butterfly in the Amazon rainforest flapped its wings a few times and two weeks later a hurricane reached Texas. Haier names its scenario brand the Three-Winged Bird with the ambition of creating new markets and new users.

Therefore, Haier has achieved three types of leadership under the Rendanheyi model:

1. Leadership in theory

   Harvard University produced five case studies on Rendanheyi in the space of five years. Nine of the world's top 10 business schools include the Haier case studies in their syllabi. In international academic conferences, the pinyin of Rendanheyi is used, like "kungfu" in English. European scholars, after examining more than 30 existing management models from around the world, concluded that Rendanheyi is a clear standout.

   James Moore sees Haier as taking a path that is vital to the future of humanity, because his idea of a business ecosystem didn't attract much interest until Haier's implementation proved its value. Six localized Rendanheyi research centers have been founded by local scholars around the world, without any Haier secondees. According to Annika Steiber, director of the Rendanheyi Silicon Valley Center at Menlo College, in the twenty-first century, there should be a universal management concept that can be followed and adopted by organizations in different countries in different ways and in varying degrees. Haier is the only organization that has truly disrupted traditional management models. Haier's model will overtake the Silicon Valley model because the latter only applies to SMEs, while Rendanheyi exemplifies the successful transformation of large enterprises.

2. Leadership in standards

   For international standards in the IoT era, including model standards, ecosystem standards, and smart home standards, all the four main international standard bodies have picked Haier as a standard-setter. The EU is now promoting Project GAIA-X, and Haier's COSMOPlat has been engaged by the project as a founding member to contribute its experience in mass customization. There are only 44 "lighthouse factories" around the world, and Haier is the sole company with two lighthouse factories in the same country.

3. Leadership in replication

Up to now, 64,560 companies from 74 countries and regions have registered as members of the Rendanheyi Boundaryless Network. According to an article in MIT's *Sloan Management Review*, Haier's model trumps those of Toyota, Apple, and Hasbro in the context of the COVID-19 pandemic. The supply chain of these companies showed signs of rigidity because of the deep-rooted organizational rigidity, while Haier's organizational model has been very nimble. During the pandemic, Haier achieved growth in North America and Japan, defying market trends. Bloomberg, the world's largest financial intelligence platform, argues that, "In a sense, Rendanheyi is no longer a term exclusive to Haier, but rather a management revolution in the IoT era to be celebrated by companies around the globe."

The Rendanheyi model has been replicated in different industries and in various countries across the world. In the catering industry, the Italian restaurant brand Convis has achieved an initial milestone of organizational change to operate as an ME. In the ICT industry, the European headquarters of Fujitsu has started a transformation toward an ME-based organization. In the textile industry, Jaipur Rugs, India's largest carpet manufacturer is actively piloting the ME model. In the industrial sector, Severstal Group, a well-known Russian industrial and investment holding company, is preparing to adopt the Rendanheyi model. International organizations such as the UNDP Asia Pacific Regional Innovation Centre also posted on their official social media account saying that the application of the Rendanheyi model can indeed have positive impacts.

In 2020, Chinese President Xi Jinping proposed "a new development paradigm with domestic circulation as the mainstay and domestic and international circulations reinforcing each other." The premise of having domestic circulation as the mainstay and dual circulations co-evolve underscores the importance of leadership. The Rendanheyi model is in a leading position because it enables co-creation among Chinese and international brands in a dynamic ecosystem, much more advanced than a simple supply chain relationship. For example, Haier's Internet of Clothing platform has attracted more than 5,000 ecosystem resource providers from nearly 15 industries, including international brands such as Procter & Gamble and Decathlon while having aggregated 65 million ecosystem users.

Marx's epitaph reads, "The philosophers have only interpreted the world, in various ways. The point, however, is to change it." Similarly, everyone is interpreting the IoT era, so how does one become an IoT business? I think we must change our world through IoT, and the path to change is what Wang Yangming calls "the unity of knowledge and action."

Some say action is easier than knowledge, and others say the opposite. For us, both views are too static. We should hold a dynamic view. The difficulty with the "unity of knowledge and action" lies in constant iterations. When knowledge is relevant and action improves to keep up, knowledge will improve and the action will improve again. I encourage Chinese companies to take collaborative actions so they can truly shape a business model that leads the world in IoT.

Qingdao, China   Zhang Ruimin

Personal Foreword

Each of the eleven books I have now written has been a very personal project for me, always arising from attempts to bring my education as a scientist and philosopher to bear on problems, issues, and events that were troubling, or at least preoccupying me, in my daily life, and that I felt were likely troubling or preoccupying many others. Each book was an attempt to offer a vision to myself, and hopefully others, of "some better way," some sense of changes that I and others could make that would improve the quality of our lives. But I feel that no other book I have written has been so personal or felt so urgent, or its subject matter troubling to so many others, as this one.

During the past four years that I have been working on this book, all of us have experienced Brexit, the Trump presidency, and the Covid-19 pandemic. Many have suffered directly from these events, experiencing disorientation, depression, financial hardship or insecurity, personal illness, and even the loss of loved ones and livelihood. Those of us in the West who pay attention to, and are aware of our vulnerability to larger scale world events, have experienced these personal challenges in the wider context of a chaotic, global upheaval that sees the prospect of a declining America, in particular, and the Western world order in general, doubt about the efficacy of democracy, indeed a declining moral order that leaves many wondering who and what we can count on. The world as we have known it seems to be spinning out of control.

Personally, my own head has been spinning during much of these past four years. I have spent far too many hours watching and re-watching the news, simply trying to understand what it all means. Why does the world seem suddenly to be falling apart? What are the forces behind it? I have suffered my own lost months simply immobilized with depression and anxiety. I have been very ill with Covid, endured the months of "lingering symptoms" that follow, and suffered the isolation and loneliness of lockdown and social distancing. I have missed the international travel and international friends that were so much a part of my life and work, and the livelihood that depended on it. I have watched my native America, where I was born and grew up, slip into a country I no longer recognize, and experienced Britain, where I have lived for the past fifty years, no longer feeling like home.

And so, like many others I believe, during these past four years I have felt disillusioned, lost many of the assumptions that framed my life, lost a sense of security about things I thought I could take for granted, and even lost the ground from beneath what had supported many of my memories. Indeed, at times, I felt I had lost the whole framework that supported my "being-in-the-world." And thus in response, as always when troubled in the past, I have written a book, this book, in an effort to work out for myself and others a vision of "a better way," a better path we might all follow, and a new framework that might guide us and make sense of it all. And as always before, I have drawn my inspiration for this book from my lifelong passion for quantum physics, and the vision from the philosophy it offers of a very different reality and a very different way we might live this in our lives and leadership.

On the surface, this is a book written for leaders, particularly business leaders, because the nature, role, and activities of business and the preferences, values, and style of its leadership lie so closely at the heart of what has brought us to this present crisis. It was American business and its well-paid lobbyists that put Trump in office, both through their wish for the tax cuts and deregulation he promised during the 2016 election, and through much longer term lobbying that created America's obscene wealth inequality that motivated so many people to jump on the Trump bandwagon. At the same time, it is mainly the money, power, and cross-border global reach business leaders now possess that makes them best placed and most responsible to lead us beyond these dark times. Business is the wealth creating engine of society and the employer, directly or indirectly, of most people. Business leaders, both directly and through their influence on the decisions political leaders make, play a huge role in deciding both the distribution of wealth and the living and working conditions enjoyed by most others. The practices, values, and preferences of business leaders hold sway in determining the quality of life for the majority, the quality of our health, and the endangered health of our planet.

I will be arguing that it is in business leaders' own interest that they now take the lead in reversing much of the damage for which they have largely been responsible. This is because the mindset that lies behind the leadership attitudes and management practices that have gutted America's middle class and put over 70 million Americans into poverty is the same mindset that is now threatening business itself. This book is primarily about changing that mindset.

But this is not just a book for business leaders. They, like the rest of us, also have personal lives, families, and relationships. They, too, are citizens of their communities, nations, and the global family, and thus a new vision for what it means to be a good person, what makes a good society, and how we can build a stable global order concerns them both as guardians of their companies and in their more private lives. And we who are not business leaders must all play the role of leaders in various dimensions of our lives, in our families, among our friends, in our communities. Indeed, I will be arguing for a vision of business in which every employee will become a leader. So the quality of our leadership also determines the health, well-being, and happiness of others, especially those we most love. The nature of leadership and the question of how to be a good leader is an issue for us all. We will see that perhaps the most powerful insight of quantum physics is that everything is connected to everything, and everyone to everyone. It is a very big deal to all of us whether companies succeed, and the means and morals by which they do so. Everything is everyone's "business." And, thus, I think this book is a book for all.

There is one more personal comment I want to make about this book. Most of the positive and exciting things that I have experienced during the past six years have been things I experienced while spending a great deal of time in China. The business model highlighted in this book was conceived by a Chinese CEO and first implemented in his Chinese company. It is not "politically correct" in most Western circles today to say anything positive about China, but if I did not highlight in what follows some of the many creative & exciting projects & initiatives coming out of China today, and the positive qualities of Chinese society I have experienced and valued, I could not have written an honest book. Just as the whole world has learned and gained great value from the achievements of Western nations, I believe that only wilful ignorance & a failure of imagination can stop the West now learning from and adapting to our own ways and purposes the many almost miraculous achievements of modern China. The *RenDanHeyi* management model I write about so extensively here is one of them.

About Myself

It may interest readers to know the personal story behind my life's work devoted to making the wider implications of quantum physics accessible to "ordinary" people. There was a much earlier time in my life when it felt like "the bottom had dropped out of everything," and it was discovering the philosophy offered by quantum physics that restored the ground beneath my feet.

Until age 10, I was raised by my devout Methodist grandparents in the Ohio countryside. I sat beside them in church every Sunday, & their simple Christian beliefs provided the focus and framework of meaning for my early childhood. But at age 11, I lost my faith in Christianity, and have never been able to find that lost meaning in any other organized religion. The vacuum that left in my young life began to be filled with a fascination I developed for atomic physics at age 13, and still more so when I read David Bohm's classic textbook *Quantum Theory* at age 15. Quantum physics became, and has remained, the driving passion of my life. I then spent all my teenage years building atomic devices in my bedroom, smashing atoms, and finding, in the philosophy offered by quantum theory, answers to all those Big Questions that young people ask. The homemade atomic devices collected many top prizes at local and national science fairs and contests, and these won me a physics scholarship to MIT. I was one of only 17 young women that entered MIT's Class of '66, along with 1000 young men.

At the end of my first year at MIT, I realized that I was far more interested in the philosophy suggested by quantum physics than in having a career as a practicing research scientist, and I was allowed to change my course of studies to pursue a combined degree in Philosophy & Quantum Physics. During the ensuing three years of my undergraduate studies, I reflected constantly on the wider philosophical implications of quantum physics, and this understanding was enriched by a specialization in Heideggerian philosophy and Heidegger's concern with the damaging implications of technological thought. I also had the good fortune to attend the seminar offered by C.P. Snow during his year as a Visiting Professor at MIT, and I had an early intuition that quantum philosophy could bridge The Two Cultures Divide for which he was so famous. I recently discovered an old video made by the BBC to describe student life at MIT in which I had appeared as President of the MIT Humanities Society, already speaking about the possibility of "a quantum society."

I continued my study of Heidegger and reflections on the wider relevance of quantum philosophy for new thinking about personal & social sciences I was exploring during my three years of postgraduate studies at Harvard while pursuing a Ph.D. at the Divinity School in Philosophy, Psychology, & Religion. I finally published my first "quantum" book, *The Quantum Self*, in 1990, offering a new, quantum framework for psychology that could replace Freud's dominant, mechanistic framework that had been inspired by Newtonian physics. Ironically, and very much to my surprise, it was the publication of that book that began my career as a management thinker.

After publication of *The Quantum Self* in England, I received a call from a professor at London's City University Business School, asking me to give a lecture about the book to his MBA students. Despite my passionate protests that I knew nothing about business at that time, he insisted, and the enthusiastic reception given to my lecture by the MBA students led the professor to recommend me to the Training Manager of Shell UK, who was looking for someone who could speak about paradigm shifts in management as part of the "Challenges for Change" course he was designing for Shell senior managers. After two years of developing my management thinking while teaching in that course, I wrote up what I had been teaching in my first book on Quantum Management, *Rewiring the Corporate Brain*. Everything else about my developing work on a theory of Quantum Management and my career as a "management guru" followed, beginning with an invitation to deliver a keynote speech at a systems thinking business conference in Boston, and invitations soon after to introduce this thinking to senior managers at Motorola and then to Shell USA's Leadership Council in Dallas. The rest is "history."

Oxford, UK   Danah Zohar

ACKNOWLEDGMENTS

I am very grateful to The Haier Group for generously supporting the research for this book, and for granting me full access to the company and its microenterprise leaders. I thank my students, Felix Wentian He and Domi Zhong Hongsheng for their massive personal assistance during my stays in China. Christopher and D'Artagnan Giercke offered me sublime hospitality at their Genghis Khan Polo Camp in Mongolia, where I spent many months working on the book. My good friend Johnson Chang provided the book and me with a peaceful home in Suzhou, where I could write sitting by the waterfall in his Chinese garden. And I owe special gratitude to my agents, Jackie Huang, of The Andrew Nurnberg Literary Agency, Beijing, and my New York Agent, Robin Straus.

CONTENTS

LIST OF FIGURES

PART I

Building Blocks

CHAPTER 1

Introduction: The Need for New Thinking

Writing in *The New York Times* during the midst of the Covid-19 crisis, Thomas Friedman said that, from the time the Coronavirus appeared onward, "There is the world B.C.—Before Corona—and the world A.C.—After Corona." This is definitely an After Corona book, and I am certain there will be many others. Most thinking people recognize the Covid-19 crisis as a turning point in our human affairs, and hope we will seize it as an opportunity for a fresh start. But the book I am offering here is different. I really believe it should be the starting point for all others.

Quantum scientist David Bohm said, "All the problems of the world are problems of thought. If we want to change the world, we need to change the way we think." If we are *really* going to create a better, wiser, and more *sustainable* post-Covid world, we will need to *think* differently, and to *organize* differently. We need to change the mindset that determines how we see and act in the world. As Peter Diamandis & Steven Kotler make clear in their eye-opening book *The Future is Faster Than You Think*, the human brain evolved for thousands of years to think about and adapt to an environment that was local, linear, and largely stable, and we used it to build organizations, social institutions, and government agencies that now find it difficult to cope with today's uncertainty, complexity, rapid change, and global interconnectivity. To build more relevant and resilient ones, we need to update the thinking that created the old ones.

Neuroscience now teaches us that our brains are "plastic," and that we can "rewire" them. The way that we experience and think about our

© The Author(s) 2022
D. Zohar, *Zero Distance*,
https://doi.org/10.1007/978-981-16-7849-3_1

surroundings and relationships actually reinforces or alters the complex system of neural connections that shape that thought and experience. Change the way we think, we change the way we do all future thinking, and what we do with it. This book offers a radically new, *total framework*, for *thinking* differently (about everything!), and thus for *organizing* differently. And it offers a radically new *organizational model* for implementing this new thinking in companies and other social systems.

THIS BOOK

This book about a new paradigm in management thinking and a new, practical model for implementing it in our personal and working lives, in our companies, in our communities and nations, and in a sustainable global order. It will offer an understanding of why and how "thinking-as-usual" is failing both business and political leaders in these new times, and it will advocate new thinking and new management practices that are so *radically* new that they turn everything we have taken for granted inside out and upside down. I call this new management model "Quantum Management," because it is rooted in the new paradigm bequeathed to us by quantum physics and its younger sibling, complexity science.

The new organizational model featured here originated as a business model designed and implemented in 2012 by Haier, China. Haier, still largely a domestic appliances company based in Qingdao, is one of China's largest and most successful global companies and the world's largest supplier of domestic appliances. In January 2016, Haier acquired (one of its many global acquisitions) the stagnating GE Appliances that the parent GE wanted to off-load, implemented its own business model there, and has turned the company into a great success, even by the usual standards of profitability, share-holder value, company ranking, and increased market share. The story of how GEA has been turned around with the Haier business model is particularly important for American readers because it proves that a very radical new model conceived by a Chinese company can work in America.

Thus, this is not a book about Haier itself which, though one of China's most successful global companies, need be of no more interest to English-speaking readers than any other successful Chinese company. It is the *Haier business model* that moves Gary Hamel and Michele Zanini to describe Haier as "arguably the world's most creatively managed company," in their book, *Humanocracy*, and its CEO Zhang Ruimin as one of the world's most innovative leaders. It is the *Haier business model* that is attracting so much attention among business leaders and leading business schools in Asia, Europe, and even America. It is the *Haier business model*, that is the subject of so many case studies and so many featured articles in the business press—most recently an article by Gary Hamel in the December 2018 issue of *The Harvard Business Review*. It is the *Haier business model* that brings 10,000 visitors a year, many of them American business leaders and academics, to the company headquarters in Qingdao. And it is the *Haier business model* that I will argue in this book gives us a practical model for implementing much needed new thinking, not just in business but new thinking about individual people and employees, new models for social and political organization, and a new model offering a vision for a very different kind of global order.

This book is also about the management *theory* that Haier Chairman & CEO Zhang Ruimin credits with largely inspiring his own thinking when designing the company's new business model. This is my own Quantum Management Theory, developed over the past forty years as part of my broad project to tease out and articulate a new paradigm (*in the full Kuhnian sense of that word*) for all thinking about everything, modeled on the defining principles and philosophy found within quantum physics. I base my argument on the fact that it was the philosophy and principles of Newton's seventeenth-century mechanistic physics that gave rise to the modern, Western paradigm and its embodiment in Taylorism, the management theory that still dominates nearly all business thinking and practice today. My argument is that the paradigm shift in physics heralds and defines a broader paradigm shift in the way we experience and think about everything—including management.

I have published three previous books within which Quantum Management Theory has evolved, but they were just books about a *theory*, and though many business leaders found it attractive, they didn't see how it could actually work for them. What is *different about this book* is that Haier, followed by Roche India & GE Appliances in America, and the American Army's own Special Operations Task Force (the "green berets"), has now embedded the theory in a practical business model, and given it life by *implementing* it in the structure, practice, and culture of the company. Haier's Zhang Ruimin had the genius and the courage to turn what was only a theory into an actual, practical business model *that has worked*. And, thus, I can present here for the first time a theory that *both* sets out the framework for a new, quantum paradigm, *and* backs this up with some solid case studies of real organizations that have implemented the theory with demonstrable success.

THE HAIER BUSINESS MODEL

I shall, of course, describe the Haier model in great detail in Chapter 4 of this book. Condensed here to just a few short words, Zhang Ruimin surrendered all power at the top of the previous Haier hierarchy. He did away with all middle management, and turned many of them into CEOs of their own, independent, and self-organizing microenterprises. All powers of decision making, hiring, & remuneration were passed to these microenterprise heads. In every sense, each microenterprise is a company in its own right, working directly with its own customers to innovate and produce its own products in response to those customers' declared needs and preferences. Microenterprise teams are paid directly by their customers, not by Haier itself, and they keep most of their own profits, passing back to Haier a proportion to pay for the larger company service platforms that provide the scale of backup service only available to a larger company. These service platforms are run by senior management. All that Zhang Ruimin himself now does is provide the vision, the inspiration, the resources, and the personal character traits that "glue" the whole operation together. Today there are nearly 4000 customer-facing microenterprises, each acting as an innovative start-up, and Haier itself is described as "a company of companies," providing the combined benefits of large company resources together with the innovative capacity of small start-ups.

That was a brief description of the *structural* aspects of the Haier transformation. There are also crucial, defining *cultural* aspects. Now that "every employee is a CEO" (a company motto), the microenterprise teams are as highly motivated and committed to the success of the team as any business people who own their own company. The usual emphasis on *products* has been replaced with an emphasis on *process* and *service*, getting high-quality products to customers with whom each microenterprise is in direct, interactive contact. The most important company motto is, "At Haier, the customer is the boss." And, perhaps most radically, Haier has redefined the metrics for success. Short-term shareholder value and market share have been replaced as indicators by growing numbers of loyal customers who constantly return for more products. Following this model, Haier was recently listed on the Fortune 500.

In both Chapters 4 and 15, as I offer detailed descriptions of the Haier model, its infrastructures, processes, and practices, I will make clear how each of these is an expression of Quantum Management principles in action.

My Own Involvement with Haier

In October 2014, I received an email from Haier Chairman Zhang Ruimin. He told me that he admired my work and that my ideas about Quantum Management had influenced much of his thinking when designing Haier's new business model and company transformation program. He invited me to the company headquarters in Qingdao to meet with him personally, to meet his senior leadership team, and to give a lecture to the top 250 people in management. During a 2 hour personal meeting, he asked me many questions about quantum physics, explained to me specific ways in which he felt his new business model was putting quantum principles into practice, and shared his enthusiasm for similarities he saw between my own quantum work and the thinking of traditional Chinese philosophy, especially Taoism, which also inspired his business thinking. After our conversation, he invited me to his private office and pointed to a row of books in the Mandarin language, saying, "These are all your books." Unknown to me, he had been ordering private Mandarin translations of *all* my books going back as far as *The Quantum Self,* "because they were so helpful with my developing vision for Haier." I was stunned! And somehow awkwardly embarrassed, not knowing what to say. Before receiving Mr. Zhang's email invitation to visit Qingdao, I had only heard vague things about Haier, as "an interesting company."

For the past 5 years, I have continued visiting Haier two or three times a year, always at Zhang Ruimin's invitation and always including a long personal conversation with him. We discuss physics, philosophy (both East & West), global politics, our favorite authors & ideas, the role that business might play in changing the world for the better. An accomplished intellectual in his own right, Zhang Ruimin is fondly known throughout China as, "The philosopher CEO."

Each of my many visits to Haier also always involved conversations and short "mentoring" seminars with the various platform leaders and many of the microenterprise teams. I have always worked particularly closely with the Strategy Platform and the Culture Platform. In September 2018, I was awarded the $200,000 Haier *RenDanHeyi* Medal "For Academic Contribution to the Haier Business Model." My fellow winners were Gary Hamel & Rosbeth Moss-Kantor, both of whom have also had a long relationship with Haier.

Shortly after my most recent book, *The Quantum Leader*, became a Business Best Seller in its Mandarin translation (2016), and I was named "China's Top Innovation Management Thinker of 2018," by the highly respected *Tsinghua Business Review*, I met with Mr. Zhang again. He told me, "Everyone in business is talking about your book. Quantum Management is now China's new Big Idea." He was pleased about this, but also deeply concerned that the book's popularity was making "everyone want to jump on board, and most of them don't know what they are talking about." He worried that this rush of unqualified copy-cats would cheapen & discredit the idea of Quantum Management. He then suggested that I write "the Bible of Quantum Management to keep the idea pure," and recommended the five-part structure described in this outline, "to include the themes of all your major books and applying them specifically to business & management." Hence the book outlined here. Its title, *Zero Distance*, is both another name for the Haier business model and a defining principle in quantum physics.

SUMMARY OF THE BOOK'S ARGUMENT AND DEVELOPMENT

At the 2019 Davos Economic Forum, many of the world's most powerful business leaders gathered there, when interviewed by the media, described an air of pessimism prevailing in their meetings and conversations. It was generally recognized, they said, that that the global community is facing very serious, in some cases existential, problems, but they were not able to think of workable solutions. The problems discussed included climate change, of course, the increased threat of nuclear conflict in an unstable world, mass migration, the prospect of massive unemployment resulting from ever new technology, populism, identity, inequality, and the economic uncertainty associated with some, or all, of these. And for the business leaders of course, there were the familiar problems associated with today's uncertainty, rapid change, and adjustments to globalization. Big problems indeed! And added to all this, we now have Covid!

My view is that the real problem leaving these leaders unable to find solutions is that the thinking they have always used when faced with problems or challenges is not equipped to deal with these very twenty-first-century ones. Indeed, their accustomed thinking, and the world it created, *caused* most of these problems. And neither does that same outdated thinking allow them to turn many of the problems into opportunities. It seems obvious to me that none of us can solve the problems or seize the many opportunities of life in the twenty-first century with thinking designed in the seventeenth century to cope with the problems and opportunities of The Industrial Age that followed. We need to "rewire our brains"!

And that is what this book is promising to offer: an understanding of *why* and *how* thinking-as-usual is failing both business and political leaders, and a description of a new kind of thinking that is so *radically new* that it will turn everything they have taken for granted inside out and upside down. I will argue that a paradigm shift that began in the early years of the twentieth century has now come fully into play in the twenty-first, that this paradigm shift is revolutionary, and that it calls for new thinking in every aspect of human affairs. This new thinking, when applied to business, will demand not only that leaders change how they manage, how they make decisions, how much power they have, and their very *role* as leaders, but that they will have to create whole new structures and infrastructures, whole new meanings and purposes, for the organizations, or social systems they lead.

As Zhang Ruimin commented on what is required, "You simply have to forget *everything* you thought was true, and start from scratch." Both Zhang's leadership philosophy, and the business model he conceived to guide his radical company transformation program, will be the central characters and role models in this book. So readers here will not have to start entirely from scratch! They will have the example of Zhang Ruimin and other leaders who have successfully followed that example to guide them, and I will provide the essential elements of the disruptive thinking they and I will argue is needed to thrive as leaders in the twenty-first century—both to solve its problems and to seize its opportunities. But much of the reinvention required will be neither quick nor easy. It requires *deep* change, and as any leadership mentor worth the high hourly fee he or she is charging to advise their clients will warn, deep change takes time. I would add, it also takes commitment and courage. The pioneering leaders I write about in this book took enormous risks, with both their companies and their own careers, and they told me they did so because, "I was deeply convinced that it was right. I had to do it."

I call the new thinking I shall advocate so strongly "quantum thinking," the leaders who practice it "quantum leaders," and the management model embedded in the successful transformation programs described in what follows, examples of Quantum Management Theory— in action! And unlike so many, chiefly New Age, authors, advertisers, and countless others, I use the word "quantum" *as an actual reference to quantum physics!!* I see quantum physics as the origin of and basis for the new paradigm that now calls for new thinking about everything in twenty-first-century life. While quantum physics itself, as practiced in the laboratory and originally conceived as describing the strange micro-universe within the atom, clearly has *nothing* to say about management*, the ideas, categories of thought, underlying principles, and philosophy that underpin it as pure physics, clearly are of wider paradigmatic signif-icance. As were the principles of Newton's physics when they were published in the seventeenth century, and thus adopted in their own work by every major thinker in every field whose ideas for the following 300 years created and defined the Modern Age. Thus Quantum Manage-ment Theory is inspired by, and draws its own principles and philosophy from, those that define quantum physics itself.[1]

The paradigm that arose from Newton's seventeenth-century physics was adapted as a "scientific management theory" by the Scottish engineer Frederick Taylor in the early twentieth century. "Taylorism" as it became known, was universally adopted by global business. Every management theory and every management practice, every management strategy and every management decision since, has borne the mark of Taylorism. And that was right while businessmen were operating in the simple, stable, predictable, and controllable world of machines and their technology.

But the Industrial Age is past, and so are the industrial machines and the mechanistic certainties that allowed business to generate great wealth and draw successful management models from them. The new technology of the twenty-first century is digital, and our new century is frequently called the Age of the Internet. Haier's Zhang Ruimin more correctly calls it "The Quantum Age." This is because *all* the new technology now forming the basis of twenty-first-century economic and scientific

---

[1] It is important to note that the *living* quantum systems that complexity scientists call "complex adaptive systems" *are* directly relevant to understanding things like companies and cities, and thus are described at length in this book. They are the bedrock science upon which Quantum Management is based.

development is quantum technology. The digital revolution itself was made possible by the silicon chip. Every digital tool or service we use today, from our computers, smart phones, smart appliances, video gaming machines, and the internet itself, was made possible by the arrival of the silicon chip. And the silicon chip itself was made possible by knowledge gained with quantum physics. As are any devices using laser technology or technologies relying on solid state systems like superfluids and superconductors. These include the new "quantum computers" that are causing so much excitement.

The revolutionary quantum technologies of the Quantum Age both offer new opportunities and create new problems, and that is why we need "quantum thinking" to seize the opportunities and solve the problems. Leaders of social systems and business organizations need to *understand the logic behind* the new systems and organizations they now lead, both how it is *different* from the old Newtonian logic of the Industrial Age, and how being able to use the new quantum logic can serve their needs and meet their challenges today. And that is why I offer Quantum Management Theory, and the thinking it presents, as a necessary leadership philosophy to guide all twenty-first-century leaders.

Theories in science must be tested by experiment before they can be accepted as valid. It is the same with new theories in management. This book therefore offers detailed case studies of three large companies whose leaders took the risk of testing Quantum Management Theory by fully implementing it as a business model to guide large-scale company transformation programs. These companies are Haier China, Roche India, and GE Appliances in America. Their success stories provide "experimental" validation of the theory and a guide for others to follow.

Haier was the first large, global company to pioneer the implementation of Quantum Management Theory, and Haier Chairman Zhang Ruimin's *RenDanHeyi* business model was the first to present these ideas in the form of a practical business model. *RenDanHeyi* is Quantum Management *in practice*, and that is why it interests me. Both Roche India and GE Appliances took their lead from the Haier model and adapted it for their own transformation programs, and the American Army's Special Operations Task Force, perhaps independently, introduced an identical transformation adapted for military purposes. Therefore, *RenDanHeyi* and its implementation at Haier form the template I describe in this book for other companies and organizations to follow. I also go further, and argue that Haier's *RenDanHeyi business* model has applications as a *social* and *political* model that could address challenges facing leaders in government and public service. And in Part II of the book, I present applications of *RenDanHeyi* that I believe could help individual people adjust to the new global realities and working conditions that are causing so much fear and confusion in our *personal* lives.

Zero Distance is not "just another business book," and Quantum Management Theory not "just another business theory." It is the first new organizational theory to offer an *overarching* theoretical framework for *fundamental* change in the way we think about management—a new *management paradigm* grounded in science and the new scientific understanding of organizational systems dynamics. Thus it offers the first *comprehensive* understanding of *why* we face the problems that we do, *why* our familiar solutions are not working, and the fundamentally new thinking we need to adopt if we are to find *better* solutions and more *creative* responses to the many new problems & opportunities presented by twenty-first-century realities.

Many piecemeal stabs have been made at suggesting new solutions for business—"the flexible organization," "agile organizations," "dynamic capabilities," "conscious capitalism," "humanocracy," "authentic leadership," "sapient leadership," "holocracy," "the Teal organization," etc. And several experiments are being made to address various problems in society. All of these are good ideas, but piecemeal solutions cannot be effective unless part of a comprehensive, larger framework that explains why there are problems that *need* new solutions and *why* the solutions being offered are *good* ones. Experiments are blind if not embedded in a comprehensive understanding of why they are being tried. Thus a senior partner in one global consultancy admitted to me after being introduced to Quantum Management Theory, "I see now that everything we have been doing with clients is shallow and piecemeal, and that we have been wasting our own and everyone else's time." Indeed, Quantum Management Theory is best understood as a *meta-theory*, within which many new management ideas can find their home.

The paradigm shift reflected in Quantum Management is so fundamental, and so relevant to every aspect of our business and social lives, that no one book, nor no one thinker, can tease out all the opportunities offered in all the fields of thought and action where it might be implemented, especially not one now in her mid-seventies. There are so many more applications of *responsible, informed,* quantum thinking! I can only hope that others will follow my lead, and write those books.

STRUCTURE OF THIS BOOK

I want to explain briefly here why I am writing the book in five parts and covering the topics that I do. Part I, Building Blocks, is necessary to equip readers with the understanding they need to make best use of the arguments and examples that follow. Parts II through V, devoted in sequence to The Quantum Self, The Quantum Leader, The Quantum Organization, and The Quantum Society (including a Quantum Global Order) represent my conviction that we don't live our lives in isolated silos of experience, and the insight from quantum physics that, "Everything is connected to everything." This supports my argument that business, its philosophy, values, culture, priorities, and decisions, is the business of everyone because it impacts on every aspect of everyone's life. Any business (or other) leader is also of course a personal individual with a private life. The quality and nature of that private life are affected by the decisions of business leaders and, in a quantum organization, the character of that personal individual is of central importance to the quality and efficacy of his/her leadership. And, of course, every leader is also a citizen, local, national, and global. And both the nature and quality of society, and the survival of our fragile planet and its global community are directly affected by the personal character and personal/professional values, and thus consequences of his/her leadership decisions. Therefore, though presented in five parts, each part of the book has implications for and further develops the theme of every other part.

CHAPTER 2

From the Newtonian Age to the Quantum Age

In the Western world at least, since the ancient Greeks, we have lived with and had all our lives, thoughts, and decisions defined by a paradigm that stresses the "reality" of separation and fragmentation. From the atoms of Democritus to those of Newton, we in the West have experienced ourselves, our organizations, and our societies as being composed of atomistic bits—body parts, minds & bodies, individuals, departments, sectors, nation states. Today's existential climate crisis is the denouement of our 2000-year-old belief that we humans are *separate* from Nature, that Nature is a resource to be *used* by us. All of our wars and injustices have been fought or perpetrated against *others* who are separate from us. In our three great Western religions, even our God is portrayed as separate from us, possessing another nature or substance, not wholly fathomable to our limited human understanding. And yet we learn from both the defining principles of quantum physics, and from their much earlier expression in ancient Chinese Taoist philosophy, that both our newest physics and one of humanity's oldest traditions tell us "there is no such thing as separation," that "separation is an illusion." Everything is connected to everything, everyone is connected to everyone else. We live, they say, in a universe and in a world of *zero distance*.

Changes in scientific understanding often herald great changes that overtake human thinking as a whole. Science draws its inspiration from often vague and tentative but wider cultural shifts, and then transmutes these into highly focused, rigorous, clear language and into powerful

© The Author(s) 2022
D. Zohar, *Zero Distance*,
https://doi.org/10.1007/978-981-16-7849-3_2

images and metaphors. In this book I will be drawing upon the principles and philosophy of our modern science (quantum physics and complexity science), their realization in our twenty-first-century technology, and the globalized world this technology has created, to explore how to navigate and thrive in this new world of zero distance. And I will argue that the paradigm of atomistic separateness is exhausted. I believe that this exhausted paradigm, so deeply embedded in our sense of ourselves and our relationships, in the thinking behind the management and organization of our companies, and in the nature of our social and political thought, is no longer sustainable. Indeed, I believe it has *caused* many of the problems our leaders now struggle to solve, many of them existential threats to our very survival.

Solutions to global challenges like global pandemics, climate change, nuclear conflict, identity, populism, inequality, mass migration, the prospect of massive unemployment resulting from ever new technologies, and the economic uncertainty associated with some, or all, of these, require new thinking on a sweeping scale. As, of course, do the complexity, chaos, uncertainty, rapid change, and global interconnectivity that demand new ways of structuring and managing our companies. It is my argument here that a sweeping change of thought on this scale cannot be achieved through tinkering with piece-meal adjustments or by adopting trendy new theories. We are moving from one entire era of human civilization to another, from experiencing lives wholly framed by a now exhausted paradigm to lives yet to be framed by a new paradigm. We are, in short, in the throes of a massive *paradigm shift*, and it is the purpose of this book to navigate us through understanding this and to outline a guide for individuals and leaders who must "learn to build their bridge while crossing it."

WHAT IS A PARADIGM SHIFT?

The word "paradigm" has become so widely used and so widely misused, particularly in business circles, as nearly to have lost all meaning. Every new business guru who introduces his or her latest management theory claims to be introducing a "new paradigm." The word has come to mean no more than a "new mindset," a "new approach," a "new model," a "new idea," a "new fad," or simply "something different." These collective misrepresentations blind us to the deep, all pervasive meaning and power of a paradigm, and thus of a "paradigm shift," and thus condition us to pay little attention or to weaken our powers of discernment when some truly revolutionary way of understanding and experiencing our lives and our world really is demanded. If readers are to gain anything valuable from the contents of this book, it is essential you begin by understanding the correct meaning of a "paradigm" and a "paradigm shift."

The word "paradigm" was first introduced into modern usage by the University of Chicago historian of science Thomas Kuhn. In his groundbreaking book *The Structure of* Scientific Revolutions,[1] Kuhn described a paradigm as, "the entire constellation of beliefs, values, techniques and so on shared by members of a given community." He was speaking specifically of the scientific community, the entire sense and understanding they shared when making their claims about the nature of physical reality, and the way this changed with the birth of Relativity Theory and Quantum Physics. He pointed out that this shared paradigm determined the questions they asked, the experiments they did, the observations they took from those experiments, and the meaning they assigned to them.

In the books I have been publishing since 1990, I have been among the first to point out that our scientific paradigm at any time in history, what our natural philosophers or scientists, or in ancient times our mythologies, priests & prophets, tell us about the nature of the universe, gives rise to a more generally shared paradigm defining every aspect of how we experience and understand our human lives. In this more all-embracing meaning, a paradigm is the full sense of reality in which we are immersed. It *is* our sense of reality and of ourselves, body, mind, and soul. Our paradigm determines not just what we think about and how to understand our human world, but also how and what we feel, how and what we experience, and even what we detect with our five senses, most especially what we see with our eyes—what we see, and what we *don't* see. It determines the questions we ask and our understanding of the answers we then are given, how we view ourselves and relate to others, what is or is not worthwhile to do with our lives, even what it means to be a bad or a good person, a bad or good leader. For the vast majority of people, it is not possible to live or comprehend life and how to live it outside the constraints of the existing paradigm of the times.

But Kuhn made the very important distinction between what he called "normal science" and "revolutionary science." Normal science operates

---

[1] Thomas Kuhn, *The Structure of Scientific Revolutions*, 1962.

within the categories and understanding of the existing paradigm. Scientists assume that they know what is true and how to deepen their knowledge of it, and the experiments they then conduct are carried out to *verify* those assumptions. Their science is mainly an exercise in ratification and self-assurance. Each new experiment can add to their catalogue of knowledge within their existing paradigm, but nothing really surprises them. Revolutionary science, by contrast, is scientific discovery that breaks the mould, that violates existing assumptions and understanding and forces the scientist to rethink everything he thought he knew—about *everything*. Revolutionary science is *disruptive*. And it is when this kind of major disruption demands that every previous assumption now be questioned, and that all data be looked at through new eyes, that the revolutionary scientist stands at the door of a paradigm shift. Normal science, Kuhn says, goes astray,

> And when it does – when, that is, the profession can no longer evade anomalies that subvert the existing tradition of scientific practice – then begin the extraordinary investigations that lead the profession at last to a new set of commitments, a new basis for the practice of science. The extraordinary episodes in which that shift of professional commitments occurs are the ones known to this essay as scientific revolutions. They are the tradition-shattering complements to the tradition-bound activity of normal science.....Each [of the great scientific revolutions of the past] necessitated the community's rejection of one time-honored scientific theory in favour of another, incompatible one....And each transformed the scientific imagination in ways that we shall ultimately need to describe as a as a transformation of the world within which scientific work was done.[2]

Ever since I published *Rewiring the Corporate Brain* in 1997, I have been arguing that new realities facing business were major disruptions of the sort described by Kuhn as heralding scientific revolutions. And in that and subsequent books,[3] I suggested that a similar revolution in business leadership thinking and practice required that we forget everything we thought we knew about business and focus our minds on an entirely new way of understanding and dealing with the challenges of the twenty-first century. In this book I want to make clear that this required

---

[2] Kuhn, ibid., p. 6.

[3] Danah Zohar, *Spiritual Capital* (2004) and *The Quantum Leader* (2016).

revolution is indeed a paradigm shift in the fullest sense of those words, and that this paradigm shift demands a totally new understanding not just of business leadership and practice itself, but also of the human individuals who work in business, the societies in which business operates, and the global community in which we all participate. As I said earlier, every business leader is a person who also needs to lead in his or her own life and personal relationships, and they are also citizens of communities and nations and members of the global community.

Thus, I make the claim that the paradigmatic transformation of business called for in this book has the power to transform the world at all levels of our human experience. The enormity of the paradigm shift required as we move ever deeper into the twenty-first century is a *total, radical, reframing* that begins at the most basic level of our five senses—what we see, what we hear, what we smell, those hidden tastes we never noticed, the feeling of another's proximity or touch. We must start again as infants just born into this world, and explore it with eyes of a child, filled with surprise and wonder.

THE EXHAUSTED NEWTONIAN PARADIGM

We all learned at school that we should study history because understanding the past would help us better understand where we are now, and what lessons can be learned about how to create a future that does not repeat past mistakes. Thus, it is good to remind ourselves of the defining features of the Newtonian paradigm from which we are now emerging, to realize how these impacted the way we have viewed ourselves and our leadership and, unfortunately, how so many *still* view the world through their filters.

The Scientific Revolution of the sixteenth and seventeenth centuries, powerfully summarized by Newton's three laws of physics, took the world by storm. Although in many ways Newtonian physics itself built on a 2000-year-old Western world view that originated in ancient Athens and drew from the monotheism of the West's religions, never before had any single body of work offered to explain Nature so succinctly. Coinciding with the Enlightenment's claims for the unlimited power of Reason, Newton promised that now, not only could we *know* Nature, but also that we could *predict* and *control* her. Knowing the starting position of any particle or object, he said, a knowledge of the forces acting upon it, and equipped with a knowledge of the three laws of motion according to which everything in the universe is governed, we could know *exactly* its future trajectory.

Fate was written not in the stars but rather in the ink with which Newton wrote his equations, and uncertainty was banished forever from our lives. Newton's physics described a world that was simple, law-abiding, and predictable. From the moment that God set the great "clockwork machine" of the universe in motion, the individual, isolated, and impenetrable atoms of which it was made would follow their predetermined destinies. There would be no exceptions, no surprises, certainly no chaos. It was a universe designed by a blueprint, with which scientists could build models and predictive charts, make flow diagrams, and forecasts. A tidy universe that all could understand fully with the objective powers of observation and pure Reason. And though we human beings and our consciousness had no part in this quite dead and lifeless drama, we had the tools fully to control it. Such promise! Such power! The greatest thinkers in fields of thought never before linked to physics took notice and were inspired to emulate Newton in their own work.

Freud, the father of modern psychology, saw Newton's deterministic forces of action and reaction at play in his three-level map of the human mind, a mind whose content and dynamics were determined by the cause and effect of early childhood experience. Newton's impenetrable, isolated atoms became the isolated individuals of Freud's "object relations theory," mere objects to others, incapable of love and imprisoned within their own projections. Freud's work later evolved into Skinner's Behaviorism that portrayed humans as so many laboratory rats and Pavlovian dogs, wholly governed by the iron laws of stimulus and response. And this in turn evolved into the computer models of mind celebrated by today's cognitive and neuroscientists. They tell us we are "mind machines" who are programmed for success or failure, social mimicry, and obedient conventionality. In none of this Newtonian psychology is there room for free will, responsibility, conscious motivation, or personal growth and transformation.

We see here the roots of how workers and employees are treated in our factories and companies today, objects and automatons who must be controlled with power from above by rules and regulations, job descriptions and assignments, often with fear, told what to do, not to be trusted with responsibility or decision making, their muscles and their minds, their "human capital," exploited for profit. And the working lives of most of them meaningless, their personal lives, emotions, passions, ambitions, and relationships "nothing to do with the job."

Newton's atoms inspired the social atoms of August Compte's new science of sociology, the atomistic individuals of Locke's and Mills' liberal democracy, and the atomistic nation states of the modern political order. Freud's atomistic and selfish individuals became the businessmen of Adam Smith's capitalism, and the laws and forces of Newton's predictable universe Smith's model for the laws and forces of the predictable capitalist markets. And finally, the Scottish engineer Frederick Taylor took both Newton's machine metaphor of the universe and Weber's Newtonian inspired "iron cage" of bureaucracy as the models for his Scientific Management Theory, known more popularly as "Taylorism."

The Taylorian company, with its all-powerful executive control from the top, its siloed functions and departments, its inflexible bureaucratic rules and regulations and chains of command, its workers and employees who are told what to do and viewed as passive instruments of production, its atomistic sense that it is an isolated island onto itself with no responsibility for community or planet, no regard for ethics or values, consumed by mindless competition in pursuit of maximum profit and share-holder value, is *still* the model used by most of today's companies. And the management principles needed to run such companies are still the management skills taught by most of the world's business schools.

Is it any wonder that the atomistic and selfish individuals who have learned they are separate from Nature & separate from others, that the existing capitalist model advocating the ruthless pursuit of self-interest, the dinosaur-like Taylorian company weighed down with bureaucratic structure and atomistic fragmentation and responsible only to its share-holders, and the atomistic nation state that pursues a variation of Trump's "America First!" motto (though perhaps more subtly than Trump himself!), have made a mess of globalization? Can it be any surprise that we now face seemingly insurmountable problems with climate change, identity, inequality, nuclear threat, etc., and can't cope with today's interconnectivity, complexity, diversity, rapid change, and uncertainty?

The Newtonian paradigm worked in its day, just as Newton's physics successfully described the world as scientists understood it then. That physics gave us the technologies of the Industrial Revolution, the bureaucracy and Taylorian management that drew from it gave us the giant factories and companies that provided that revolution with its wealth-creating base, and the selfishness and greed of atomistic individualism focused the energy associated with some of the worst of human motives for purposes that at least produced a higher standard of living for larger numbers of people than perhaps ever before. But we realize today all this was at a very great cost, and it doesn't work anymore. It created problems that its own models and mindset cannot solve, and these problems now pose an existential threat to the whole human project. The Newtonian paradigm has exhausted its usefulness, and even its relevance. Something new is needed, an entirely new paradigm is needed.

In science itself, Kuhn points out, the conditions for a paradigm shift occur when experimental data turn up an "anomaly." That is, a result that simply cannot be explained within the framework of the old paradigm. Scientists then begin to ask new, "out of the box" questions that might make some new sense of the inexplicable results. For our present western culture, that anomaly has taken the form of the Covid-19 crisis and the total inability of the existing system and cultural values to meet the life-threatening and economy-busting needs it presented. As Anne-Marie Slaughter described the spontaneous self-organization of new structures, systems, and values in response to the crisis, "The Coronavirus, and its economic and social fallout, is a time machine to the future. Changes that many of us predicted would happen over decades are instead taking place in a span of weeks."[4]

One of the unsettling claims made in Kuhn's book was that a new paradigm can never be fully accepted until all the believers in the old paradigm die off. Hopefully, his pessimism was misplaced and there may now be a critical mass of leaders who can embrace a new paradigm and rise both to its challenges and opportunities. And fortunately, there is a new physics, quantum physics, to give this new paradigm its solid conceptual foundations and an overarching framework for helping leaders understand how to build a new and more sustainable personal, business, political, and economic culture within it.

---

[4] Anne-Marie Slaughter, *New York Times*, 23 March 2020.

THE NEW QUANTUM PARADIGM

Schrodinger's cat is the mascot of the new physics. He was conceived by Erwin Schrodinger, one of the five men who established quantum physics, to illustrate some of the apparently more bizarre and "mind boggling" features of quantum reality.

Schrodinger's cat lives in an opaque box, and the fact that we can't see inside this box is an important part of the story. Inside with the cat is a fiendish device, triggered by the random decay of a radioactive sample that determines whether he is fed good food or poison. If a decay particle hits one switch on the device, the cat gets food. If it hits the other, he gets poison.

In the everyday world of common sense and Newton's physics, one switch or the other would be triggered, the cat would eat *either* good food *or* poison, and would be *either* alive *or* dead. But Schrodinger's cat is a quantum cat, so things don't work out that way. In the quantum world, all possibilities, even mutually contradictory ones, coexist and have a reality of their own. These coexisting quantum possibilities ensure that the cat is fed *both* food *and* poison simultaneously, and he is *both* alive *and* dead at the same time.

Of course we never see alive/dead cats, and we can never catch Schrodinger's cat in his double act. If we open the box to look at him, we will find that he is *either* alive *or* dead. And this is another curious fact about the quantum world: it is our *looking* at the cat, our *observing* him, that determines his fate. According to quantum physics, there is always a dynamic, cocreative relationship between we, the observers, and what we observe. Our very involvement in the act of observing determines the kind of reality that comes into existence. Just these two examples alone from the strange new world of quantum physics—that multiple realities coexist simultaneously, and that it is human observers who influence which of them will then appear as a fact or as an actor in the everyday world of human affairs—have very large implications for the role and responsibilities of leaders. We will see many others as we go along.

A radically new way of thinking runs through the scientific work of the twentieth century. New concepts, new categories, a wholly new vision of physical and biological reality mark a sharp break with nearly everything that science held dear or certain in these past three hundred years. The transition to this new thinking, which I call "quantum thinking," has been so profound that it constitutes a Second Scientific Revolution calling, perhaps, for a new scientific method. I shall be arguing in the following chapters that this same quantum thinking will bring about a management revolution, calling for seismic changes in the structure, leadership, and culture of our companies and other social organizations.

Newtonian science was hierarchical. The physical world, like the Taylorian company, was structured into ever-descending units of analysis: Molecules are more basic than complex compounds; atoms are more basic than molecules. Newtonian models of relationship and organization structure power and efficacy on the same ladder of ascending and descending authority. Power radiates out from the center or down from the top.

But the biological "complex adaptive systems" described by complexity science are non-hierarchical. Everything in these systems is connected to everything else and every element of the system is of equally vital importance to the successful working of the system as a whole. Complexity science adapts the principles of quantum physics to living systems. So the systems that complexity science describes are in fact "living quantum systems," and it will be the application of the behavior of complex biological systems to complex human social systems that will form part of our guide for bringing the lessons of the new physics to necessary changes in the leadership and structure of companies. Indeed, Quantum Management Theory is best understood as being a companion to the Santa Fe Institute's pioneering work on complexity economics and other social systems that function as "complex adaptive systems."

Newtonian science stressed continuity and continuous, linear change. The new physics is about abrupt movements and rapid, dramatic, nonlinear change. It is a tale of quantum leaps, catastrophes, and sudden surges into chaos. The constant and the predictable give way to uncertainty and unpredictability. In the hands of quantum or chaos-and-complexity theorists, Newton's clockwork universe becomes a gambling casino where scientific method must give way to a Monte Carlo method, a computerized rolling of the dice and the calculation of odds.

As we saw, the old science portrayed a physical universe of separate, atomistic parts bound to each other by rigid laws of cause and effect, a universe of things connected by forces and causes. Quantum science gives us the vision of an entangled universe where everything is subtly connected to everything else, where things can be understood only *in relationship*. Influences are felt in the absence of forces or signals; correlations develop spontaneously; patterns emerge from some order within.

Where the Newtonian scientist reduced everything to its separate, component parts and a few simple forces acting between them, the quantum or complexity scientist looks for new properties or patterns that emerge when parts *combine* to form wholes. A universe where nothing new or surprising ever happens is replaced by a self-organizing universe of constant invention. The quantum scientist knows that this fact, or that part, cannot be isolated from its environment, or context. Holism replaces reductionism, and wholes are known to be greater than the sum of their parts. Organized simplicity gives way to self-organized complexity. And, as I have long argued, the quantum scientific paradigm is now giving birth to a more general, all-embracing new quantum paradigm in human affairs.

All the new technologies we use in the twenty-first century are quantum technologies. The silicon chip on which our computers, and all other digital devices, rely, was made possible only through a knowledge of quantum physics. The iPhone lying at my elbow just now, the smart TV I will watch when I finish my day's work, and the internet on which I will check the day's latest news flashes, are quantum technologies. Laser surgery, CAT scans, PET and MRI scans, the medical technologies that diagnose our illnesses and extend our lives, are all quantum technologies. Superfluids and superconductors, the new physics of power systems and the quantum chemistry of materials science—all harness the secrets of quantum science. And now quantum biologists are telling us that our bodies rely on quantum processes within their cells, and neuroscientists are finding quantum processes at work in our brains. The flocking patterns of birds in flight and the photosynthesis of plants rely on quantum signals and processes, and complexity scientists tell us that our cities do, and our companies could, operate according to the same quantum laws as the universe itself. We live in a Quantum Age now, within a newly emerging quantum paradigm, and the companies and organizations that will succeed, and the leaders who will manage them, must be quantum companies and quantum leaders. We must all master quantum thinking. And hence I offer this book.

Readers will *not* be asked to understand quantum physics itself. That requires very advanced mathematical understanding and is only of practical use to other scientists and to people developing new technologies that rely on it. My purpose in this book is to outline the *paradigmatic implications* of quantum physics, the "big ideas" that make a quantum paradigm different from the old Newtonian one, and how these apply to the challenges and opportunities facing and available to leaders today. This can be done clearly, in simple language that non-scientists can easily understand.

This book is written in five parts, but these are "quantum parts." This means that every theme in the book is an element of the larger whole, every theme is connected to every other and is necessary to understanding the full implications of every other. It is a book addressed to leaders, but as we shall see, I believe that each of us is a leader at some level of our lives, the true masters and makers of our own individual lives, and many are the leaders of families, companies, communities, and nations. And thus, the new paradigm being offered in this book is a new paradigm for living, thinking, learning, leading, and organizing ourselves in our shared world, which each of us helps to create and for which each of us is responsible.

CHAPTER 3

Defining Ideas of Quantum Physics

Quantum physics was born to describe the curious and common-sense denying micro-universe within the atom. Today, physicists tell us that it is actually the most accurate way to describe *everything* that exists, including ourselves. They tell us that we live in "a quantum world." This world is made of energy, not "bits of matter," and everything and everyone that exists in our world is actually an evolving pattern of dynamic energy. You and I are patterns of dynamic energy, and our companies are dynamic energy systems. The quantum world is also made of relationships, and everything and everyone is in relationship with, is "entangled" with, everything and everyone else. This is "quantum holism." The quantum world is indeterminate, and thus unpredictable, creatively "feeling" its way into the future through self-organization. It is a world where questions are more important than answers, and we people who ask those questions "co-authors of reality."

These, and other key defining elements of the quantum world are spelled out in greater detail here, and contrasted with the defining elements of the earlier, Newtonian physics and Newtonian paradigm. These basic quantum concepts and principles are the necessary building blocks for understanding Quantum Management and its place in the wider quantum paradigm, and thus readers may need to refer back to them while going through the book. I believe this is basic science that

© The Author(s) 2022
D. Zohar, *Zero Distance*,
https://doi.org/10.1007/978-981-16-7849-3_3

every twenty-first-century leader should know, especially business leaders, and I will be spelling out the relevance and wider leadership implications of these quantum concepts throughout the book.

QUANTUM INDETERMINISM

The most powerfully revolutionary feature of Newtonian physics was the certainty it offered. If everything in the physical universe was controlled by three inviolable, mechanistic laws, then by using those laws we could, infallibly, predict the future trajectory of any moving particle or unfolding event. Furthermore, if we knew how to employ those laws of motion ourselves, we could *control* the outcome of events. It is little wonder that, as the decades and centuries passed, this Newtonian determinism became an attractive model for everything from the behavior of individuals and societies to that of markets and companies. But in the rapidly changing, complex, and apparently chaotic world of the late twentieth and then twenty-first centuries, relying on the deterministic certainty of behavior and events to guide decision-making has become a hindrance rather than a help. Decisions based on "the best laid plans" just keep blowing up in our face.

I have said that the new quantum paradigm turns everything we thought we knew upside down and on its head. And one of the many revolutionary discoveries of quantum physics is that there is no such thing as certainty. When an electron makes a quantum leap from one energy orbit to another inside an atomic system, there is no predicting when that leap will take place, or how big the leap will be. And if the nucleus of a radioactive atom emits a particle, there is no telling when this decay event will be. There don't seem to be any laws controlling events in the radically contingent quantum universe. Things just happen as they happen. We don't see them coming, and we have no idea where they are going.

Quantum events are probabilistic. Some are more likely than others to happen. Given a large enough number of events, we can predict certain *patterns* of outcome. Schrodinger's wave equation (see below) describes all *possible* outcomes of a quantum event, now and in the future, but this is only a set of bookmaker's odds. We can rarely predict anything useful about the future behavior of a single quantum event. Newton's vision of a universal clockwork machine gives way in quantum physics to a universal roulette wheel, or a game of dice. This outraged Einstein, who protested, "God does not play dice with the universe!", and he and others tried to argue that the uncertainty was a result of our limited knowledge, not a feature of reality itself. But countless experiments proved him wrong. Radical contingency really is a fundamental feature of our world.

Within the categories and values of the exhausted Newtonian paradigm, quantum indeterminacy appears as a threat or a negation of everything science has offered us, but it is the very foundation of what the new quantum paradigm sees as positive. It is precisely because the outcome of quantum events is indeterminate that its uncertainty underpins the potentiality, or the "what might be," of an evolving system or situation. It holds out the possibility of unlimited creativity and innovation. Because the many variables of a quantum system begin as unfixed or ambiguous, the system is free to evolve in co-creative dialogue with other systems, with its environment, or with conditions prevailing in human affairs. It frees our hands to be spontaneous, or flexible. Thus, just as knowing the iron laws of Newton's physics allowed leaders of the Machine Age to thrive on certainty, understanding, and learning to work with the principles of quantum physics can help leaders of our twenty-first-century Digital, or Quantum, Age, thrive on uncertainty.

HOLISM

Like the word "quantum" itself, being "holistic" has acquired so many uses in the popular vocabulary that it has lost most of its original, and really powerful meaning. But just as any proper understanding of the broad, new quantum paradigm requires that we know quanta are packets of energy, and a single quantum is the smallest amount of energy required to make anything happen in our universe, which is itself made of energy. A useful understanding of quantum holism is necessary to living, acting, and leading effectively in what is now the zero distance, Quantum Age.

Newtonian physics, and all the social, business, and political models inspired by it, is atomistic. Taking atoms, which are separate and isolated, as the basic building blocks of the universe, the atomistic thinker believes that any whole can be broken down and analyzed into separate parts (its "atoms") and the forces acting between them. True knowledge about what anything is, or how it works, is thus achieved by isolating the thing and then reducing it to its constituent parts. The whole thing is always thought to be just the sum of its parts. The human body is a brain, plus lungs, plus a heart, plus kidneys, etc., and a human being is a mind, plus a body. Thus, a top doctor becomes a brain specialist, a lung specialist, a kidney specialist, etc., and a patient suffering an illness is referred to the relevant specialist. Until very recently, and now only with a few recognized exceptions, a patient suffering from stress is sent to a psychiatrist or psychologist, but another suffering with ulcers is sent to a gastrointestinal specialist. Western medicine has no whole-system understanding of mind/body complex.

By contrast, quantum physics, which holds that quanta of energy are the basic building blocks of the universe, teaches us there is no such thing as separation, that every quantum of energy in the universe, and everything made of quanta, is "entangled" with everything else. Nothing really is *anything* identifiable or knowable except in relation to the whole of the system of relationships with which it is entangled. This is because quantum "parts" acquire many of the properties they have *through* those relationships (see **Contextualism**, below). And they have the potential to have *different* properties if they then find themselves in a different relationship. Furthermore, each quantum part has the potential to have *further* properties when it is in relationship to other parts. The very combination of parts in any system of relationships gives that combination *more*, or *different*, characteristics or properties than originally possessed by the parts. *A quantum whole is always larger than the sum of its parts.* This is the quality known as quantum *emergence*, and it makes the constant creation of something new a feature of the quantum world. Life is an emergent property of certain inorganic chemical elements combining in a given relationship, a human being is an emergent phenomenon resulting from a relationship of body parts, and consciousness itself is thought to be an emergent phenomenon of brain processes, quite likely in relationship to those of the body.

Thus quantum holism maintains that the whole is more primary than any parts of which it is constituted. A holist always looks at things or systems in aggregate, and knows that any true understanding of them rests on understanding the relationships between them. This has far reaching implications for how we understand teams and organizations.

BOTH/AND: WAVES AND PARTICLES

One of the big challenges to Newtonian physics was its inability to say whether light is a stream of particle-like photons, or a series of wave-like photon patterns. Some experiments indicated one thing, but then other experiments indicated the opposite. William Bragg, a Noble prize-winning British physicist whose distinguished career spanned the late nineteenth and early twentieth centuries, expressed this confusion when he said, "Light seems to behave like a wave on Mondays, Wednesdays, and Fridays, and like a particle on Tuesdays, Thursdays, and Saturdays." Quantum physics answered the conundrum effectively by saying, "Every day is a Sunday." Light is *both* wave-like *and* particle-like, and to different degrees, always *at the same time*. This is called wave/particle duality. And it is true of every quantum entity: all matter in the universe can always behave as though it has both wave-like and particle-like properties.

The both/and nature of quantum reality also extends to positions in space and time. Where both Aristotelian and Newtonian logic insist that a particle is *either* here *or* there, that it has interacted with another particle *either* now *or* then, experiments in the quantum laboratory have proven that particles and their interactions are spread out all across space and time. Particles can be *both* here *and* there, interactive events can be *both* now *and* then. And this same quantum logic applies to our statements, decisions, and emotions. A statement can be *both* true *and* false at the same time, a decision *both* bad *and* good at the same time. And we all know that we can *both* love *and* hate a life partner or a friend at the same time. Those who speak the Mandarin language also know that a word or a phrase can always mean this *and* that (and many other things besides!), and any Indian will tell you, "Yes, we drive on the left, *and* we also drive on the right." We will see later that the both/and nature of quantum logic raises important questions about the preferred nature of corporate planning and decision-making, and makes us think twice about "one best way" or "one best product or service."

As physicists now tell us we live in a quantum world, we know that all things have quantum properties. Thus wave/particle duality is *literally* true to a very small extent even of large entities like ourselves, or our companies. But if we extend the both/and nature of waves and particles as a principle of how we think, then it can also serve as a powerful metaphor for better understanding the dynamics of our human relationships and the nature and potential of our companies or other organizations. In some circumstances, it can be best to think of these as having the characteristics of overlapping waves, co-mingling and co-creating with whomever or whatever is around us. Yet in other circumstances or ways, it can be best to stand out, or stand back, and behave as though we are particles that have boundaries and can act as independent individuals.

QUANTUM NON-LOCALITY

However, just to make this new understanding of wave/particle duality still more challenging, even particles are not entirely separate in the quantum world. The fact that every particle *also* has a wave nature that can be entangled with the wave nature of other particles, means that even apparently separate particles can be *nonlocally correlated*, their movements or characteristics acting in mirror-like synchrony with those of others.

If a light source emits two, different photons in opposite directions, and a scientist then measures each of them when they have traveled to the far ends of a very long room, he finds that the polarities of the two photons are synchronized, the polarity of one is always opposite to the polarity of the other. No force or signal has passed between these photons to inform them about the state of each other, there is no hidden string or spring connecting them, and no one has informed them beforehand which polarity to adopt. The photons just seem to "know" what each other are doing. When this "quantum non-locality" was first predicted, Einstein was outraged, called it "ghostly and absurd," and protested it would mean that photons have telepathic powers. It was indeed the feature of quantum physics that he hated most, even though he had been one of those who first discovered the new science. But in the late 1970s, experiments proved the existence of non-local correlation beyond any doubt, and it was soon explained that, though the photons as *particles* were separate when measured across a distance, as *waves* they were entangled, and no amount of "distance" had any meaning. And this would apply even if the photons had traveled to opposite sides of the universe before being measured.

Today, quantum non-local correlations are known to be part of our everyday world. Non-local correlations between electrons in their eyes now explain the once great mystery of how birds maintain their flocking patterns during migration, and these correlations also play a key role in plant photosynthesis. They may well explain many forms of human communication like crowd behavior, the beautiful, dancer-like synchrony of football players' movements during a match, or even things anecdotally reported such as telepathy and precognition. Being such a critical defining feature of quantum systems, including much of the quantum technology upon which twenty-first-century industries rely, it is quantum non-locality that perhaps stands out as the flagship on our voyage into today's zero distance world where having something local is no longer an issue.

CONTEXTUALITY: RELATIONSHIPS MATTER!

When we learned middle school science, we were taught that the first step of the Scientific Method is that you isolate the thing you want to study from its environment. Built into this instruction is the assumption that a failure to isolate will confuse or contaminate our knowledge of the thing itself. Things are only purely or truly themselves when separated from other things. But quantum science stands this whole methodology on its head. It tells us there is no such thing as separation, that everything is in relation to, is "entangled with," everything else, and that therefore the very concept of isolation is wrong-headed. If a quantum physicist wants to know the nature and properties of any particle, or any element of a system, he knows that he must know what surroundings it is in, what it is in relationship to, what is its role in the whole system. This is the principle of *quantum contextualism*: things never "are just what they are," but rather, things "are what they are in relationship with." The nature of a thing, the *identity*, of a thing is determined by its context, its relationships.

This contextual nature of quantum reality is made clear in its boldest form in the outcome of what is probably the most famous experiment in quantum physics, "the two-slit experiment." This is the experiment that proved the dual wave/particle nature of light. In the laboratory, a beam of photons is directed toward an opaque barrier, and this barrier has two slits, or "gates," either one of which the scientist can open or close. If just one slit is opened, the photons pass through as a stream of particles and go "click, click, click" on a particle detector (a photomultiplier tube) that has been placed behind the barrier. But if the scientist opens *both* slits, the photons pass through as a series of waves and make an interference pattern on a wave detector (a white screen that has also been set up on the other side of the barrier.) Light is both wave-like *and* particle-like at the quantum level of reality, but it manifests as either wave-like *or* particle-like at our everyday level of visible reality, depending upon the context—i.e. whether its environment is a single open slit or two open slits.

This contextual, or relationship-dependent nature of quantum things and events also turns on its head another sacred truth of ancient Greek philosophy and Newtonian physics, causality, or The Law of Cause and Effect. When we want to know why something has happened, we are accustomed to seeking its *cause*. We ask, "What caused this argument?"

"What caused my company to fail?" "What caused the financial recession?" Built into every "Why?" that we ask is the assumption that a cause lies behind the event or the effect we are questioning. But the discoveries of quantum physics tell us that such causal thinking is wrong-headed. There are no *causes*, quantum scientists tell us, there are only *relationships*.

Indeed, according to quantum physics, reality itself exists because there are relationships. Relationships, we are told, *make* reality. Of the two basic types of particles of which everything in the universe is made, bosons and fermions, bosons are themselves *particles of relationship*. The Four Fundamental Forces that bind the universe and everything in it together—gravity, electromagnetism, the strong and weak nuclear forces, are made of bosons. And the things they bind together are all made of fermions. As Plato said, wherever we have two or more "things," there will also always be present the relationship between them.

So a basic principle of the quantum paradigm is: Don't ask what cause is, or should be, present here, but ask instead, what is the relationship that exists, or needs to exist, in this situation? To achieve what we want or to improve our conditions, we don't add or alter causes, but rather we add or alter relationships. It is obvious to most of us that the quality of our personal lives is dependent upon the nature and quality of our relationships, and the health of a community or society depends upon the quality and extent of its network of relationships. And when we discuss the nature of a quantum company or organization, we will see that all human organizations are, in large part, systems of relationships, indeed systems of relationships *within* larger systems of relationships. Just as it is true in physics that relationships make reality itself, it is the quality of its internal and external relationships that makes a company a good or bad company, and that determines whether it will be a successful or a failing company. Thus *systems thinking* will be seen as a critical skill of quantum leadership.

A Universe Made of Energy

Like the Greek philosopher Democritus, Newton asserted that everything is made of atoms, and the Newtonian atom was visualized as a tiny, solid, material object very much like a miniature billiard ball, its boundaries hard and impenetrable. Newton said that atoms were the ultimate building blocks of the universe and everything in it, and as the Newtonian scientific paradigm became the general paradigm for all Western thinking,

Newton's atoms became the metaphorical building blocks and structural models for things as diverse as plants and animals, the human psyche, human relationships, societies, markets, and companies. But the discoveries of quantum physics and quantum field theory have blown atomism out of the water.

According to quantum science, the universe and everything in it, is in fact made of energy. The very source and foundation of the quantum universe, the **Quantum Vacuum**, is itself a still field of energy, like a very calm, mirror-like sea without waves, the field of all fields. And then all existing things—elementary particles of "matter," stars, planets, everything living and dead on our Earth including ourselves, our relationships, our companies, etc.—are oscillating "waves" of energy on some field, which is itself a field upon this background "sea." Every existing thing is a dynamic pattern of energy "waving" upon the Quantum Vacuum or on one of the many other energy fields that emerge from it. "Matter" itself, including what we take to be our own very material bodies, is in fact just extremely dense, highly compressed, patterns of energy. The universe is not made of material atoms, as Newton said, but rather of "quanta" of energy. A "quantum" of energy, the smallest packet of energy that can make anything happen or exist, is in fact the irreducible building block out of which everything is made. Atoms themselves are made of quanta.

As we go through the remaining chapters of this book, the revolutionary fact that everything and everyone is in fact a dynamic wave pattern of energy oscillating on the common, universally shared, background energy sea of the Quantum Vacuum will figure largely in our understanding of the new quantum paradigm, and how this changes everything we have ever thought about anything. This includes the promised new understanding of what it means to be human, and how we human beings live, work, lead, and manage our companies. Indeed, how we understand what a company *is*.

A UNIVERSE OF "REAL" POTENTIALITY

In normal discourse, when we speak of a person's or a system's "potential," we mean something that lies in the future, a promise of some ability or use that is yet to show itself, and we might say, "This student is not performing up to his potential," or "There is vast potential in our workforce." Both statements imply there is a lingering ability or resource yet to be realized or discovered. "Quantum potentiality" does have some of this same meaning, but it refers still more powerfully to properties of a quantum system that are present in the here and now, properties built into the system's identity, and thus to properties that must be considered as active players in any given situation involving the system. A quantum system's potentiality is an explanatory factor in how a system behaves, the affects that it has on other systems, or its role in an unfolding situation. Thus, in quantum physics, potentiality is as "real" as what we call reality.

The quantum physicist David Bohm described two orders, or levels, of reality that he called the Implicate Order and the Explicate Order. As their names suggest, the Implicate Order is hidden, but always implied, and the Explicate Order is what is actually seen, what is manifesting now, i.e., what is explicit. In Bohm's model, The Implicate Order is the realm of quantum potentiality, where all things are possible, and the Explicate Order is the realm of everyday perception and experience, where only one of an infinite array of potentialities rises to the level of what we normally call reality. Thus, like the Quantum Vacuum itself, The Implicate Order is a sea of possibilities and the Explicate Order the waves that stand out upon that sea. And just as the sea and the waves upon it are one continuous medium, so the Implicate potentialities of a "thing" are within, are the ground substance of, its Explicate manifestation.

In the example of Schrodinger's alive/dead cat that we read about in the Introduction to this book, in the Implicate realm (inside his unopened box) the cat is *both* alive *and* dead at the same time, just as the quantum nature of light (a beam of photons) is wave-like and particle-like at the same time. But when we view the cat in the Explicate realm by opening his box, he is *either* alive *or* dead, just as the light becomes either a stream of particles or a series of waves when it enters the Explicate realm by passing through one or two open slits in the opaque barrier.

In fact, there are not just two distinct possible potentialities for either Schrodinger's cat or the beam of light while they reside in the Implicate realm of being, nor for any other quantum "thing," but rather each has an almost infinite array of possible outcomes for how it will manifest in the Explicate realm. Everything existing in the Implicate Order exists as a wave of superimposed, often contradictory, potentialities, each displaying a range of probable outcomes, and this "probability wave," or "wave function" is described in the famous "Schrodinger's wave equation." Everything in the universe, including you and me and even any company that we might manage, has a wave function. Each of us, at one level of our being, is a wave of potentialities waiting to manifest as "real" in one way or another.

Until the twenty-first century, most quantum physicists believed that only *one* potentiality could ever manifest, that for some unknown reason the Schrodinger wave function "collapsed" as many potentialities entered the Explicate Order and became one actuality. And this apparent "collapse of the wave function" was the great unsolved mystery, perhaps, some thought, even the tell-tale incompleteness or wrongness, of quantum theory itself. But today, the vast majority of physicists accept that the wave function doesn't actually collapse after all. Many follow the Many Worlds view that *all* potentialities manifest as real outcomes, but that each does so "in a different world," that reality itself splits into different worlds every time a wave function is confronted with an array of different probable outcomes. Thus Schrodinger's cat is alive in one world and dead in another.

Other physicists, myself included, believe the Many Worlds view to be a metaphysical nonsense. I prefer David Bohm's view that the wave function spreads out into one, *fully realized*, visible outcome made most probable by its interaction with the surrounding environment, and into an accompanying array of other, *partially realized*, outcomes, all remaining in an interactive dialogue with each other and thus all having an active influence on the situation. It is in this Bohmian view that potentiality is always a hidden side of actuality. What we *are*, or are doing, now is always *entangled* with what else we *can* be, or *might* be doing. I will be following this Bohmian view throughout the book, and it plays a significant role in how I will describe the nature and dynamics of a quantum self, a quantum organization, and a quantum society.

HEISENBERG'S UNCERTAINTY PRINCIPLE: QUESTIONS *CREATE* ANSWERS

Both philosophers and scientists wonder at times how much we can ever know about fundamental physical reality. They ask whether ambiguity and uncertainty are inherent features of the real world, or is our knowledge about reality always incomplete, for some reason always necessarily limited? Heisenberg's Uncertainty Principle, the most famous principle in quantum physics, addresses exactly these questions. And it is important that leaders know about it because it has wide implications for how we understand and manage our organizations.

Much like the new science of behavioral economics says about the market, quantum reality is a strange, uncertain, shadowy realm. The more we try to pin it down and make rational models of it, the more it eludes us. The Uncertainty Principle tells it must always be so; because quantum reality itself is indeterminate, we must always content ourselves with partial truth and ambiguity when trying to know it.

Newton's physics said that a particle always has both position and momentum. It should always be *somewhere*, and always traveling at a definite speed. But due to the strangeness of the quantum world, we can never know *both* at the same time. If we measure, or focus on position, the momentum becomes fuzzy and indeterminate; if instead we measure momentum, then the position eludes us. It is the same with all the other complementary pairs of properties that particles can possess: waves and particles, energy and time, or continuity and discontinuity. Fixing our attention on any one property of any pair always makes the other property become fuzzy and indeterminate.

David Bohm later pointed out that it is the same with our conscious attention in human situations. If we conduct an interview with a job applicant, for instance, we can ask them a series of detailed, factual questions and compile a written report of their skills and past work experience, but when the applicant leaves the room we won't have gained much sense of them as a personality. Or, if instead, we conduct the interview as an informal chat intended to gauge what kind of person they are, they will then leave the room with our knowing few actual facts about them. In our organizations, we often find we must choose between laying down rigid rules and tight structure, or allowing things to creatively self-organize. Tight structure gives us control, but it loses us the benefits of innovation.

The other, and perhaps most important, lesson leaders can take away from Heisenberg's Uncertainty Principle is that the questions we ask give us the answers that we get. If we ask different questions, we get different answers. More importantly, we can see that asking good questions is like dropping a bucket into a well of potential answers, and then bringing some of those back to the surface with our rope. But given the co-creative relationship in quantum physics between the observer and the observed, between the question and its answer, we can see that the art of asking good questions is more like dropping that bucket into the sea of quantum potentiality and then bringing up a bucketful of new reality. Questions don't just *fetch* answers; questions *create* answers. And for this reason, we will see later that a quantum organization is an organization that fosters and encourages questions—and questioning!

A PARTICIPATORY UNIVERSE

One of the reasons for so many people feeling powerless today is that we feel we have little or no influence or control over how events in this world unfold. Even in democracies, citizens often have the sense that their vote doesn't really count, that either the "system is rigged" or the politicians they elect won't do what they have promised anyway. In Newton's physics, there were grounds for this sense of powerlessness on a cosmic scale. There simply was no place in his mechanistic universe for human beings, our consciousness, our intentions, our hopes, or dreams. Conscious creatures like ourselves were accidental bystanders in a universe wholly governed by the iron, deterministic laws of the clockwork universe. We could stand back and observe a world "out there," but our observations had not the slightest effect on what we observed. The material world had its own reality, and obeyed its own laws, quite apart from what observers see or do, or indeed whether there even are any observers.

The discoveries of quantum physics changed all this, putting human consciousness and intention squarely at the center, not only of how the universe works, but even of what comes to exist in it. We have already seen that the way a scientist sets up his experimental apparatus determines the result his experiment will produce. The quantum observer stands *inside* his or her observations, and those observations themselves play an active role in bringing about the very reality they look at. According to quantum science, the observer and what he or she observes are one, co-creative, partnership in what *gets* observed. In a sense not yet fully understood, the quantum observer *makes* the world of his or her observations.

The unobserved world of the Implicate Order is a plethora of possibilities. We have already seen that Schrodinger's wave equation describes an infinite array of possible states into which any quantum entity may emerge. All this possibility becomes actuality only when the wave function comes into relationship with something in the environment that then makes one of its potentialities stand out as an existing thing in the Explicate Order—the world of daily reality. And the mere act of measurement—making an experimental observation, asking an experimental question, is one thing that teases a quantum entity into existence. Further, the *kind* of measurement that is made determines *which* kind of actuality will be plucked from the sea of infinite possibility. In other words, the observer *sees* what the observer *looks for.* As we learned from

Heisenberg's Uncertainty Principle, the questions we ask give us the answers that we get.

Thus, quantum physics tells us that we live in a *participatory universe* in which our questions, our projects, our experiments, our decisions, even our character, make the world we live in. This has enormous implications for our role *in* the world and our responsibility *for* the world, and we will explore these more fully in later chapters.

CHAPTER 4

What Is Quantum Management?

"Taylorism," the basis for all modern management theory, took its inspiration and its organizational model from the ideas and principles that defined seventeenth-century Newtonian physics. Just as Newton saw the universe as a giant machine, so Taylor urged the organization should function as a well-oiled machine, divided into atomistic separate "divisions," controlled from the top, and organized with well-defined bureaucratic rules. Quantum Management, by contrast, takes its inspiration from quantum physics and the basic principles according to which all quantum systems organize themselves. It proposes that the organization is best understood as a conscious, living system, as a *biological system.* Living quantum systems (all of organic life, including ourselves) are called "complex adaptive systems" (CADs), and are featured in the breakthrough work of complexity science. Complexity science itself is an offspring of the larger quantum paradigm. CADs are holistic, constantly evolving and redefining themselves through co-creative dialogue between the constituent elements and co-creative dialogue with the external environment. CADs are also self-organizing, and any imposition of control from outside or from "the top" alienates the constituent parts and destroys the creativity of the system. Thus, we will see in the next chapter when we look at the implementation of Quantum Management Theory in actual business practice that it demands both hands-off, non-directive leadership and the removal of stifling bureaucracy.

© The Author(s) 2022   41
D. Zohar, *Zero Distance,*
https://doi.org/10.1007/978-981-16-7849-3_4

Because Quantum Management is dealing with human systems, a necessary part of the theory argues that the purposes, values, aspirations, and motivations of people working in an organization, and the emergent organizational culture, must be seen as part of its system dynamics. This is an important way in which both quantum physics itself and Quantum Management differ from Newtonian physics and Taylorian management. In ancient Greek philosophy, Aristotle's theory of causation included a Final Cause, or purpose, when explaining any action of event, and the notion that even physical systems have purpose embraces the implication of associated motivations and values. But in both modern Western philosophy and in Newton's mechanistic physics, which assumed a Cartesian separation between mind and body, physical systems were thought of only in terms of their form, function, and outcome. In Taylorian management, the company has the form and function of a machine, and its only desired outcome is the generation of profit. Quantum physics, by contrast, eradicates the sharp boundary between mind and matter, between the outcome of an experiment and the consciousness, or purpose, of the scientist who conducts it. Thus we will see that a quantum company leader *begins* by asking, "What is our purpose? What are our values? What motivations must drive our people?" and that purpose, while always including the necessary outcome of generating a profit, is based on wider moral and ethical considerations that derive from the company's responsibility to its employees, customers, and the surrounding environment, both social and natural (Fig. 4.1).

HUMAN SYSTEMS THRIVE BEST AS NATURAL SYSTEMS

The Taylorian company, like everything else in the Newtonian paradigm, saw itself as an artificial human construct distanced from Nature and its ways. Indeed, these companies viewed Nature as a *resource*, something to be conquered and exploited, something to be used. They also saw themselves as islands onto themselves, each company pursuing its own best profit interests and oblivious to both the needs of its own employees and to those of the surrounding communities (local, national, and global) and to any impact on the earth's environment. Even customer needs were a resource to be manipulated and exploited. And the company at its best was a well-oiled machine controlled by a central mechanism (command and control leadership from the top and mediated through a system of tight bureaucratic structures and rules). Everything and everyone in

QUANTUM SYSTEMS	CAD'S
Spontaneous Organization	Self-Organizing
Indeterminism	Bounded Instability
Emergent	Evolutionary
Holistic	Holistic
Contextual	In Dialogue with Environment; Adaptive
Potentiality	Evolutionary Mutations
Wave Function "Collapse"	Outside Control Destructive
Heisenberg Uncertainty Principle	Exploratory
Create New Realities	Recontextualize Environment
Negative & Positive Cosmic Forces	Order Out of Chaos
Driven Towards Complexity	Evolutionary; Driven Towards Growth
Emergent	Emergent
Decoherence	Outside Control Destructive

Fig. 4.1 Features of quantum systems and complex adaptive systems

the Taylorian company was in its place, and that place was determined by its usefulness to the single-minded pursuit of maximum profit and shareholder value (Fig. 4.1).

But now we see these Taylorian companies struggling, and often failing, in a world defined by uncertainty, rapid change, and an undeniable connectivity with supposed externalities like climate and economic instability, health pandemics, and the socio-economic conditions in "distant" regions and countries—all of which affect customer choice, demand, and availability. Internally, these companies are also struggling with employees, often now better educated, demanding not just better pay and working conditions but also intangibles like purpose, meaning, and more scope to realize their own potential. Employee attrition rates are high and expensive and strikes disruptive. Companies designed to create and maintain siloed separation internally and assuming a safe distance from everything around them cannot remain sustainable in today's world of Zero Distance.

The quantum paradigm teaches us both that everything is entangled with everything else and that all things are systems, systems within systems, within systems. We human systems are not distinct constructs set apart from and different to Nature, but rather in every way part of Nature and bound up with the health, balance, & and vitality of natural systems themselves. If natural systems become unbalanced and fall ill, our human bodies fall ill, and then those same human bodies, now in the role of employees and customers, cease to meet the needs of companies and the economies that rely on them. And so the companies "fall ill." When companies fail, jobs and tax revenue are lost, economies suffer, the quality of individual lives and the social structures of communities suffer, and the entire human ecosystem comes under strain. Everything is connected to everything, every element of the system depends upon the balance and health of the system as a whole. Nature "knows" that, and our company leaders need to learn it, and respond accordingly.

Quantum Management recognizes that human systems like companies function best when led, managed, and structured to function like natural, biological systems. Its defining principles for achieving this are the same defining principles that make CADs adaptive, sustainable, and creative. These are the eight quantum principles outlined in the previous chapter and then expressed as they are in all living quantum systems. The promise of Quantum Management is that if human systems like companies follow the organizing principles of CADs, they, too, will achieve sustainability and creative evolution by adapting to both internal and external system cues through co-creative dialogue between elements of the internal company system (employee needs, skills, and potential, leadership, company structure and culture, R&D research) and elements of the external environmental system (technological developments, the socio-political environment, the earth's environment, available resources, customer needs, and market potentialities). In short, quantum organizations can be managed in a completely scientific way.

The Defining Principles of Quantum Management

- **Self-Organizing**: The quantum universe itself is self-organizing. There is no top-down "blueprint" that laid out a program for cosmic creation and evolution. Each new creative relationship that is formed evolves out of already existing relationships and then takes its shape in response to the surrounding environment. There is a direction, or "way" ("purpose") of cosmic evolution that leads to the creation of ever greater complexity, more order, and more information. Closer to home, the complex adaptive systems (CADs) that complexity science has discovered underpin all organic life, including our own human bodies, form themselves according to their own inner logic, and then evolve in a self-organizing, adaptive way that ensures both survival (sustainability) and growth, or creativity. Each element of the system is "attuned" to all other elements and constantly adapts to both internal system changes and needs and to external factors in the surrounding environment, such as temperature, available sunlight, and available resources. These organic CADs embrace all the basic design principles of quantum physics itself and are, for all practical purposes, living quantum systems.

As I said above, so long as a CAD is allowed to live and evolve in its own self-organizing way, it will always sustain itself and grow in accordance with its designated life-span. That is its "purpose." But if such a system is subjected to any kind of outside control, the constituent elements of the system become "alienated" from each other and the system loses its own self-organizing capacity. It then becomes ill, and usually dies. There is no bureaucracy in Nature, no top-down control.

Complexity theorists are now applying the principles of CADs to human systems like the economy, companies, and cities, indicating that these all function best when left to self-organize and evolve in a naturally adaptive way. This is critical to Quantum Management Theory as it discusses the leadership, structure, and management of quantum companies, quantum societies, and quantum cities, and advocates ridding these systems of top-down control and bureaucratic structure. This means that one important principle of quantum leadership is, as I have said: *hands off!*

As we will see more deeply in later chapters, the key elements in human systems are the purposes, values, and motivations of their human constituents. If these are positive, they will pump positive energy into the system and ensure its sustainability and growth. The system, say a company, will be internally harmonious (coherent) and will naturally and flexibly adapt to challenges and opportunities in its external environment. If, however, the purposes, values, and motivations driving a company's activities are negative, the resulting negative energy being poured into the system will lead to internal disharmony (decoherence) and its external adaptive capacity will diminish. Thus any attempt to implement Quantum Management Theory in a real company (or city or society) will involve work with purposes, values, and motivations—both in leadership circles and in every individual employee (or citizen). Such things, obviously, are aspects of a company's culture, and therefore in the creation of a quantum company, building a strong and positive company culture is a priority consideration.

- **Holistic, System Thinking**: We have seen that in the quantum universe, everything is connected to everything, "entangled" with everything, and a principle of Zero Distance applies in every quantum system and in the cosmic quantum system as a whole. We are always part of a larger, systemic whole, and both the driving principles and the needs of that whole are within each of us. If we want to be in tune with ourselves, we must be in tune with the larger whole, and in its own self-organizing wisdom, that whole will be in tune with our own real needs. We are always "elements" of a system, and if we are to lead our lives in a way that ensures sustainability and growth, we must do so with system intelligence.

In the case of companies, the internal system comprises all people who work in the company, their skills, knowledge, and intelligence, *and their potential*—for constant adaptation, discovery, creativity, and growth. The sustainability and growth of the company are ensured only if the best interests of all who work in it are ensured—their health and safety, their remuneration, and their ability to find meaning in their work that ensures productivity and loyalty to the system. The whole company system suffers if any member suffers, and all members will suffer if the company system as a whole fails to achieve sustainability and growth. Quantum holism and systems thinking gives real meaning to the expression, "We are all in this together."

But any company system is also part of, is embedded within, larger, external systems. The Taylorian notion that a company is an island onto itself and that its leader need only consider the interests of its shareholders is as out of date as Newtonian atomism itself. A company's external systems (the trendy word is its "ecosystem") obviously require consideration of customer satisfaction and loyalty, which depend upon both product and service quality and affordability. But post-Covid experience is bringing home now to even the most tunnel-visioned business leaders that other externalities like the health and stability of society, indeed the health and stability of the entire global community, the vagaries of climate change, population migration patterns and regulations, global stability and cooperation, and a need for some degree of cooperation even with competitors all have a direct impact on a company's viability and success. Some business leaders are almost screaming today, "I have a company to run. Don't tell me it is my business to save the world!" But it is a central argument of this book, indeed a central *reason* for this book, that in the Zero Distance world of our Quantum Age, the way leaders run their companies does have a very large role to play in whether our world system as a whole will experience sustainability and growth or suffer illness, and possibly death.

So yes, it is the primary responsibility of a business leader to run his/her company and to make it profitable, but holism tells us the *way* this is done, the purposes, values, and motivations embedded in the company culture and then reflected in company decisions and performance, the questions about who and what the company serves, and what role the company is playing in the larger ecosystem, all come back to impact on company success and profitability. Just as the whole company thrives only if each person who works in the company thrives, and vice versa, so too a company will realize sustainability and growth only if the whole world system of which it is a part thrives. "We are all in this together."

- **Relationships Matter (Contextualism)**: We saw in the last chapter that the quantum universe is not a universe of cause and effect, but rather a universe both created and governed by relationships. And I commented there that instead of asking, "What caused our problem?" company leaders should ask, "What is wrong with our relationships?" If company strategists have a desired outcome or goal, they should ask, "What relationships do we need to build to achieve this?" In today's interconnected and interdependent world that makes an everyday reality of zero distance quantum entanglement, close, cooperative, win/win relationships are necessary to system success—both internally and externally. Thus Quantum Management calls upon companies to rid themselves of borders and boundaries (siloed departments and functions), rid themselves of hierarchy, and rid themselves of the stranglehold of bureaucracy— to break out of Weber's "iron cage.". I am reminded of the stirring lyrics of a Door's song that cry out, "Break on through, break on through, break on through to the other side!" This, too, has structural implications for how to implement Quantum Management. How do we design a Zero Distance company?

- **Experiment!** (**Heisenberg's "Ask Questions"**): In quantum physics, remember, questions create their own answers. I, the questioner (a scientist making a measurement), exist in the Explicate Order of here and now actuality. But my question will pluck out one possible answer from the infinite potential of the quantum Implicate Order. Ask a different question (set up my measuring apparatus in a different way), and I will get a different possible answer. Thus, the more questions I ask, the more answers, or new actualities/outcomes, I will create. Asking a question is like dropping an empty bucket into a well and then bringing up a bucketful of water.

  All science itself is driven by the activities of ceaselessly asking questions and then seeking answers to these questions through ceaseless experiments. Drawing from this lesson, scientific Quantum Management advises people in companies constantly to ask many questions. These questions may take the form of thought experiments in forming an array of possible decisions or strategies, or they may be actual experiments with new products, services, markets, or supply chains. Pursuing multiple questions in this way not only stokes creativity and innovation, but of course it also spreads risk. If a company puts an array of products or services out to an array of trial markets, it is not "putting all its eggs in one basket." The same is true with imagining an array of possible decisions or strategies. The future is uncertain, black swans are frequent, and market taste can be fickle. Better to have ready cache of responses to these uncertain outcomes, thus thriving on uncertainty rather than fearing it. Achieving this is the central reason that leaders are now talking about making their companies agile. This Quantum Management principle has implications for the best way to structure a quantum company, which we will explore in greater depth in the next chapter when we discuss how to implement Quantum Management in a practical business model.

- **Get the Energy Right**: The quantum universe and every existing thing within it, including ourselves and our social systems, is made of energy. My argument in this book is that companies are energy systems. Any energy system can get blocked or out of balance, and this can happen in companies. In Chinese traditional medicine, the human body is viewed as a "*chi*" or energy system, and the purpose of acupuncture treatment is to clear blockages in the flow of *chi*, and thus to restore health. We cannot apply acupuncture needles to our company systems, but we can do the equivalent by recognizing the "map" of energy flow in a company, noticing vital points in the system where this energy may be blocked, and then working out why it has become so. In the universe itself there is both a source of negative, destructive energy, entropy, which pulls systems apart and dissipates their order into chaos, and a source of positive, creative energy that causes new relationships to form and then out of these new order and new information to be created. In thermodynamic systems, order is born out of chaos, so even negative energy, if properly channeled and transformed, plays a creative role. We will see in Chapter 6 that psychologists and counselors who do "shadow work" realize that less attractive features of our personalities can be sources of positive transformation.

In human social systems like companies and societies, the motivations that drive our behavior are the energy drivers of the system. Negative motivations like greed, fear, or anger can dissipate a company's energy system and thus cause dysfunction, and when we look in detail at The Scale of Motivations in Chapter 8, we will see that such negative motivations dominate the cultures of business-as-usual companies. But in quantum companies where all employees are aligned with the company's own sense of positive purpose and higher values, greed can become inner power, fear can become mastery, and anger can become a desire to cooperate. In short, by getting all members of the company system practicing/promoting a collective sense of purpose and values, negative energy can be transformed into positive energy, and dysfunction into synchrony and success. The company then functions as a CAD, becoming both sustainable and creative. Bringing about such energy transformation and thus smooth system energy flow is a critical priority of Quantum Management. It requires both initial and then constant attention to raising and keeping employee and leadership motivations on the positive end of the scale, always noticing and understanding when and why these fall back into being negative.

It is also the case that companies share an energy field with their customers or users, and even with the wider societies in which they are doing business. If employee morale or motivation is low, this negative energy will impact on customer response and satisfaction, both through poorer customer service and lower quality goods or services. Equally, because all people who work in companies are also members of wider society, social disquiet, unrest, or a sense of collective depression will impact on company morale and thus function. Companies may be able to combat such social contamination by creating a strong internal culture of cooperation, trust, and positive achievement, and then this in turn can flow back into society as a healing force, just as one very positive, upbeat person can energize and motivate a group of listless people. Remember, in our quantum world, everything is connected to everything, and thus everything impacts everything else.

- **No Unimportant People**: As is equally true in the participatory quantum universe, in individual quantum systems, and in CADs, every element of the system has its unique and important role. It has its purpose in the system. If any element were missing, the system would be different, and might become dysfunctional. Try to imagine an atom without protons, or a human body without kidneys. They would not survive. As complexity scientist Geoffrey West says, "Changing just one component of a CAS without fully understanding its multilevel spatiotemporal dynamics usually leads to unintended consequences."[1]

The equivalent principle in Quantum Management is that there are no unimportant people, no "less important" jobs. This is just one important sense in which quantum companies are non-hierarchical. The CEO would be lost without his/her PA, without his/her secretary or driver. Their office would be an unsightly and dusty mess without its cleaner, and trips to the toilet would be unpleasant if these were not cleaned. Everyone in the company would go hungry without the cook, and the cook could not function unless there were people to wash the dishes. And ironically, it is often these "little people," these "invisible people" that know or notice things their "superiors" don't. They overhear conversations, they witness events and behavior, sometimes they even envisage solutions to problems or have ideas that would make the whole company system function more effectively. If included in the company's mission and sense of

---

[1] Geoffrey West, *Scale*, p. 204.

purpose, if their value and their potential are recognized, they can be a glue that holds the company together. And the same is true in a quantum society. If "the people" are sound, the society will prosper.

• **A Sense of Purpose**: The quantum universe has a clear sense of direction. By constantly creating new relationships between constituent elements, it is always creating new order and new information, always growing richer and realizing new potentialities. CADs, too, have a clear sense of direction. They want to sustain themselves while constantly evolving, or growing. The Quantum Management equivalent of this drive toward growth is found in a company's sense of purpose. Why does this company exist? What is this company *for*? What is its mission? Whom or what does it serve? Companies that have a clearly defined sense of purpose that answers such questions have integrity and meaning. Their people, though numerous, and their activities, though varied, share a common culture and common goals, they "pull together" like the metallic elements in a magnetic field. A sense of purpose permeates every person, activity, service, and product in a company in the same way that the ground state energy field of the Quantum Vacuum permeates every existing thing in the universe. It is the "sea" upon which all boats sail, with their compasses pointing to true North. Like the Vacuum itself, this is a sea of potentiality, the font of the company's growth and evolution into the future. It is also the brand with which customers or users will identify and to which they will give their loyalty. In a quantum society, too, it is a shared sense of meaning and purpose that binds the society together and drives its energy. It gives its flag meaning and grounds its many customs.

Finally, as I said in the Introduction, Quantum Management is not just another theory of management. In the first place, it is a new *paradigm* for management. But it is also a philosophy of life and a new philosophy of leadership, founded on values and moral principles, a way of life, that underpins an entirely different way of thinking about what it means to be a person, an employee, a leader, a citizen. It changes how we view the organization, and even how we think about the nature of work itself.

Newtonian	Taylorian	Quantum	Quantum Company
Mechanical	Company: a Machine	Adaptive System	Conscious Living System
Atomistic	Siloed Functions	Holistic; Entangled	Networked Organizations
Deterministic	Bureaucratic; Rule-Bound	Spontaneous; Self-Organizing	Self-Organizing
Particle OR Wave	Particle-Like; Division of Labor	Both Particle AND Wave	Employees: Individuals And Team Members
One Best Way	One Best Way; Simple Point of View	Superposition of Multiple Potentialities	Multi-Functional Teams; Many Points of View
React to Forces	Reactive	In Dialogue With Environment	Responsive; Agile; Adaptive
Observers Passive Witnesses	Employees Passive; Units of Production	Participatory Universe	Employees Co-Creative Partners
Isolated	Company Isolated from Environment	Contextual	In Dialogue With Environment Customers; An Ecosystem
Absolute	Leader Knows Best; No Questions	Heisenberg; Questions Determine Answer	Encourages Questions

Fig. 4.2 Newtonian physics and Taylorian companies vs quantum physics and quantum companies

- QM is *meaningful* management;
- QM is *dynamic* management;
- QM is *agile* management
- QM is *ethical* management;
- QM is *purposeful* management;
- QM is *zero distance* management (Fig. 4.2).

CHAPTER 5

Implementing Quantum Management: The *RenDanHeyi/*Zero Distance Business Model

Haier, China was the first large, global company in the world to imple-ment Quantum Management Theory, in its own *RenDanHeyi* Manage-ment Model, and its undoubted success in doing so has proven that the theory can work in practice, in a real company. Other compa-nies, discussed later in this book, have now followed Haier's pioneering example and adopted Quantum Management as implemented by their own adaptations of the *RenDanHeyi* model. Because no theory has much value unless it can be implemented in practice and produce real results, it is important we look closely here at the origin and nature of *RenDanHey* as an example of Quantum Management in practice, and view it as a generic organizational model drawing from Quantum Management theory that can be adapted for use in many spheres. Indeed, my faith that implementing *RenDanheyi* is a positive and meaningful way of changing the world for the better, is what this book is about.

Haier is the world's largest supplier of domestic appliances and a leading actor in the Internet of Things (IoT) sector, directly employing more than 75,000 people in China alone, and another 27,000 globally, but today the company is better known for the revolutionary *RenDan-Heyi* Management Model than for its appliances. Indeed, because of the almost infinite expansion allowed by that model, Haier has now moved well beyond simply manufacturing appliances into products and services such as clothing, food, agriculture, biotechnology and health

© The Author(s) 2022
D. Zohar, *Zero Distance,*
https://doi.org/10.1007/978-981-16-7849-3_5

care, and this expansion is continuing. While traditionally managed Taylorian companies have realized an annual growth of 1.1% during recent years, since fully implementing *RenDanHeyi* in 2012, Haier has realized a 23% annual growth. And while, with the exception of the big e-commerce companies, nearly every large retail company in the world suffered major losses and contraction during and as a result of the Covid-19 crisis, the unique features of its *RenDanHeyi* model saw Haier back in full production by mid-February 2020, and achieving growth as the crisis played out while others were contracting.

Haier's CEO, Zhang Ruimin, who conceived the *RenDanHeyi* model—and who is cited by Corporate Rebels as "arguably the leading management strategist of modern times"—claims it has universal application in any industry (see Chapter 15, which explores in more detail how Haier itself implements *RenDanHeyi*). My own claim for *RenDanHeyi* is broader still than that. I believe that the defining, *generic* principles of the model—a network of self-organizing, self-governing, and self-motivating micro-units serviced by platforms and united in a common purpose and by common values and a common strategic vision—offer a revolutionary organizational model, per se, particularly suited to the realities of the Quantum Age.

In following chapters of this book, I will be illustrating how it suggests a new way to realize more potential in ourselves as individuals, a new way to organize and govern cities and societies, even a new way to educate our children, and perhaps the basis for a new kind of global order. I also believe that the organizing principles of the *RenDanHeyi* model combine the best qualities of both East (collectivism and harmony) and West (dynamic individualism), while discouraging their less beneficial extremes, thus making it a potential vehicle for greater East/West understanding and collaboration.

THE MODEL

RenDanHeyi (roughly pronounced as "RenDanHyoy") is translated by Haier to mean "the value to the employee is aligned with the value to the user," and this emphasis on an alignment between people who are partners in a win/win relationship is critical to the deeper philosophical roots of the model. A play on the famous Taoist mantra *Tian Ren Heyi*, "Man aligned with Heaven," this emphasizes the model's deep commitment to alignments of various kinds, reflecting the Taoist view that when

Man is aligned with Heaven, and then brings the power of this alignment to his projects and activities on Earth, such alignment brings maximum benefit and harmony to the whole of humanity. This basic harmonizing principle, found in all ancient China's philosophies, is the root of a thousand year old Chinese preference, still very much alive today, for win/win solutions in matters of both business and diplomacy, something I believe is not properly understood about China in the West today.

Tian Ren Heyi and its Heaven/Man/Earth Triad as an inspiration for *RenDanHeyi* may also explain why Zhang Ruimin himself was also drawn to look for inspiration and guidance in science, particularly quantum physics and complexity science, while conceiving his model. Taoism holds that there is one Way (the *Tao*) for all things in the universe, just as modern science holds that all things in the universe follow the laws of physics, although both the Tao and the laws of quantum physics themselves constantly adapt as the systems in which they operate evolve. As the subtitle of complexity scientist's Geoffrey West book, *Scale*, expresses it, "One law for the universe, organisms, cities, and companies." Perhaps doctors' advice to politicians during the Covid-19 pandemic to "Follow the science!" is good advice to company leaders also. The whole premise of this book is that it is, and *RenDanHeyi* does so.

RenDanHeyi also expresses the very Taoist and quantum insight that we live in a Zero Distance world of entanglement where everything is connected to everything and that no part of a system can thrive unless all parts of the system thrive. In this case, *RenDanHeyi* is saying that the employees (*Ren*) of a company, indeed the company itself, cannot thrive and enjoy value unless the customers/users (*Dan*) it serves thrive and enjoy value from (are aligned with, *Heyi*) their products and services. Having borrowed the term from the writings of Peter Drucker, the *RenDanHeyi* Model is also known as the "Zero Distance Model," as befits any Quantum Management model.

Just like Quantum Management itself, *RenDanHeyi* embraces a philosophy of leadership, a whole philosophy of life, and a set of values. The driving philosophical principle underpinning *RenDanHeyi* is a deep respect for human dignity, the autonomy of the individual, and a belief that all autonomous individuals are unique and each has the potential to create his or her own distinctive value if allowed freedom to do so. Newtonian/Taylorian companies, which treat the employee as a tool or resource of management, there to do its bidding as told, rob employees of this dignity, autonomy, and potential. This both defeats the possibility of employees finding meaning, joy, or a sense of purpose in work, and denies companies all that lost potential, including lost motivational potential, resulting in less innovation and lower productivity. The entire structure of *RenDanHeyi* is designed to implement this wider philosophical view in practice. We will look at the generic characteristics of each of its defining principles now, and see how it is that each represents quantum principles in action.

BOTTOM-UP REPLACES TOP-DOWN

Zhang Ruimin says that his motivation to derive a new management model was his strong belief that traditional management theories are no longer relevant today and must be reinvented. Taylorism, and Adam Smith's praise for the division of labor which it incorporates, were designed for the age of the machine, steam engines and internal combustion engines, and the more simple, atomistic, and deterministic, thus predictable, age made wealthy by that kind of technology. Machines are designed by blueprint, consist of simple, separate parts, and operate according to simple, fixed rules, just as companies and other organizations intended to function as no-surprise machines are governed by design from the top and structured according to the iron rules of bureaucracy into siloed functions enabled by workers who will do as they are told, like good machines themselves. But as we have seen, the twenty-first century is an age of uncertainty, rapid change, and interconnectivity, the age of the Internet and the Internet-of-Things (IoT) (everyday objects embedded with devices that enable them to communicate via the Internet), and this new age is enabled by quantum technology and all its associated complexity. Also, today's employees are better skilled and better educated, and have far more potential to offer their companies than serving as mere robots.

Quantum technologies such as the Internet, like the physics on which they are based, eradicate borders and boundaries with their essential interconnectedness, give rise to unplanned self-organization on which it thrives, and have infinite potential constantly to generate emergent, unpredictable disruptions. This demands a management model that is itself sufficiently flexible and adaptable to absorb uncertainty and the shocks of constant disruption and to thrive on the opportunities they offer. This is what makes Zhang Ruimin say that, "In the future, all management must be Quantum Management," and why *RenDanHeyi* is an excellent means to implementing it.

- *Goodbye to Bureaucracy, Middle Management, & Borders*: Although many business leaders agree with management guru Gary Hamel's saying that bureaucracy "saps initiative, inhibits risk taking, crushes creativity, and is a tax on human achievement,"[1] they maintain it is a necessary evil for managing large companies, and continue to embrace its stranglehold, and the monster is growing. While the number of employees in big companies has increased by only 44% in recent years, the number of middle managers has grown by 100%. Most employees working in companies with a workforce of larger than 5000 are buried under eight levels of middle management. They are also assigned to fragmented, siloed functions and expected diligently to follow instructions as these filter down through the hierarchical chain of command. Power comes from the top and the employees, stifled by all that middle management and its endless rules, regulations, and forms, are treated as mindless robots. The result is not just squandered employee talent and potential, but also employee stress and boredom, low morale, lost man hours, and of course, low productivity and growth. Over the past 12–14 years, as we have just noted, the average annual growth in these bureaucratic monstrosities has been only 1.1%, while, by contrast, over that same period of time, Haier's *RenDanHeyi* implementation has delivered 23% annual growth, with increased annual revenue of 20%.

    The first rule of *RenDanHeyi* is to get rid of all bureaucracy and clear out the middle managers. Make the organization lean and agile. The whole idea of linear management goes out the door with this, including all power coming from the top. At Haier itself, today, there are only two layers of management between the CEO and front-line employees. Next, get rid of the siloed, monopolized functions and their borders between employees and replace them with multi-functional, cooperating teams empowered to make decisions, take responsibility, draft strategies, conceive products and/or services, cooperate with each other, and communicate

---

[1] Gary Hamel, "The End of Bureaucracy," *Harvard Business Review*, November–December 2018, p. 52.

directly with customers/users. After firing 12,000 middle-managers, Haier divided itself into 4000 independent "micro-enterprises," referred to as MEs. Those now unwanted middle managers were given the choice to join the new model as entrepreneurs running their own MEs, or let Haier help them find jobs elsewhere. But countering that original loss of so many jobs, the *RenDanHeyi* transformation has since created tens of thousands of new jobs.

• *Self-Organized, Self-Motivated, Self-Rewarding*: In quantum systems, any kind of outside influence or intervention "collapses the wave function," i.e., eliminates potentiality. In complex adaptive systems (living quantum systems, including human bodies and human social systems), outside intervention or top-down control destroys the interconnectedness/holism and creativity of the system, eliminating natural evolution (growth) and limiting sustainability. Thus in *RenDanHeyi*, bosses do not assign people to the independent teams, or micro-enterprises (MEs), do not tell teams what or how to do, do not dictate how teams are composed, or give them fixed goals they must achieve. Instead, the teams are self-organized and self-selecting and work toward more long-term, all-embracing targets.

At Haier, each micro-enterprise has the "Three Rights" normally kept by senior management in a hierarchical company: (1) the right to set its own strategy, decide its own priorities, how to achieve its targets, and what partnerships it wants to make; (2) the right to hire its own employees, assign them their roles, and decide on cooperative relationships; (3) the right to set the pay rates of each team member and how to distribute bonuses among them. As is the case with sub-atomic particles within the atom, each member of an ME team is able to change their identity (role/function) to stand-in-for or replace another when challenges or opportunities facing the team system require this. Indeed, even MEs can come and go, as some fail and new opportunities arise.

At Haier itself, which has a company purpose to make everyone an entrepreneur and to give each employee the opportunity to achieve his or her full potential, each of these self-organizing micro-enterprises is a small independent company in its own right, with its own CEO, offering its own products and services, owned by its members, creating and communicating with its own customers, motivated both by a wish to see their company succeed and, thus, to bring value to their customers/users, and rewarded both by a sense of personal achievement and by their ability to keep most of their own company profit and share it among themselves as they choose. Most employees at Haier are paid directly by their customers rather than by receiving salaries from the company. At Roche Pharma India (Chapter 18), the independent, self-organizing sales teams found reward in the greatly enhanced sense of meaning and purpose their jobs now had, and in their personal ability to decide and design the services they could offer to doctors and their patients.

Again, at Haier, there are three types of MEs/micro-enterprises: (1) market-facing MEs that deal directly with users wanting the company's range of traditional appliances, though constantly transforming these products in dialogue with changing customer needs and newly available technology; (2) "incubating MEs" that are constantly extending exploring new business opportunities and extending Haier's product and service lines into new areas such as e-gaming, biotechnology, health care, etc., and (3) node MEs that supply component parts, or services like marketing or human resources to the market-facing ME's. Others connect traditional Haier appliance products like smart refrigerators or smart wine coolers to other companies offering food or wine products so that these commodities can be delivered to users in rapid time. These kinds of collaborative activities, and even partnerships based on "temporary contracts" with other companies have now been hugely extended with Haier's recent move into offering its users "scenarios" and "Eco-System Brands," which I will discuss below.

Generically, I believe the *RenDanHeyi* model of small, independent, self-organizing micro-entities or teams can be adapted to how community services can be offered in cities, to how both local and national health services can be provided, to how national and global infrastructure projects can be organized, and to how learning opportunities in schools and universities could be hugely broadened and kept both up to date and relevant to students' differing interests. We will explore some of this in later chapters.

- *Independent But Aligned*: On the surface, dividing a company or any other organization into thousands of independent, self-organizing entities might sound like a recipe for fragmentation and anarchy. But the *RenDanHeyi* model makes Haier a coherent, well-coordinated organization that ensures cooperation and alignment between all 4000 of its operating micro-entities. A strong, central operational system was designed for the entire conglomerate as a first priority. Senior management ensures a company culture that sets common standards and values, common operating procedures, and kpis (key performance indicators) for every ME and its members, and delivers an ever-evolving common strategic direction for the company as a whole. A network of service platforms, each also independent and owned by the platform entrepreneur, and each bringing together more than 50 MEs, act as facilitators for coordinating cooperation between the differing MEs, arranging collaborative discussions, and making them aware of joint entrepreneurial opportunities.

Platform owners thus serve the MEs with such facilitation, and also provide the wider service benefits, including start-up resources when needed, of a large company to the much smaller MEs, which then function more like start-ups. They guide and facilitate, but never command. But platform owners are also entrepreneurs in their own right, selling their services to the company's vast internal market, having their own growth targets, and the responsibility of looking for ever more opportunities to create new MEs.

Another level of system coordination is provided by "integration nodes" that exist within each platform. These ensure an integrated supply of component parts from all manufacturing MEs in the company, provide new competence skills to MEs about such things as smart manufacturing and big data marketing information, administrative services, etc.

These central coordinating structures provide the always necessary, Newtonian "particle aspect" of any quantum organization, while the self-organizing independence of the individual MEs provides the "wave aspect"—thus giving *RenDanHeyi* the dual benefit of any quantum system's both/and, wave/particle duality.

- *The Customer/User Is Now the Boss.* *RenDanHeyi* insists that the core competency that any organization must have is an ability to create value for its customers/users. Organizational purpose and success begin and end with a continuing ability to meet ever-evolving user needs. Thus the model requires Zero Distance between the employees who make, sell, and service products and the users who buy them. "Employees must know their users better than they know themselves," says Zhang Ruimin, and this in turn requires a constant, co-creative dialogue between them via every means available—telephone, internet surveys and conversations, user feedback mechanisms, face-to-face meetings, and even home visits where relevant. The user should always feel the employee is "at his/her service," contactable, and interested.

RenDanHeyi assumes that users are partners of the organization, sometimes even becoming employees themselves, whose feedback and suggestions inspire new product and service developments, thus stoking the fires of innovation. Some adaptations of the model, such as Haier's own, allow for users to share the profit or advantages of a suggested new product or service, themselves becoming user-entrepreneurs. This is an implementation of the co-creative quantum relationship between the observer and the observed which tells us that in observing and questioning reality, *relating to* reality's potential, we make reality "happen," we turn the possible into the actual. Through observing, discussing, and relating to user needs and suggestions, the employee and the user together cocreate innovative realities.

- *Relationships Make the Organization*: We have seen that our quantum universe is literally made of relationships, and thus it is relationships that make reality. There are even "particles of relationship," called *bosons*, described by quantum physics as the "glue" that holds everything together. All four of the Fundamental Forces—gravity, electro-magnetism, the strong and weak nuclear forces—are *made* out of bosons, and in a proper understanding of how the universe works, the word "force" itself must really be understood as "the presence of a relationship." And built into the term *RenDanHeyi* itself, too, is this understanding of a fundamental, defining relationship between the employee and the customer/user similar to the role feedback loops play in cybernetic theory. Thus any company or organization implementing the *RenDanHeyi* management model sees that its fundamental organizing principle must be the building of Zero Distance relationships.

In the big e-commerce companies like Amazon and Alibaba, multiple independent companies are serviced by common e-platforms, but there is no relationship between the various companies served, and each has only transactional relationships with its own customers. We have seen that *RenDanHeyi* makes an "up close and personal" relationship between the micro-enterprises and their users a first priority, but it also mandates cultivating cooperative, co-creative Zero Distance relationships between all the company's micro-enterprises. At the very least, there should be shared knowledge throughout the networked system of what others are doing. There must be opportunities for cross micro-enterprise discussions and a sharing of ideas to cross-fertilize innovation throughout the system. There must be a cultural sense of belonging together for the shared purpose of creating value, for the user, for themselves, for each other, for the company as a whole, and for all the other players in the company's system of relationships—share-holders, the community, the planet, etc.

- *Open Innovation*: Most companies and other organizations are very secretive about their research for innovation. Innovative ideas are seen as company capital, and everything is done to stop possible competitors "stealing" it. But *RenDanHeyi*, which sees the value of all relationships, calls for building a strong, co-creative relationship between company "insiders" and those "outsiders" in the surrounding environment. So Haier, for instance, does not just build Zero Distance relationships with its users to mine their needs and thoughts for innovative ideas, but instead goes much further in seeking the creative help of the entire outside community.

Both known problems facing company R&D, as well as appeals for "bright ideas" about new products or product features, are posted on social media for all to see and respond to. Sometimes as many as three million people respond to such requests for creative input that relates to a given problem with an existing product or the opportunity to create a new one. The company also communicates regularly with 400,000 "solvers," both individual experts and expert research institutions as it seeks advice, feedback, and ideas that will further innovation. Those individuals or institutions whose input is used in a successful new product or service are then rewarded with a share in any profit that will be realized. Some even join the company as heads of new ME's.

This "no borders" approach to innovation and creativity means that *RenDanHeyi* sees every citizen as a fellow partner or fellow entrepreneur, thus implementing the quantum principle that, because everything in our universe is entangled, because everything and everyone is part of everything and everyone else, there are no "outsiders," there are no "strangers." We are all part of one, larger, cooperative, and co-creative system. Gary Hamel observes that by putting its product development process online and thus open to all, "Haier has reduced the time from concept to market by up to 70%."[2] Imagine the benefits to global health if all the many institutions in the world's many countries that were seeking to discover and then to manufacture a vaccine for Covid-19 had followed the *RenDanHeyi* model!!

- *From Fear to Experiment and Innovation*: Psychological studies have shown that fear is the central motivation driving employees in large, bureaucratic companies and other organizations. A fear of making mistakes. A fear of upsetting the boss. A fear of rocking the boat. A fear of being fired. Thus most established companies follow the motto, "If it works, don't fix it." But this makes them essentially conservative and risk-averse, and risk aversion stifles innovation. Our quantum universe as a whole, and the living organisms within in it that we call complex adaptive systems, take risks all the time. They thrive on risks because the creative function of risks is built into their nature. Risks are experiments, risks are recce missions into the Future, they are the key to evolution and growth. And being itself a quantum model in practice, *RenDanHeyi* creates a system structure that accepts and thrives on risk.

Each *RenDanHeyi* micro-entity, because there are so many of them, is free to be an exploratory "finger into the future," behaving like one of the multiple "virtual transitions" that an atomic system throws out in preparation for a move to a different energy state. Each such virtual transition explores one possible path to the future state, and even if this is not ultimately the path the system will take, the virtual transition nonetheless has real effects in the real world as it conducts its trial run. Similarly, each of Haier's many ME projects may or may not succeed in the marketplace. If they do not, they are allowed to fail, without the larger company system suffering any significant consequences. But the failed experiment itself enriches the total system with the experience and knowledge gained through the experiment, and thus was worthwhile. Haier always gains from experimentation, while celebrating diversity and even thriving from any adversity that arises.

---

[2] Ibid., p. 57.

- *Ecosystems: A Superposition of Possibilities.* We have seen that the quantum universe is a system of systems. Even each individual quantum wave function is a system of superimposed possibilities, each a rich new reality waiting to happen. And these new realities come about as elements of the system form new relationships. *RenDanHeyi's* employment of ecosystem alliances gives a quantum company this same almost infinite potential to branch out by turning possibilities into new, combined realities in every direction. Many possibilities for many different ecosystem alliances and thus new opportunities are created with each new relationship. This gives a quantum organization the possibility of constant, endless growth, and even perhaps "eternal life."

  When Haier first introduced *RenDanHeyi* by dividing the company up into thousands of smaller micro-enterprises, it found that a kind of dog-eat-dog, zero-sum competition emerged between them. Each thought only of its own possible success. So very soon into the company's transformation, an ecosystem model of win/win cooperation was encouraged. It was quickly noticed that users very seldom came shopping for just one appliance, but rather that someone who purchased a new toaster would soon after, and perhaps simultaneously, order a new microwave and/or a new iron. Similarly, within Haier's own internal market, a market-facing ME needing a component part from one manufacturing ME also needed another from a second, and so on. MEs quickly learned that if they teamed up to form temporary partnerships, they could offer more "total solutions" to users, saving the users searching and shopping time and benefiting themselves from a combined market. Today, Haier is a network of cooperating ME's, sometimes as many as 400 at a time, forming temporary alliances to give users these desired total solutions. As in quantum holism itself, the whole (shared profit derived from the larger market) is greater than the sum of the parts (sold individually, one at a time).

  In 2019, Haier went even further with developing the ecosystem idea by introducing its new Eco-System Brand. Discovering as it went along that users liked buying its own products in combinations that would fill a multiplicity of needs, the company began offering whole "scenarios," such as its "balcony scenario." Originally thinking that people would use their balconies as a place to locate their washing machines, they soon discovered users would like to add a sofa, perhaps a mini sound system, even a piece or two of sporting equipment. The idea for the "balcony scenario" evolved from this, but that required reaching out to other companies, like the sporting goods company Decathlon, with the offer of a temporary contract to supply any such items as part of the new balcony scenario "product," and the whole combination was offered as an Eco-System Brand. The partnering companies negotiate a temporary contract through which each partner makes some profit from every item included in the scenario package (see more in Chapter 17). Now the borders fell, not just between individual functions and ME's within Haier, but between Haier and other companies. Haier now sees itself more as the "hub" of a vast multi-company network than as a mere "company," and the scenarios/Eco-System Brand benefit is key to its long-standing preference to aim for growing numbers of loyal customer numbers rather than concentrating on market share as a criterion of success. As Zhang Ruimin sums up this logic, "By fulfilling users every need, we are cultivating life-long users that will stay with us."

As in the quantum universe, with *RenDanHeyi*, everything is connected to everything and the whole system gains from a network of win/win solutions. In (Chapter 2), we looked at the quantum concept of "emergence," through which an entirely new reality arises from a relationship of constituent parts. We can now say that a quantum company like Haier "emerges" out of the relationships within its ecosystem. Indeed, each individual enterprise, through its relationships to the others in *RenDanHeyi*, acquires new, emergent possibilities. All both sustain themselves and grow at the same time. Now functioning like living organisms, they become "living companies." I will imagine this happening between nations on a global scale in (Chapter 22).

A Different Kind of Leadership

The Newtonian/Taylorian CEO or other leader is a powerful figure who has all the answers and calls all the shots, and he/she leads the organization from the top. But such power goes with the now-mistaken Newtonian understanding of force, something that works *on* people and events, something that can manipulate and control them. There are more questions than answers in today's world, and no one person can know all the answers and call all the shots amidst the complexity and disruptions that accompany the exponential technological changes and chaotic events we all experience now. A quantum/*RenDanHeyi* organization is designed to thrive on chaos, uncertainty, and rapid change, but to do so, it turns the familiar Taylorian pyramid of power on its head. Instead of the leader and senior management at the top, and employees at the bottom, the inverted *RenDanHeyi* pyramid puts employees at the top and management at the bottom. The leader gives up all power and instead assumes a role of service, offering support, resources, vision, and inspiration to those whom he/she leads. As Lao-tzu says in the *Tao te Ching*,

> The best soldier is not soldierly;
> The best fighter is not ferocious;
> The best conqueror does not take part in war;
> The best employer of men keeps himself below them.[3]

A complex system has many events happening all at once, and often these are disruptive. In today's complex market, there is a plethora of constantly changing or evolving user needs, in turn influenced by emerging technologies, socio/political events and, as we have just experienced, occasional global pandemics. There will be more as the challenges of climate change emerge. It takes "many hands on deck," with those hands at a Zero Distance from user needs, supply chains, and potential partners with whom necessary alliances can be made to keep up with all this complexity, and those many hands must have the power to make quick, local decisions and alliances as necessary. It was precisely because Haier had the very agile *RenDanHeyi* structure, with its 4000 MEs and their ability to form spontaneous alliances quickly, in place, that it could be one of the very few big retail companies to thrive during the Covid-19 crisis. But it needs a very special kind of leader, a quantum leader, to guide such a complex network of independent, self-organizing entities.

All human groups and organizations need leaders. People do look to leaders who can keep the "tribe" or the "ship" steady and who can provide a compass they can follow, both morally and in practice. But the *RenDanHeyi* leader sees power as a supportive relationship and an ability to *be related to*. He/she *listens*, heeds suggestions, alternative views, and constructive criticism. Such leaders lead with their persons, with their

---

[3] *Tao te Ching*, No. 68.

example, with their clearly expressed ability to "walk the talk," and have cultivated *power within* rather than *power over.* They have faith in the potential of those whom they lead. They trust their employees or citizens, and of equal importance, these employees or citizens know they can trust them.

Leaders are often referred to as "the captain of the ship," but we have seen that the *RenDanHeyi* organization is a fleet with many ships, each with its own captain and crew and its own, local mission to accomplish. So the *RenDanHeyi* leader is more like the "admiral of the fleet" who provides an overall strategic vision, a "central operational system," services and resources for the many ships in the fleet, and a guiding spirit that inspires, motivates, and maintains a harmonious coherence among all the many crews as each self-organizes its own mission and alliances—and does all this as with "an invisible hand," exercising force not *on* people but, rather, *through* people. He/she serves the fleet and its crews rather than controlling them, and sees him/herself as a Servant Leader.

The whole of Part III of this book is about the nature, challenges, and strategic and creative thinking of the quantum leader, and the whole of Part IV is more about the nature of the quantum organization, with case studies of several companies that have implemented Quantum Management thru the various adaptive possibilities inherent in *RenDanHeyi.* But first I think we need a still deeper understanding of the philosophical roots and vision of the quantum/*RenDanHeyi* model and how these release deeper potential for each of us as individuals, whether we serve our organizations as employees or as leaders.

CHAPTER 6

The Tao of Quantum Management

Zhang Ruimin has made clear that, when drafting the *RenDanHeyi* business model, his thinking was inspired both by his life-long interest in Taoism as a model for leadership, and by quantum physics as articulated through my own work on Quantum Management Theory. One of my arguments in this book is that the wider adoption of quantum thinking, and of *RenDanHeyi* as a business, social, and political model would provide an important bridge between East and West. For all practical purposes, I believe that the Western science of quantum physics is simply the Eastern philosophy of Taoism expressed in equations and verified by experiment. The implications of each for the nature of reality and for the way that we humans can best conduct our affairs, and thus for leadership and organizational thinking, are largely the same.

Understanding the striking similarities and worldviews of Taoism and quantum physics, and the way they have been integrated and implemented through *RenDanHeyi* may help both East and West understand how they can learn from each other and perhaps work more harmoniously together in building a new world order. Much of the current, mutual misunderstanding and suspicion felt by both China and the West stems from the fact that the entire thinking structure of the two cultures is radically different, and each sees the other through the lens of its own thinking. Now that life, business, and global relations in the twenty-first century require a quantum world view held by all, there may be a convergence of understanding and collaboration.

© The Author(s) 2022
D. Zohar, *Zero Distance*,
https://doi.org/10.1007/978-981-16-7849-3_6

Western scientists discovered quantum physics, but they have never understood it. Einstein called it "schizophrenic physics" and "Alice-in-Wonderland physics," others called it "absurd." But the Chinese have understood the quantum vision of reality for over 3000 years. It is embedded in ancient Chinese philosophy, particularly Taoism and then in the Taoist influence on Neo-Confucian philosophy centuries later. And still today, the Chinese people naturally think in a quantum way. Even the Chinese language, Mandarin, with its emphasis on patterns and relationships and its comfort with paradox and ambiguity, invites its users to "think quantum."

Perhaps the most challenging feature of both quantum physics and Chinese thinking for Western people to understand is their understanding of polarity and duality, such as particle/wave or matter/energy duality in quantum physics—which mirror the *li/qi* duality in Chinese philosophy. In Chinese thinking, everything in the universe, including ideas, is structured in pairs of polar opposites, like *yin/yang*, but for the Chinese these are *complementary* opposites that, like the two sides of a coin, could not exist without each other. Each is essential to an understanding of a thing or an idea, and it is from out of their co-creative dialogue that existence or meaning emerges. *Yang*, the strong, or light force, could not exist or function without *yin*, the receptive, or dark force, and the creative relationship between the two. Similarly, *li*, the structuring principles of the universe, would have no purpose without *qi*, the energy, or creative force and its potentiality, that *gets* structured. Similarly, in quantum physics, particles could not exist without waves, nor actuality without potentiality. Both are co-present and co-active in any thing or event.

Thus the *I Ching*, or Chinese *Book of Changes*, which offers commentary on sixty-four hexagram patterns, actually consists of thirty-two pairs of complementary opposites, and to fully understand the "image" or "judgement" of any one hexagram, the reader must refer to those of its two, component and complementary trigrams. The *I Ching* was actually the inspirational model for Niels Bohr's famous "Principle of Complementarity." Struggling to understand wave/particle duality from any Western perspective, Bohr, a Danish physicist and one of the five founding fathers of quantum physics, turned to his familiarity with the *I Ching* for a model that could mirror this "weird" reality. Similarly, two other quantum physics' founders, Wolfgang Pauli and Erwin Schrodinger (of

"Schrodinger's Cat" fame), turned to their knowledge of Chinese philosophy in an attempt to understand their own new discoveries. Schrodinger actually became a Buddhist.

This need to attempt an understanding of quantum physics in terms of Chinese thought was necessitated because, in Western thought, polarities like strong and weak, or light and darkness, are *conflicting* opposites. Strong is the opposite of weak, light the opposite of darkness. Similarly, in Western management thinking, management and labor, or the leader and employees, are seen as essentially different and very often in conflict, just as in Western societies, the interests and identity of "I" or "We" are seen as often in conflict with "others," or "them." It is essential for any proper understanding of Quantum Management, or its implementation through the *RenDanHeyi*, that readers think of such polarities in Chinese, rather than Western, terms. I think it no accident that it was a Chinese CEO who conceived and implemented the *RenDanHeyi* management model, and quite natural that China's prime minister would recommend this as the ideal business model for all Chinese companies to adopt. Indeed, Quantum Management has now become so widespread in China that the Chinese are calling it "Chinese Management."

Because all of twenty-first-century technology is quantum technology, this indigenous quantum thinking is giving the Chinese a natural competitive edge. Consider Huawei's advanced 5G telecommunications system, the fact that the Chinese have launched the world's first quantum satellite, and the very advanced work that Chinese scientists are doing to develop quantum computers. I will point out in later chapters that we can see echoes of *RenDanHeyi* in China's bold, international Belt and Road infrastructure project, and even in an *ideally practiced* model of the way the modern Chinese government structures the organization of its state. Let us look at the philosophical and cultural roots of this.

During the past 3000 years, Chinese civilization has evolved in dialogue with three great philosophies: Taoism, Confucianism, and Ch'an (Zen) Buddhism. Being the oldest of the three, there are shades of Taoist thinking in each of the other two, and then in the tenth to sixteenth centuries, the defining elements of all three were integrated in an emerging and unifying Neo-Confucian philosophy. The greatest of the Taoist thinkers was Lao Tzu, whose *Tao Te Ching* is one of China's most formative books, and also a book now familiar to many in the West. Lao Tzu described the nature of the universe, the place of human beings within it, and the natural Way for human beings and their leaders to live in harmonious alignment with both "Heaven" and each other. The greatest of the Neo-Confucian philosophers was the sixteenth-century Wang Yangming, who adhered to basic Taoist ideas but elaborated much more on the nature and natural inclinations of the self, the source and nature of morality, the relationship and duties of individuals to society, and the principles of harmonious governance. I have found Wang Yangming's philosophy very close to the quantum philosophy I have spent my own life trying to articulate.

Taoist Principles and Quantum Management

- *Made of Energy, Governed by Principles:* Newton's static and predictable, materialist universe is made of separate, isolated atoms that are impenetrable and unchanging. Designed and structured as a machine is designed and structured, as a collection of separate, moving parts, this universe is controlled from above by the iron laws of physics, Newton's three Laws of Motion. The Laws of Motion themselves were decreed by a God who is outside the system and wholly other than anything inside it. This view of the universe gave rise in Western culture to a view of society consisting of atomistic individuals with no intimate relationship to each other and only a transactional relationship to society, mediated by laws and social norms. In the Taylorian company, it gave rise to companies modeled as machines, structured into atomistic, siloed divisions and functions, and ruled from above by the dictates of a CEO who, like the Western God, is wholly other than and outside the system. The atomistic employees of the Taylorian company have no direct relationship to each other and only a transactional relationship to the company, mediated by the CEO's rules, their assigned roles in the company structure, and their dependence on the company for a salary.

Taoist philosophy, by contrast, like quantum physics, portrays a dynamic and evolving universe made of energy (*qi*) and impregnated with a network of self-organizing and harmonius, symbiotically related patterns (*li,*), or principles, that then give a sense of direction to the self-organizing creation and behavior of all things. These patterns, like the laws of quantum physics, emerged from within the system itself, and define a sense of direction, or Way, for the evolving universe to unfold. It is important to stress they are *principles*, not *rules*. All things, including ourselves, are *guided* by these principles, but not *controlled* by them.

The principles of the Way are a *pattern* which can be expressed in many different ways, not a *structure* in the Newtonian sense, which limits expression or action to just one, limited direction. In Quantum Management, this same idea is implemented by the central operational system of the *RenDanHeyi* model, that gives a company its sense of a common direction and culture, and each self-organizing team or microenterprise targets to aim for, while at the same time allowing them the freedom to work out their own best way of doing so in direct dialogue with their customers/users and the entire ecosystem environment. And, true to both the Taoist and quantum insights that everything is energy, the *RenDanHeyi* model treats a. company as an energy system. Zhang Ruimin even refers to Haier's microenterprises as "energy balls."

- *No Force; "Non-Action"*: We have seen that Newton's physics portrays a universe designed at the top and tightly controlled by forces and his three Laws of Motion. Thus the Taylorian company is governed by rules imposed from the top, and force (sanctions, punishments) is used to ensure these rules are obeyed. But both Taoism and quantum physics warn of the destructive effects of any force or control imposed on a system from the outside. The very essence of Taoism is its principle of "non-action" (*wu wei*), the insight that the greatest effectiveness is achieved when one "goes with the flow," harmoniously aligning oneself and one's actions with the natural Way (*Tao*) of events rather than forcing one's will upon them. Lao Tzu writes,

Even the best will in the world, when forced,
    achieves nothing.
The best righteousness, when forced,
    achieves nothing.
The best good-form when forced
    does not come out right.[1]

And we know that in quantum physics, any outside interference with or measurement of a quantum system "collapses the wave function,"

---

[1] *Tao te Ching*, No. 38.

robbing the system of its multiple possibilities, just as outside control imposed on a complex adaptive system (living quantum system), interferes with the internal self-organization and robs the system of its creativity. Thus Quantum Management teaches that the CEO must give up control, and power should be distributed to self-organizing teams throughout the company system. The *RenDanHeyi* business model implements this by giving powers of decision-making, hiring, and remuneration to the independent microenterprise teams, and has them working directly with customers/users and with each other. The quantum leader governs with a light touch as though heeding Lao Tzu's advice to, "Govern a large [company] as you would cook a small fish: lightly."

- *Everything is Connected to Everything:* We have seen that Newton's universe is composed of separate, isolated atoms that cannot get inside each other and can relate across the distance that separates them only by the imposition of some force. And thus the Taylorian company is composed of separate functions and separate siloed departments, management is separate from (above) employees, and employees are separate from customers. By contrast, both Taoism and quantum physics tell us that "separation is an illusion," that we live in a world of *Zero Distance* where everything and everyone is entangled with everything and everyone else.

One Taoist master compared the universe to a multidimensional network of jewels, each jewel containing the reflections of all the others, and said there is no obstruction or distance between one "thing-event" and another. Lao Tzu taught that the whole universe is within each thing or person in it, and each thing or person is within every other. In quantum physics, the entangled wave patterns of every quantum entity ensure this same thing, and thus apparently distant particles are in fact connected *nonlocally.* The quantum universe is like a large hologram, in which the entire hologram is implicit in each small section of it. So as in Taoism, quantum physics also tells us the entire universe is within each atom or thing. And the *RenDanHeyi* Quantum Management model, also called the Zero Distance Model, sees every microenterprise in the company in a cocreative relationship with every other, with its customers/users, and with other companies in the ecosystem. Thus the whole company is in every part, and every part is implicit within every other. There are no borders.

- *A Participatory Universe:* Just as Western culture and Western grammar distinguish between the subject and the object, Newtonian science distinguishes between the observer and the observed, and the Taylorian company, often seeing itself as an island, distinguishes between what is "inside" the company, and what is "outside." In Newton's materialistic universe, there is no place or role for conscious beings like ourselves. We can only stand back from afar as outsiders and view reality, often as its pawns or victims. But just as quantum physics tells us that the observer and the observed are one, that the way we observe, question, or act *within* reality *co-creates* that reality. So, too, Taoism tells us that the *Tao* is within each of us and each of us is within the *Tao*, and that it is our acting in alignment with the *Tao* that can influence the course of the *Tao* itself. Both the Taoist and the quantum person are agents of cosmic possibility, makers of reality. And because they make the world, they are responsible for the world. The story of the universe is our story, and our story is the story of the universe.

Quantum Management argues that the company is inside the community and the world, and the community and the world are inside the company. Together they make the world and thus, through their relationship, they are responsible for the world. We have seen that in the way that Haier itself implements the *RenDanHeyi* model, not only is each microenterprise inside every other, but both the customer/user and the community are literally inside the company, sometimes indistinguishable from employees, and the company is inside them (their lifestyles, health care, etc.). It is these cocreative relationships that are constantly giving birth to new, emergent realities—new products and new opportunities for growth.

- *Always in Context.* In Newton's physics, a thing just is what it is, no matter what its surroundings or relationships, and we have seen that Taylorian companies behave as though they are islands onto themselves, oblivious to the world around them and thus often damaging both their own bottom line and the surrounding environment. Indeed, Western thinking in general tends to solve problems by isolating them as best possible. "Just forget about everything else and concentrate on what is important here," or the admonition, "Get to the point!"

In Taoist thought, which insists everything is in relationship with everything, and it is understood relationships make reality, the larger surroundings of a word, an action, or an event are seen as shaping them. Thus Chinese thought is always "situational" or "contextual." You can never know the meaning of a Chinese pictogram except through its relation to others in a sentence, never understand an action or an event unless you know "the whole story," and never make a decision without exploring all the factors bearing on it and all those it might bear upon. I can't count the number of times I have stood for more than half an hour on a Beijing street corner with a group of Chinese friends while they consider every possible factor influencing their decision before they hail down a taxi cab to take us to a restaurant. Once seated in the restaurant, they seem to avoid any further long-winded decisions by simply ordering everything on the menu!

And we have seen that "contextuality" is one of the defining principles of quantum physics. A quantum entity or quantum system always *is* what it is depending upon its context, upon what it is in relationship to. Change the relationship, you change the entity. Quantum Management thus always calls upon a company to consider all its relationships, both internal and external, because these will affect the outcome of strategies and decisions and indeed the very health of the company. Business, and any business decision, always happens within a context. In the *RenDan-Heyi* model, this awareness of context and its power accounts for the "no borders" slogan and a company culture that stresses relationships and understands how *all* internal and external factors shape the company and its health. And its reliance on a network of interconnected but at the same time independent microenterprises, each operating in a different context, allows a company implementing it to spread both risk and opportunity.

- *Spontaneity.* Everything in Newtonian physics and the modern Western mindset that arose in response to it fights the very idea of spontaneity. The promise of Newton's physics was that, if we know the starting position of a particle or situation, and we know the forces acting upon them, we can know everything, predict everything, and control everything. Forced control is thus in the Western DNA, and of course it reigns supreme in the Taylorian company, with its reliance on top-down control and rigid bureaucratic structure. In times of uncertainty and rapid, unpredictable, disruptive change, these companies find themselves like heavy, lumbering dinosaurs trying to navigate themselves through a delicate and shifting terrain.

But both Taoism and quantum physics have always known that complete knowledge is unobtainable, prediction unreliable and often impossible, and control destructive.

Taoism has always taught that the *Tao* itself, the Way that universe unfolds as it evolves, is always changing, and the only successful way to thrive in this world is to remain spontaneous and rule with a light touch, creatively *responding* to the flow of unpredictable events rather than by *reacting* to them with forced control. "The *Tao* in Nature does not contend, yet skillfully triumphs. Does not speak, yet skillfully responds. Does not summon, and yet attracts. Does not hasten, yet skillfully designs."[2] The Taoist leader triumphs "by accepting, incorporating, and supporting change. Our cooperation with the forces in Nature makes us a part of those forces. Our decisions become astute because they are based on a dynamic, evolving reality, not on fixed or wishful thinking."[3]

Quantum physics and complexity science, too, describe an indeterminate, ever-changing and self-organizing Nature, and counsel spontaneous adaptation to the evolving flow of events rather than any attempt to forcefully control them. Quantum Management calls upon the leader to surrender control and to lead with attitude, character, and example rather than forcing his/her will upon the organization as it spontaneously responds to surrounding challenges. The *RenDanHeyi* management model builds an "autopoetic" organization that can continuously self-generate and spontaneously adapt and evolve to ever-changing external circumstances. A quantum company is light, guided by patterns and principles that allow it to surface freely on the currents of market-influencing events as a butterfly does on the currents of the wind.

Thus we can see that China's 3000 years of thinking and culture, originating in and always incorporating Taoist principles, has well prepared modern China to thrive in the Quantum Age. Chinese scientists have an edge with innovative quantum technology because they have a natural, intuitive feel for the laws and principles underlying its development and use. And Chinese business leaders have that same natural, intuitive feel for how quantum organizations work. At the same time, the Western world is now handicapped with a mindset geared to simple, predictable, controllable, and atomistic/mechanistic systems in an age defined by complexity,

[2] *Tao te Ching*, No. 73.

[3] A.L. Wing, *The Tao of Power*, p. 12.

unpredictable, rapid change, and global interconnectivity and in which control is self-defeating. I am not expecting the Western world suddenly to become Chinese, but if we do not become quantum, we are destined to further decline and perhaps oblivion. We in the West *discovered* quantum physics. It is imperative we now develop a quantum mindset that can *understand* it, can *live* it, and thus find our own way to thrive on the challenges and opportunities it presents. The rest of this book is a guide for doing that.

PART II

The Quantum Person/Employee

The *RenDanHeyi*/Quantum Management organizational model sees as its main purpose the release of human potential. In their book *Humanocracy*, Gary Hamel and Michele Zanini call for more "people centered companies" and urge that people be treated as *people*, not as company "resources". And a 2020 KPMG survey found that the top concern right now of 71% of CEO's is how to get the best out of their people. But I think we need to go deeper to give such appeals and concerns their real meaning. We need to ask what it is that we mean by "a person", and explore exactly what *is* human potential. And we need to understand how we saw people and human potential in the old paradigm such that we ever thought it effective (or moral!) to treat them as "resources" or mindless robots in the bureaucratic corporate machine. What do both leaders and employees need to learn about the true nature of each other as people so that they can work together as equal partners in co-creating their companies' futures? These are the questions we will explore in the next set of chapters.

CHAPTER 7

I Am the Universe

Zhang Zai (1020–1077 AD), one of China's most important Neo-Confucian thinkers, has written, "Heaven is my father and Earth is my mother, and even such a small creature as I finds an intimate place in their midst. Therefore, that which fills the universe I regard as my body and that which directs the universe I consider as my nature. All people are my brothers and sisters, and all things are my companions."[1]

One of the "big questions" that humanity has been asking since we began asking questions is, "Where do we come from?" What is our place and our purpose in the wider scheme of things? Was all of creation made for our benefit, as the Western religions claim, and thus we are the masters of the universe and the rightful inheritors of all the earth's resources? Are we instead just some inexplicable afterthought in a wholly materialist universe governed by the deterministic laws of physics, or the accidental byproducts of random evolutionary forces, as Newtonian and Darwinian science have described us? Or has Taoism got it right, and our existence is in fact an integral and necessary part of both an evolving universe and a living earth whose futures we help to write? Once again, we will see, quantum physics agrees with the Taoists.

According to quantum science, our universe began with a Big Bang about fourteen billion years ago. No scientist can yet say with authority what existed before the Big Bang, but grounded speculation suggests

---

[1] Jung-Yeup Kim, *Zhang Zai's Philosophy of Qi*, Chapter 1.

© The Author(s) 2022
D. Zohar, *Zero Distance*,
https://doi.org/10.1007/978-981-16-7849-3_7

that the creation of our universe was part of a cycle of creation and destruction that saw universes being born from infinitely condensed "singularities" that exploded, then expanded for some billions of years until they began to contract and finally, once again became infinitely dense singularities. Grounded speculation also suggests that ours may not be the only universe that resulted from the last Big Bang, or that there may have been other Big Bangs, and thus we may in fact live in a "multiverse." But for purposes of this book, let us just concentrate on the one universe within which we know that we dwell!

The first thing created after the Big Bang was the Quantum Vacuum, a field of potentiality that remains today and acts as a force that lies within, and acts upon, every existing thing in the universe, including ourselves. The Vacuum has a misleading name, because it is not empty, like a vacuum flask, but rather infinitely full with the potential existence of everything that ever was, everything that is, and everything that ever will be. It is a field of pure, unexcited energy, and is called a Vacuum simply because it has no discernible qualities or characteristics. In our quantum universe, qualities and characteristics are the result of *excited* energy, and it is only when the "zero point" field of the Vacuum gets exited that "things" emerge which possess qualities or characteristics. Thus the Quantum Vacuum can be thought of as a still sea underlying all existing things, and all existing things, including ourselves, as waves upon that sea. Indeed, the word ex-ist means "to stand out from," as a wave stands out from the sea. All existing things, including ourselves and our companies, are patterns of dynamic energy "written upon" (excitations of) the Quantum Vacuum.

Because the Quantum Vacuum contains the potentiality for everything that exists, or ever will exist, it contained the potentiality for what became you and me. In truth, each of us has existed as a potentiality within the Vacuum since that first split second that it was created after the Big Bang. Each of us has been here through the whole long history of the universe itself so far, and so each of us is really very old—fourteen billion years old! We were here when a perturbation of the Vacuum's stillness gave rise to the Higgs field and the Higgs boson, which then gave rise to matter (its mass), and then as matter formed first into elementary particles, then fiery gases, then stars, then planets, and, in our case at least, then life on earth. As the *Tao te Ching* tells this story, "The One gave rise to the two, the two to the three, and the three gave rise to the ten thousand things."[2] And we are among the ten thousand things.

Thus each of us carries the whole history of the universe, the Quantum Vacuum, and the whole panoply of its infinite potentialities within us. Our bodies are made out of stardust and both our bodies and our minds obey the same quantum laws and forces that govern everything else in the universe. And our subconscious minds, at least, know this and remember it all. This is the source of our quantum intelligence, or *gangying*, as the Taoists call it, that I will discuss in more detail later, and the reason why we *do* have the ability (and the responsibility) to govern our companies and our societies with those same principles that underpin the successful functioning of the universe, Nature, and our own living organisms.

I Am Nature

Not only did Newtonian physics assert that we humans play no role in the wholly material, mechanistic universe, but the Western religions also maintain that neither are we any part of Nature. The Western Bible tells us that God created the natural world for our benefit, and gave us domain over all of Nature. Nature is our "resource," to be used for our own benefit as we think best. This lingering attitude still exists in the minds of many today, including those of many business leaders, and of course underpins the activities that have now led to our climate crisis. But Darwin's Theory of Evolution challenged it, and the quantum world view asserts very clearly that we are fully part of both the universe and Nature. We can see this very clearly in the "archaeology" of the human brain, the seat of both our personhood and our thinking.

By nature, the brain is quite conservative. It carries the whole history of the evolution of life on this planet within its complex structures. Its architecture is like the twisting alleyways and jumbled buildings of a very ancient city—layer upon layer of archaeological history built one on top of the other and all somehow being "lived in".

In the simplest layer of our bodily organization,— the part corresponding to the lowest archaeological level of the ancient city—we find structures like those of the single-celled animals, such as amoeba. They have no nervous system; all the sensory and motor functions of these

---

[2] *Tao Te Ching*, No. 42.

animals exist within one cell. Our own white blood cells, as they scavenge for rubbish and sweep up bacteria, behave in our bloodstreams much like the amoebae in ponds. Simple many-celled animals like jellyfish still have no central nervous system, but they do have a network of nerve fibers that allow communication between cells so that the animal can react to its environment in a coordinated way. In our bodies, the nerve cells in the gut form a similar network that coordinates peristalsis, the muscular contractions that push food along the gut. More evolved animals develop increasingly complex nervous systems.

As evolution progressed, a primitive brainstem developed in the lower skulls of multicelled animals, such as fishes and reptiles. Indeed, the human brainstem is even called the "reptilian brain." With the arrival of mammals, the brain grew more complex layers,—first the primitive mid-brain of the lower mammals, ruled by instinct, then the midbrain of higher mammals like tigers and wolves, ruled by instinct and emotion, and finally the cerebral hemispheres of the forebrain that we share with the higher monkeys, with their more sophisticated computing ability and increasing social skills. The prefrontal lobes, those "little grey cells" that we identify with the human mind, but shared in their less developed form by the higher apes, have evolved most recently, and are essential to rational ego abilities. Yet drunkenness, the use of tranquilizers, great stress, violent emotion, or damage to the higher forebrain result in regression to primitive, more impulsive, less calculating types of behavior found in lower animals.

So despite the increasing centralization and complexity of the nervous system as it evolves, even in human beings the most primitive nerve nets remain, both within our expanded brain and throughout the body. And we live and think with it all, with the instincts of the snake and the wolf, the emotions of the apes, and on our better days, with the rationality of humans. Yet we share 98% of our genes, our minds, and our emotions with chimpanzees, so at this stage of our evolution, we are only 2% human. It is little wonder then, that we behave irrationally so much of the time, and make such a mess of things! Our computational abilities have now created a highly complex world that has outgrown our own capacity to live in it intelligently.

This presents us all with a personal challenge and a purpose. If just 2% of being human has got us this far, another mere 1% or 2% of brain evolution might make us able to cope with life in the twenty-first century. In terms of natural evolution, that would require tens of thousands of years, but we know now from modern neuroscience that our brains are "plastic," mutable, changeable. We have the capacity to rewire them and grow them in dialogue with our own thinking and experience. We can speed up our own brain evolution. We can think and experience ourselves "more intelligent," and the way we manage our companies and other social organizations can contribute to that. I believe that is the promise of "quantum thinking," and why I hope that at least 10% of those in leadership positions might grow into it. As international law professor Richard Falk expresses it,

> The human species has a special co-evolutionary capacity and responsibility. Unlike other species, we are aware of our roles in the world and bare the burdens of awareness...As humans, we can respond to the pain of the world by devoting our energies to various kinds of restorative action, building institutional forms and popular support for a dramatic reorientation of behavior.[3]

---

[3] Richard Falk, *Explorations at the Edge of Time*, p. 36.

CHAPTER 8

I Am a Particle and a Wave

The iconic American hero is the lonely cowboy, sitting astride his horse in the midst of a vast prairie and dependent on no one but himself to brave and survive the elements. His modern equivalent is the Superhero, who has special powers that enable him to single-handedly save the world, and the Taylorian CEO is a kind of cowboy or Superhero who bears sole authority and responsibility for running his/her company. Western society is based on this concept of the all-important individual, the "atom of society," whose power to pursue his/her interests and protect his/her rights through the personal vote is the cornerstone of Western democracy. We have already seen that this sacred individualism is rooted in the atomism of early Greek philosophy and then enshrined as a defining principle of Newtonian physics. Western society is particle-like.

By contrast, when I suggested to one of my Chinese Ph.D. students that China boosts its soft power in the West by conceiving a Chinese Superhero and having him star in a block buster movie, the student protested that such a movie would not be Chinese. "We don't believe in Superheroes," he protested. "We recognize that heroic deeds are performed by teams working together, like the doctors in Wuhan, or by the Chinese people all acting in cooperation, as we did by wearing masks and obeying the Lockdown during the Covid crisis." The modern Chinese government's stop priorities are protecting the safety of the Chinese people and maintaining harmony in society, and few Chinese people put their own personal interest, or "rights," before the best

© The Author(s) 2022
D. Zohar, *Zero Distance*,
https://doi.org/10.1007/978-981-16-7849-3_8

interest of all. This Chinese collectivism is rooted in the still influential Confucian philosophy that stresses the place and duties of the individual within family relationships, and the responsibilities of citizens and leaders to society as a whole. China is largely a wave-like society.

But quantum physics tells us that entities are *both* particle-like *and* wave-like, possessing both an individual identity and potential while at the same time evolving that individuality and expanding that potential through their relationship to other entities and to the environment as a whole. Discrete "individuals" play their active part in the system dynamics, but always as "team members" of the system, just as in the *RenDanHeyi* management model the "independent" microenterprises pursue their own targets and interests while these are always being reinvented through their relationships to other microenterprises and to the company system and the larger ecosystem as a whole. Thus, we would expect a quantum society to be both particle-like and wave-like (see Chapter 19), and the quantum persons who are its citizens to have this same dual nature. Let us look at how each of us is *both* an individual who stands out from the group *and* a person defined by our relationships within it, both a "particle" and a "wave" at the same time, and what this means for both employees and leaders of companies.

Both an Individual and My Relationships

At this moment, if I direct my attention toward myself, I feel very certain that I exist as an individual, that there is something it is right to call "me." I know that I am the person who went to sleep in my bed last night and woke up there this morning. I know my name, remember most of my personal history, and have my distinct physical appearance that others can recognize. Individuals like me, whether of the human or subatomic particle variety, make things happen, and I have my own very particular responsibilities. It is an individual that I develop my character, as an individual that I possess integrity, and as an individual that others can rely on me. It is an individual that I must sometimes be "field independent," stand against the crowd, when my values or intuitions demand, and as an individual that I make the unique contribution that only I can make. Quantum physics tells me that, like every other existing thing in the universe, I am a unique excitation of the Quantum Vacuum's cosmic energy field, an important and irreplaceable "happening" in the history of events. As Ekhardt Tolle has written, "You are here to enable the Divine Purpose of the universe to unfold. That's how important you are."[1]

As a mother and grandmother I have a distinct role in my family and things that only I can do, I am at the center of certain family and social events, and my distinct eccentricities add some spice and variety to the tapestry of family life—and are the source of many family "stories"! As one of my young grandsons commented recently in my defence, "If we were all the same, we would get very confused. And we would be very boring." If I were not "me," my entire family would be different because, while my individuality is important, my being "me" plays a defining role in all others in the family being who they are. I am not just an isolated "particle" free to be and do as I like, but also a "wave" whose being and doing affects both the kind of individuals others in the family are and what they do.

We have seen that quantum physics proves that in our quantum world, everything and everyone is related to, "entangled with," everything and everyone else, and that it is their place in this vast network of relationships that determines both the identity and the behavior of each thing or person. Relationship makes reality. Every existing thing and person is in fact a dynamic, wave-like pattern of energy "written" on the background energy field of the Quantum Vacuum, a wave on the sea of cosmic energy that permeates all things and people. And just like neighboring waves on the sea, we overlap and combine, we amplify or reduce each other. We each contain the same "seawater," and are stuff of the same substance. This is the quantum basis of the Taoist insight that each of us contains within ourselves the entire universe and everything within it. "I" am "you," and "you" are "me," and it is through our relationship that we create both ourselves and our shared world. There are no "others," no "strangers," and there is Zero Distance between each of us.

Thus, each employee in a company is both a "particle" and a "wave," a unique and irreplaceable individual *and* an integral, defining part of the company. No matter what his or her role, no matter how seemingly large or small that role, every employee matters because of his or her individual potential and contributes that potential to the making of the company system. All employees and all roles are in a defining relationship with all others, and together they create the company system. There are no

---

[1] Eckhardt Tolle, *The Power of Now.*

"others" because there are no borders. There are no less-equals because all are stuff of the same substance. There are no less important job roles, no unimportant people, because all, in their uniqueness, are integral and defining elements of the company system. If the employees were different, and their relationships different, it wouldn't be the same company.

THE CREATIVITY OF OUR RELATIONSHIPS

To understand the creative potential of personal and company relationships, we could use the metaphor of a jazz jam session and contrast it with the performance of a solo artist or that of an orchestra. The solo artist, of course, shines on his own, and can have his own brilliance. He draws his creativity from reserves within himself and performs with reference only to his personal interpretation of a musical score. The orchestra is more like a bureaucratic organization, the player of each instrument performing his or her part of the score according to the guidance and interpretation of the conductor. Both the soloist and the orchestra stick to the score and surprise us only with their style and the manner or emotional tone of their interpretation. But participants in a jazz jam session do not follow a set score and there is no conductor. Instead, each one plays his or her instrument in an improvised response to the tone and rhythm of the previous one and with a shared, relational sense of their as yet together to be played whole. The participants *create* the piece they are performing *as they perform it*, and in a self-organizing, responsive relationship to each other and their shared project. The result is something fresh and surprising, a whole now unimaginable from the sum of its parts. This is the nature of all creative relationships, be they marriages, families, or companies. By spontaneously responding together to each other and to the way that each other spontaneously responds to challenges, opportunities, and the surrounding context of events, the participants in these relationships are constantly reinventing themselves and each other, and bringing something new into the world. The created whole is always greater than the sum of its parts.

Thus none of us is, by nature, either a selfish or entirely self-sufficient, isolated particle, nor simply a wave-like member of a collective relationship that diminishes the importance and responsibility of our individuality. Each of us is, rather, a quantum person who is *both* an individual in our own right, worthy of dignity, respect, and room to exercise our free will and to develop our potential, *and* a wave-like participant in our relationships, partially defined and created by spontaneously responding to others in those relationships, drawing value, nourishment, and even identity from them, while at the same time nourishing, adding value to, and cocreating further potentiality for both ourselves and others. It is this particle/wave duality of the quantum person that makes our friendships, marriages, teams, and companies meaningful, fulfilling, and creative. Each of us, as individuals, and through the relationships that we engage in, makes our family, makes our company, and makes our world. And we are responsible for what we make. But, as we will now see in the next chapter, this relational creativity can only emerge because each quantum person, both as an individual and as a partner in a creative relationship, has multiple potentialities and an adaptive ability to play many possible roles.

CHAPTER 9

I Am a Multitude

Walt Whitman has written, "Do I contradict myself? Very well, I contradict myself. I am very large. I contain multitudes."[1]

One of the most powerful insights of quantum physics is that we live in a world of multiple potentiality. Nothing *is* just simply what we see before us now. The quantum wave function (described mathematically in Schrodinger's wave equation) is a superposition of multiple potential "realities"—for instance, photons being both particle-like and wave-like at the same time, both now and then at the same time. Which of these potentialities then gets "real-ized" at our level of reality depends upon how the scientist observes (measures) the wave function with his experimental apparatus. This is the grounds for the quantum insight that everything is "contextual"—a thing always is what it is in relationship to its environment.

For organizations, we saw how a more full realization of all, or at least more, of a company's ways to access the many potentialities in the market is facilitated by the *RenDanheyi* structure of having multiple teams or microenterprises, each tapping into a different customer base with a different product or service, or using the many skills of its employees in different ways. But this same opportunity is available to each of us in our personal lives. And it is one way of getting Zero Distance between our

---

[1] Walt Whitman, *Song of Myself*, No. 51.

© The Author(s) 2022
D. Zohar, *Zero Distance*,
https://doi.org/10.1007/978-981-16-7849-3_9

working lives and personal lives, making both richer and more effective. A kind of *RenDanHeyi* for the self.

In his book on Taoism, *The Watercourse Way*, Alan Watts speaks of "that eternal series of surprises that is myself."[2] I can illustrate this multiple, contextual nature of the self with an example from my own family. When our daughter was nine years old, my husband and I attended a parents' evening at her school. She had many teachers, and we spoke with her Latin teacher first. He was very discouraging. "I really don't know what to do with Anna," he said. "She constantly disrupts the class with her chatter, her homework is always messy, and she is not polite." But then her English teacher spoke very differently. "Anna always makes such good contributions to our classroom discussions, and her poems are so powerful that I have sent them to the school magazine for publication. I wish all my students were like her!" Different teacher, different child.

We have all had the experience of feeling and behaving differently in different relationships and social situations. This is especially true of the person we seem to be at work and the way that we and others see us at home. And most of us have a tendency to say, "I can really be myself here," in some particular context, falsely believing that we have a "true self" present in only some situations, who then, in other situations, "puts on" the mask of a less true persona when deemed appropriate. We are particularly anxious to reject unwanted or uncomfortable "shadow" sides of ourselves of which we feel we should disapprove, often repressing these so strongly that we become unconscious of them, or at least declaring passionately, "That is not what I am really like!" But in fact, all of these selves are "me," and all of them are equally genuine. Each of us is a multitude, and each of our multiple personalities is in fact present, and having an influence on, any particular situation or relationship we happen to be in at a given time. Like everything else in this quantum world of ours, the quantum self is "both/and," not "either/or."

This both/and nature of the quantum self speaks directly to the question of identity that has become such an issue today in society and international politics. People are feeling that their identity is threatened by an "invasion" of others unlike themselves who move into their neighborhoods or who cross their national borders. The whole populist movement that has swept America and Europe owes much of its existence to a fear

---

[2] Alan Watts, *The Watercourse Way*, p. 114.

that these "others" will destroy our identity. Brexit was a fear in the UK that our national identity was eroded by being "swallowed up" by Europe and European immigrants. The ultranationalism that accompanies this populism is a fear that our national identity is threatened by globalism. We must build walls! We must strengthen our borders! But we have seen from our earlier discussions that, in the entangled quantum reality of our universe, where everything is connected to everything, where the entire universe and everything and everyone in it is inside each one of us, there are no "others." The "other" is simply an unrecognized or split off part of myself. And now we can see from the both/and nature of the quantum self, that multiple, coexisting identities are in fact what each of us is made of. The notion of the human self as a separate, atomistic island onto itself, is now as discredited by science as the old, Newtonian view that the universe is composed of separate, discrete, and impenetrable atoms. Each of us is a multitude.

We can visualize the reality of the multitude that each of us is by looking at a figure inspired by a diagram of "quantum potential" drawn by the physicist David Bohm to illustrate what happens to the wave function of a quantum entity when that entity is observed or measured. The wave function carrying a superposition of multiple potentialities does not "collapse" into just one single reality when observed, as quantum scientists used to believe. Instead, it is now known that the wave function simply "decoheres," or spreads out as a rich and varied spectrum of these once superimposed potentialities. When observed, it becomes an array of various, partially expressed, "sleeping," or wave-like, realities and one fully expressed, particle-like reality that is the object of that particular observation (Fig. 9.1).[3]

In this diagram, each of the many peaks of energy shown has the potential to be observed as a particle if it is evoked by a different observation, but all of the peaks share the "space" within them as a common, wave-like feature. Though only the highest peak manifests as an observable particle, that particle actually contains within itself the common, wave-like, reality represented by all the peaks. When the scientist measures the one, visible, particle, its broader, and invisible, wave-like aspect is fully "implied within" the one reality being detected. And it is the same with the quantum self. The child that her English teacher praised was present

---

[3] Paaavo Pylkkaanen, *Mind, Matter, and the Implicate Order*, p. 167.

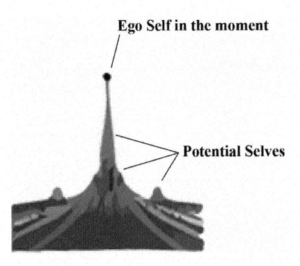

Fig. 9.1   Multiple potentialities of the self

in her Latin classroom, if only the Latin teacher had had the wider sensitivity to sense it, and the skill of a teacher who could evoke it. A skillful leader can do the same for an employee who seems "not up to the job," or for the immigrant who "does not belong here."

We will see in Chapter 14 that the celebration of diversity is one of the twelve principles of quantum leadership. In fact, the celebration of the diversity within each of ourselves is a principle of quantum living. The more numerous the sides of ourselves that we recognize and cultivate, the more fully we become ourselves. The more "strangers" we welcome in our neighborhood, the richer and more vital we and our community become. Even the rejected "shadow" sides of ourselves have a potential to add to the richness of our life experience and to the value we can bring to our relationships. Indeed, the Swiss psychologist Carl Jung believed that much of our creativity is hidden away in the shadow. It is the *yin* within the *yin/yang* self. The shadow sides of ourselves are simply damaged potentialities that were distorted by painful childhood experiences. If we face them, own them, and heal them, they can be integrated into the broader array of our positive sides and qualities and give greater life to all. The employee who functions poorly on one team, in fact has skills and qualities that will add great value to another.

Zhang Ruimin has said that as an employee creates his/her product, they thereby also create themselves. In the *RenDanHeyi* management model, every employee adds to their skill set and confidence as they creatively respond to user needs. It is the same in a *RenDanHeyi* model of the self. Every time we expose ourselves to a new experience or a new idea, every time we stretch ourselves or go outside our comfort zone, every time we see that another's "difference" is actually an unrecognized part of ourselves, we bring forth or strengthen those potential, different sides of ourselves, or evoke new ones, and we become more who we truly are. And when we "introduce" these different "me's" to ourselves and others by bringing more of them into each present situation or relationship, we integrate who we truly are. Such self-creation and self-integration is the essence of possessing integrity, of being "authentic." We are more present to ourselves and others. We feel more "real" to ourselves, and more trustworthy to others. We simply are *more*.

CHAPTER 10

I Make the World

The essential creativity of human beings runs as a theme throughout our history and culture. We see ourselves as "man the maker" and, in modern scientific terms, date the origin of *homo sapiens* back to the day that man made the first tool. We feel that our creativity somehow separates us from the lower animals and defines our humanity.

In Western religious terms, our creativity has sometimes been seen as the *reason* for our humanity, the *raison d'etre* of human existence. This theme appears, for instance, in the Jewish mystical tradition, which argues that God made man because he needed a partner in creation,[1] and in the philosophy of Henri Bergson, who believed that the whole purpose of the evolutionary process was God's "undertaking to create creators." In Chinese philosophy, the triad Heaven–Man–Earth, sees Man as the bridge who can bring the Way of the Tao to earth and then create a civilization here that will reflect the way of Heaven.

We certainly feel this about ourselves in small ways as we go about our daily lives, and if we reflect on our behavior, we can see that a "creative urge" motivates much of it. Simple things like children's first paintings or fascination with Lego bricks; the later wish to build models, carve soap, make clay pots and baskets; the adult love for do-it-yourself and the wish to decorate both ourselves and our homes are all basic expressions of the same drive that motivates others to write poems or symphonies or to

---

[1] Gershon G. Scholem, *Zohar: The Book of Splendor*.

© The Author(s) 2022
D. Zohar, *Zero Distance*,
https://doi.org/10.1007/978-981-16-7849-3_10

articulate new spiritual views. And of course scientific discovery and the technological innovation so vital to today's society and business depends on the constant creativity of scientists and employees.

In past, apart from religious accounts, any explanation for human creativity, or indeed any full account of exactly what creativity *is*, remained somewhat mysterious. Any sensitive person could notice the difference between an article made by a human craftsperson and those made by a mechanical assembly line turning out thousands of identical objects, but it was not easy to explain why craftspeople are creative and machines are not. The same question lies at the heart of our current wish to design AI systems that can mimic, or even exceed, human ingenuity. Ironically, the explanations now being offered by quantum physics, neuroscience, and complexity theory indicate that creativity is not unique to human beings.

Discoveries being made in thermodynamics as early as the 1980s demonstrated that living systems can get around the limitations of the Second Law of Thermodynamics, which claim that, due to entropy, everything in the universe is running down, or falling into disorder. Ilya Prigogine's Nobel Prize-winning work on "dissipative," or "open systems," demonstrated that some systems, including all living systems, can *create* order which is both stable and dynamic,[2] and Prigogine's discovery led directly to the rise of complexity science and its description of the complex adaptive systems (CAD's) that I have already referred to so often in this book. CAD's are creative, stable, adaptive, and evolutionary, describe how all living systems succeed, and we have seen that their science is now being applied to human social systems. It is because we humans are, by our nature, CAD's, and CAD's are, by *their* nature, creative, that we have a natural mental and biological impulse, or urge, to be creative. CAD's are, of course, the inspiration for the design of Haier's *RenDanHeyi* management model, and provide the scientific basis for Quantum Management Theory.

Discoveries in neuroscience during these past fifteen years tell us even more about the nature of our creativity. It has become almost common knowledge by now that the human brain is not hard-wired. We don't just grow new neurons and new neural connections until we have reached an age of maturity that equips us to deal with the everyday challenges of life in our culture. Our brains don't stop growing at some age limit like

---

[2] Ilya Prigogine and Isabel Stengers, *Order Out of Chaos*.

eighteen or twenty. Instead, they are "plastic," possessing the capacity always to grow new neurons and ever more complex neural connections throughout our entire life span. And we do so whenever we are faced with a new challenge or are responding to some new experience for which we were not previously equipped, responding to something that stimulates us and makes us "think." Our brains themselves have infinite potential. And because of the mutually creative observer/observed relationship in quantum physics, this gives us both the infinite potential to create an ever richer world, and an infinite potential to create and recreate ourselves.

I Make Myself

The *RenDanHeyi* management model rests on the assumption that, as employees recreate their products, they will recreate themselves—add to their knowledge, acquire more skills, realize more of their potential to serve the company. On a still wider scale, this is also the assumption of the quantum world view. In the *participative universe* described by quantum physics, as observers make reality with their observations of it, they are at the same time making themselves. As we have seen, the observer/observed relationship is a cocreative relationship. In the same way, as quantum persons make the world with our questions, decisions, and actions, each of us also recreates ourselves. We are not victims of reality; we are its makers. We are not victims of our fate; we make our fate. This self-creation happens inevitably to some extent during the years of childhood and growing up, or if we have to face some challenge in the course of life that requires a new learning experience. But we can also do more to grow ourselves and enrich our lives. By doing the kind of things mentioned in the previous chapter—extending and varying our experiences, adding to our learning, going outside our comfort zone to listen to and reflect on views different than our own, celebrating diversity in every way possible, finding meaning in our work. And the resulting, constant, self-creation is not just "a way of life," it is in fact possibly the essential purpose of our lives, the duty of our lives.

Just as Chinese philosophy has always stressed the moral duty of self-cultivation, quantum philosophy sees self-recreation as a moral principle of the good life. The universe constantly evolves toward ever greater complexity, and thus the creation of ever more order and information. As creatures that are fully part of the universe and its Way, it is natural that we do the same. In the quantum world view, which sees every person as possessing infinite potential, it is surely the built-in purpose of our human lives to develop as much of that potential as possible. And as both *RenDanHeyi* and Quantum Management argue, it should be a built-in purpose of the companies we work for to enable us to do so. By enriching ourselves through constant self-creation, we will be enriching our companies, our world, and even the fabric of reality itself.

WE ARE RESPONSIBLE FOR THE WORLD

Since it is we who create ourselves and the world in which we live, it is we who are responsible for these selves and this world. In the end, we make the world through the choices that lead to our decisions and our actions. But this leads to the obvious questions: how are we to know right from wrong? On what authority are we to base our moral and other choices? These questions are particularly urgent at a time when there appear to be no clear or agreed-upon moral or behavioral goal posts to guide us, when a spirit of "anything goes" or "whatever is good for me" seems to reign supreme in both personal and business life. As my daughter said to me when she was fifteen, "It is very difficult to be my age today. You and Dad are always changing your minds about what it is ok for me to do or not do, and none of the other adults in my life seem to know what they are doing either. I just have to make the whole thing up for myself as I go along."

Until two generations ago, people in the Western world, at least, would have looked to their religious beliefs for moral guidance and what was required of them to be a good person. Afterall, God's will was clearly spelt out in the Bible or the Koran, and all we had to do to make the right choices was obey. But today, the vast majority of people in the Western world who adhere to any religious tradition, if they do so at all, do so for social or identity reasons. Young people like my now fourteen-year-old grandson find religion totally irrelevant, "useless and boring," as he describes it. If they believe in anything, it is science, and science has not been very good at articulating a moral perspective. And yet in the East, particularly in China, an understanding of how the universe works, the Way (*tao*) of the universe, was the very basis of human morality.

As we saw in Chapter 5, Taoism taught that each of us has the whole universe within us. Confucian philosophy, which held that human nature is essentially good and that there is a natural moral or ethical resonance between Heaven and the human, believed that we are born with *liangzhi*—a "moral intuition" or "understanding" of the Way (*tao*) of the universe, and that we can strengthen this through moral self-cultivation. Thus the reason that self-cultivation was a fundamental principle of Chinese philosophy, and is still a strong value in modern China today. Self-creation is seen as the way we become fully human, and capable of mirroring the harmonious coherence of Heaven here on Earth. As the great contemporary Chinese philosopher Tu Wei-Ming expresses it,

> The precondition for us to participate in the internal resonance of the vital forces in nature is our own inner transformation. Unless we can first harmonize our own feelings and thoughts, we are not prepared for nature, let alone for an "interflow with the spirit of Heaven and Earth." It is true that we are one with nature. But as humans, we must make ourselves worthy of such a relationship.[3]

If readers have understood the argument of this book so far, they will know that Quantum Management's insistence that companies (and other forms of social organization) must become complex adaptive systems if they are to succeed is based on the quantum understanding that we are fully part of nature and the universe, and that what works best for them will work best for us. Thus, just as the *I Ching* advises the leader that "the way to success lies in apprehending and giving actuality to the Way of the universe (*tao*)," Quantum Management advises leaders that the way to success is to follow the principles of quantum physics and implement them in their organizations. And the same applies to the moral and other decisions we make in our personal lives.

Our Western word for *liangzhi* is, of course, "conscience." We view conscience as our moral compass and see it as an unfailing inner perception of right and wrong. In my own past work, I have associated conscience with our SQ, or "spiritual intelligence," and have argued that we have this ability to know and understand the way and meaning of the quantum universe because our own bodies and our minds follow the same physical principles by which the universe itself works. Our own, mental and biological, quantum fields resonate with other quantum fields in nature and the universe. It is important to understand that the principles driving the self-organizion of the quantum universe are not rules or "commandments" like those spelt out in the Bible, but

---

[3] Tu Wei-Ming, *Confucian Thought*, p. 9.

instead *principles and values* that can guide the decisions and actions made by our free will. This quantum nature of ours can be thought of as "the central operational system" that guides our moral choices and decisions, just as a quantum company's central operational system guides the self-organization of employee activity.

This argument, very similar to that made by traditional Chinese philosophers for the origin of *liangzhi*, was the basis of my deriving the Twelve Principles of SQ from the twelve defining qualities of complex adaptive systems (living quantum systems). Those same Twelve Principles appear in Chapter 13 of this book, adapted as the Twelve Principles of Quantum Leadership. The first of the Twelve Principles of SQ, or Quantum Leadership, is "Self Awareness"—knowing who I am, what I truly believe in, what I value, what my real purpose is. Reflecting on these things gives me access to knowing that I am part of nature and the universe and what are the "good" human values and purposes that reflect this. As the great Confucian philosopher Mencius wrote, "For a man to give full realization to his heart is for him to understand his own nature, and a man who knows his own nature will know Heaven."[4] Further access to distinguishing "good" or "moral" decisions and actions from "bad" ones results from knowing the "good" and "bad" forces that lead to either creation or destruction in the universe and nature.

According to quantum cosmology, there are two opposing forces in the universe—coherence, the creative force that brings things together through the power of relationship and creates order, and entropy, the destructive force that tears things apart and creates chaos. These could be the cosmic origins of what we call Good and Evil. Life brings order out of chaos through living systems (complex adaptive systems) that are internally coherent and harmonious, thus stable, adaptive, and evolutionary. All living systems, like the quantum systems that make up the material world out of which they arise, are essentially creative because they are always larger than the sum of their parts. They *add something* to what existed before. They are also self-organizing. In conscious human beings, this principle of self-organization is expressed through our free will. *We* make the decisions, *we* take the actions that make the world in which we live. It is *we* who can make it a better world and ourselves better people. And the laws of physics can guide us.

---

[4] Quoted in Tu Wei-Ming, ibid., p. 61.

Quantum physics tells us that the world is created by the formation of relationships and destroyed by the destruction of relationships, so our moral work takes place through the kind of relationships we are within ourselves and the relationships we make with others. Actions or decisions that create disharmony within ourselves, or between ourselves and others, that put us "at war" with ourselves or others, that *destroy* relationships, are aligned with the destructive force of entropy, and are thus "bad" actions or decisions. Actions or decisions that create inner harmony or harmony with others, that *build* relationships, are aligned with the creative force of the universe, and are thus "good" actions or decisions. This is true both in our personal lives and in the actions and decisions we may take as employees or leaders. If we build good and harmonious relationships with others, other individuals, other companies, other nations, we are adding to the desired greater coherence of both the social world and the material universe. If we build bad ones, we fragment them.

This insight, plus the quantum insight that, as everything is connected to everything, everything is *part* of everything, that there really *are no others*, leads to the simple, guiding principle of quantum morality that itself mirrors the Golden Rule: When in any relationship, do onto others as you would have them do onto you—because those "others" *are* you. And for leaders of companies or nations, quantum morality would fully reflect the "moral imperative" of the philosopher Immanuel Kant: Always behave in a way that it would be alright if all others behaved that same way.

Building good human relationships is, of course, not the only way that our adult creativity can contribute to greater order and coherence in our world and in the universe. Each kind of "making" that we do brings something new into the world—making a good meal, making a beautiful article or creating a beautiful space, making an innovative tool or product, making a great company, making knowledge through discovery, are but a few. And, because we have the gift of language, we can make (and destroy) things by relating words. Words brought together to convey truth are creative, and therefore "good" relationships; lies and misinformation are destructive, and therefore "bad" relationships, words of love or compassion "good"; those conveying hatred or cruelty, or simply cold disregard, are "bad," etc.

Thus moral choices, and decisions between "good" and "bad," grounded in what quantum physics now tells us about the universe, are in no way radically different from those grounded in "the wisdom of the ages"—the world's great philosophical and spiritual traditions and the wise advice of those inspired by them. But the quantum world view does offer a new language for speaking these old truths, and a new source of authority—ones that might appeal to those so currently unmoored by the amorality, materialism, selfish individualism, and lack of any higher meaning licensed or occasioned by the bleak and corrosive Newtonian world view, and unable to find guidance in the seeming irrelevance of the old language and its sources of authority.

As a summary to these past five chapters that have presented how quantum physics invites us to understand the nature of a person, I will quote these words from Tu Wei-Ming. Tu draws his authority from the Confucian tradition, but the very same conclusions are drawn from the authority of quantum philosophy:

> A human being is an active participant of an agelong biological line, a living witness of an historical continuum, and a recipient of the finest essences in the cosmos. Inherent in the structure of the human is an infinite potential for growth and an inexhaustible supply of resources for development. A person's selfhood embodies the highest transcendence within its own reality; no external help is needed for the self to be fully realized....The self is the center of a network of relationships in the human community and must recognize that it is an integral part of a holistic reality...[To quote Mencius,] "All the ten thousand things are there in me. There is no greater joy than to find, on self-examination, that I am true to myself."[5]

---

[5] Tu Wei-Ming, ibid., pp. 60–61.

CHAPTER 11

The Motivations That Drive Me

I may think I have found my purpose, but whether it is a life-enhancing purpose or perhaps a destructive one, and whether I then successfully live it, depends upon the motivations that drive my choices and actions. Human beings and organizations are energy systems. Our motivations determine how this energy flows through the system and how it is channeled. Everyone in business now realizes that raising employee motivation is key to employee productivity. But we need to look at *which* motivations are productive.

When we have negative motivations (such as fear, greed, anger, and self-importance ("ego"), our system energy flow gets blocked and distorted, with damaging or destructive consequences. Studies show that 94% of employees and/or leaders in traditional, Newtonian organizations operate from these negative motivations. When they are driven by more positive motivations (exploration/curiosity, cooperation, self-mastery, creativity, and service), both employees and their organizations thrive, as will be illustrated by later discussions of companies that have implemented Quantum Management. Haier's *RenDanHeyi* "Three Self Model" includes "self-motivation," and thus working or leading with a positive motivation is important to following the model. Having positive motivations is critical to realizing our greatest human potential, and companies that have positively motivated employees will realize their own best potential. This chapter presents a scale of motivations that outlines 8 negative motivations and 8 positive ones. Reflective exercises will be

© The Author(s) 2022
D. Zohar, *Zero Distance*,
https://doi.org/10.1007/978-981-16-7849-3_11

offered to help the reader recognize the motivations from which he or she is acting, and then suggestions are made for how to move from a negative motivation to a more positive one.

Any great shift of consciousness or culture requires first that we understand both the negative consequences of staying where we are and the motivations that have put us there. Why are we here in this predicament now? Just exactly where are we starting from? And then we need to envision the future. What shift are we trying to make? What are its attractive features? And what motivations would we need to get there? This need to understand motivations and how to shift them is critical to a more contented and successful personal life and to outgrowing the crises facing today's business culture.

The study of human motivations is as old as our ability to reflect on one another's behavior. It is a primary quality of our intelligence to ask "why?", and motivations are what we describe when trying to explain our own or another's behavior. Abraham Maslow's Hierarchy of Needs was the first attempt to present an organized scale of all motivations, from the most basic to the most lofty. Maslow's scale of needs has been widely used in business ever since. He listed survival as the most basic motivation, then a need for security followed by a need to belong or to be loved. These are his "deficiency needs." For what he called "higher needs," he described self-esteem, self-actualization, and peak experience.

In the years since, Maslow's hierarchy has inspired many attempts to develop motivation theory further, with psychologists, doctors, and scientists like R.B. Cattell, Ian Marshall, David Hawkins, and Daniel Goleman publishing more elaborate lists of motivations and different scales or hierarchies. I have decided to present Marshall's scale here because it has evolved together with my own earlier work on SQ (spiritual intelligence), and this will prove essential when we come to understand how a motivational shift can happen. This scale offers a new way of systematically diagnosing the motivational and emotional foundations of where a culture or an individual is now, and then suggests how we can shift the present, negative motivational state to a more desired future one.

THE SCALE OF MOTIVATIONS

Ian Marshall was a practicing medical psychiatrist and psychotherapist, with a Jungian background and learning. His scale of motivations was derived from over forty years of clinical observation of patient behavior and response. As we can see, the scale pictured below draws from Maslow's Pyramid of Needs, but extends Maslow's original six motivations to sixteen, eight positive ones and eight negative ones. These are arranged in a hierarchy from −8 to +8 and have the unique property that the positive and negative legs of the scale mirror one another. Thus +3 *self-mastery*, mirrors and is paired with −3 *craving/greed*; +1 *exploration* mirrors and is paired with −1 *self-assertion*, and so on. This has great implications for how to use the chart, as I will discuss in a moment (Fig. 11.1).

As implied by the numbering, it is better to have a motive of +3 than one of −1, but it is also better to be at −1 than at −4. Our personal effectiveness increases, and our behavior improves or has a more positive outcome as we progress up the scale. An individual driven by *fear*

Fig. 11.1 The scale of motivations

Scale of Motivations

(+8) Enlightenment

(+7) World Soul

(+6) Higher Service

(+5) Generativity

(+4) Situational Mastery

(+3) Power-Within

(+2) Gregariousness

(+1) Exploration

(0) Openness

(-1) Self-Assertion

(-2) Anger

(-3) Craving

(-4) Fear

(-5) Anguish

(-6) Apathy

(-7) Guilt & Shame

(-8) Depersonalization

(−4) will adopt far more reactive and defensive strategies than a counterpart who is driven by *self-assertion* (−1). This has clear implications for how bold we will be in our actions and for risk-management in companies. *Fear* leads to behavior that is risk-averse, or perhaps desperate; *self-assertion* may lead to overconfidence or carelessness.

In fact, not just our decisions and strategies, but the even deeper cognitive processes underlying them, alter as we move up or down the chart. It is clear that motivations drive behavior, but they also drive thinking. Each motivation is a whole mindset, embracing assumptions, values, aspirations, strategies, relationships, emotions, and behavior. If I have a fearful mindset, everything looks like a threat, whereas if I am ego-driven with self-assertion, I may hugely overplay my hand. A person motivated by *anger* (−2) will use a very different decision-making process than one who is driven by *gregariousness/cooperation* (+2). The angry person will be preoccupied with blame and a desire for retribution, and will seek strategies that bring this about. He/she feels set against an opponent or enemy. The cooperative person will be concerned with finding a balanced analysis of any problems and a desire for consensus. He or she sees the other as a prospective partner, and appropriate strategies will follow.

Therefore, any move up or down the scale of motivations also represents a shift of outlook and behavior. The visions, goals, and strategies I adopt will be radically different depending upon my underlying motivations, whether I am an employee or a leader. We can see from this that any growth or transformation process aimed at altering behavior (habits), attitudes, or emotions is bound to fail if it does not address the motivations at play in any situation or relationship. *Shifting motivation is the only stable way to shift behavior* and to ensure that both we and our companies are functioning at peak performance.

As I describe each of the motivations in turn, I do so in their positive and negative, mirrored pairs. Thus we shall move both up and down the scale simultaneously, letting each negative motivation come just after its positive equivalent. This is because the goal of all our actions should be to shift ourselves from the negative to the positive. We want, of course, our actions and decisions to have a beneficial effect for ourselves or others, and *nothing good can ever come from negative motivations*.

0, Neutral: The position of neutrality is not itself a motivation. It is either our starting point as infants, or our life-changing cross-over point from being driven by negative motivations to acting from more positive ones. It is like the neutral position in a car's clutch system, free and ready to go, but with no direction yet determined. Many of us awaken fresh in *neutral* each morning, before the memories, images, and emotions from the day before rush in to fill our consciousness. It is like the *tabula rasa*, described by the philosopher Descartes—the tablet on which nothing is yet written.

+1, *Exploration*: *Exploration* is associated with curiosity, a sense of wonder, and an open, willing attitude to whatever life throws in our path. It is very common in young children. It reflects a desire to know our way about a scene or a situation, such as that first exploration we do when we arrive at a new tourist or residential destination. These people are in open dialogue with their environment, they look and listen and they easily engage. *Exploration* is a recognition that we need to know, to learn, to explore, and that it will be fulfilling to do so. It involves us in reading books, papers, and magazines—anything that will teach us more and allow us actively to engage with our environment. It makes us good students and willing, attentive employees. People driven by this motivation are usually interested in music, art, and film. They love traveling to new places and are enthusiastic to solve new problems or to meet new challenges. They like to know how things work, and they pursue knowledge and learning for their own sake. All their strategies will be bent on reaching out, on extending their skills, knowledge, or area of activity. They will be drawn to innovation because it excites them, and they will greet adverse circumstances with a "What can I make of this?" attitude. *Exploration* is a necessary motivation associated with the self-creation we discussed in this chapter.

−1, *Self-Assertion*: This motivation is associated with thoughtlessness, unbridled competitiveness, too much pride, self-centeredness, and aggression. David Hawkins comments that there is enough energy in this motivation to drive the United States Marine Corps. Like the Marines, these people are always "charging over" some hill, imposing their will and structure on the environment, "taking no prisoners." Their attitude toward learning and knowledge is manipulative. They try to assert what they already know, or they engage in learning as a means to strengthening their already entrenched position. Thus they are not open to learning things that do not further their ends. In the end, this is self-defeating.

+2, *Gregariousness/Cooperation*: We human beings are social animals. We need to relate to others and usually gain great nourishment from doing so. The bonds that we form with our fellows and culture through our gregariousness are bonds of fierce loyalty often based on shared values as well as shared goals. A gregarious person usually seeks company, preferring it to being alone. He or she likes people, and enjoys doing shared social or work-related activities with them. These people make good team members, and have a strong *espirit des corps*. Cooperative people are good at seeing the other's point of view, and harbor a natural respect for it even if they disagree. This makes them very good negotiators, but also good at drawing out creative ideas in others. They are good listeners.

−2, *Anger*: We all recognize anger in others. Angry people are usually very "cold," carefully holding their emotions in check, or very "hot," letting their anger spew all over the place. They feel bad and they blame someone or something for this. Bad things in life are someone's fault. As David Hawkins puts it, "Anger as a lifestyle is exemplified by irritable, explosive people who are oversensitive to slights and become 'injustice collectors,' quarrelsome, belligerent, or litigious."[1] They often feel spiteful and seek strategies of revenge.

+3, *Self-Mastery/Power Within who has self-mastery*: We usually associate personal power with the ability to move or dominate others: "power-over." But power-over is external power. A person has it because he or she owns something, occupies some position of authority or influence, has a strong body, "is somebody." A person acting from −1, *self-assertion* seeks power-over as a means of using others to make himself feel strong or important. Unless wielded from a higher motivation, most power-over usually creates winners and losers, and the conflict that results.

The only person the man or woman who has *self*-mastery and is motivated by *power-within* really seeks to have power-over is him or herself. These are people who are centered in themselves, at peace with themselves. They know whom they love and what they value and they act from this level of love and/or values. They have *integrity* in the strict sense that they are whole people, as well as showing behavior that is filled with integrity. They may also be rooted in their skills, or, if they are athletes, in their well-trained minds and bodies. The very pleasurable sense of "flow" when performing at our physical or mental best is the correlate of *power-within*.

---

[1] Ibid., p. 82.

People who have *self-mastery* are trustworthy. We know where they are coming from and know that that is from a place within themselves that we can trust. They have a recognizable personal style derived from deeper commitments, and they have a strong felt-sense of their own identity. These people can be counted on to fulfill any responsibility they take on.

−3, *Craving*: The Buddha said that craving is the root of all suffering. Most of the Seven Deadly Sins are sins of craving. Craving expresses itself as perpetual restlessness, a sense of never having enough, of there always being something more to want or need. Driven by a sense of inner empti- ness (the exact opposite of *power-within*), these people constantly adopt strategies of grasping. They are greedy people, who are never satisfied. Most feel they "are owed," that someone, somewhere didn't give them what they needed or never gave them a break. They want things, but often they don't think they should have to pay for them. Their greed makes them materialistic if it is a greed for money or things and it makes them jealous if it is a hunger to be loved. *Craving* is of course the basis of all addictions—over-eating, gambling, alcoholism, drug-addiction, etc., and the strategies of the craving person are always the strategies of an addict: Craving people may not be trustworthy where the object of their craving is concerned, betraying anything or anyone (including themselves) that frustrates satisfaction. Because they are impulsive, they are often deeply irresponsible.

+4, *Situational Mastery*: The man or woman that has reached +3, *self- mastery/power-within* is centered in deep personal values. But when our motivation reaches *situational mastery*, we find ourselves rooted in wider, interpersonal values and skills—especially those of a profession, a tradi- tion, or a system of understanding distinctive of wider thinking or some shared vision. A master stone mason wields with his hammer all the skill and all the power of master stone masons throughout history. He draws on his craft's collective pool of wisdom and skill. A master-level execu- tive leads with an easy air of authority and inner self-assurance. He or she has an *instinct* for good strategies and decisions. There is a sense of inner discipline and of "flow" in a master's behavior and decisions. At the level of *situational mastery*, we see the bigger picture or are in tune with a larger pattern, and thus our strategies are more complex and more long-term. We'll seek long-term objectives and constantly reframe those objectives as we take in new information.

David Hawkins claims that very few people in our culture get above the level of *situational mastery*. Only 8–10% achieve it. We find among them most people who have reached the top level of their profession or craft—senior doctors, higher executives, first violin players in an orchestra, champion sportsmen, leading scientists. Winston Churchill and Franklin Delano Roosevelt were master politicians, Marie Curie was a master scientist.

−4 *Fear*: *Fear* is associated with anxiety, suspicion, a sense of being threatened or of being too vulnerable. It is the very opposite of being master of the situation. Acting from this motive, I seek always to protect or defend myself. I see others in my environment as threats or enemies. I tend to see opportunities or challenges as possible threats (because I doubt my ability to deal with them). I tend to withdraw from people (those whom I feel threaten me) or the environment, I become timid. I don't volunteer and I don't take risks. *Fear* isolates me from the moment and costs me my spontaneity. Hence the expression, "frozen with fear." Driven by *fear*, both employees and business executives become risk-averse and closed to any kind of innovation or exploration.

* * *

We get to a place with the next eight motivations where we begin to find the exceptional people, either the supernormal especially gifted or the subnormal especially injured or damaged. These are the realms of greatness at the one extreme and of psychiatry at the other. No more than 4% of the general population is driven by these higher or lower motives. These are the people whose personalities differ from the normal, perhaps up to the extreme of incipient madness. These include border-line manic-depressive (bipolar) individuals, or those individuals prone to but not actually in schizophrenic breakdown, who are known as schizotypal. There is a well-recognized correlation between these personality disorders and creativity. The same qualities that give rise to unusual behavior confer unusual vision or exceptionally sensitive temperament. For such personalities, the risks of great catastrophe are balanced by the chance of great genius.

+5 *Generativity*: *Generativity* is a special manifestation of creativity. It is creativity driven by love or passion. A painter *loves* color and his art,

Einstein said that he loved physics, Isaac Newton felt great awe and love for the universe he wished to explore. This love or passion gives generative people a sense of playfulness about their creativity. They *enjoy* it and identify with it. The work is the life.

Situational masters (+4) draw out the potentiality within their shared tradition. They are the leading expressers *of* a tradition. *Generative* people create *new* traditions, new paradigms. They love and are drawn to the unknown or the unexplored and their creative gifts allow them to give new shape to the unformed. *Situational masters* play "finite games." They play within the boundaries. *Generative* people play "infinite games." They create new boundaries.[2]

−5 *Anguish*: Hamlet's famous soliloquy, "To be or not to be, that is the question," is the cry of an anguished man. Unlike grief or mourning, which is a necessary and healthy reaction to loss, anguish arises from a sense of being lost or helpless for what to do or what to decide. It comes from a sense of blocked potential. Our generative process itself is blocked. We wring our hands and feel despair. We feel stuck, caught in the moment, with little prospect for movement. Anguish often results from incurable tragedy, like having a damaged child, being a sportsman who has lost physical agility, or being an infertile woman who had desperately wanted children. Retirement can bring it on, or immersion in a situation that we feel we can't handle. Anguished people have no strategies because their very anguish arises from the fact that they can't see any. Everything seems impossible. This is, of course, an important component of depression. But although the anguished person is suffering, they have not lost all hope, as is the case with −6, *apathy*.

+6, *Higher Service*: Higher service is the motive that drives the servant leader, the highest and most dedicated form of leadership possible. Any great leader serves something from beyond his or her self, but the servant leader serves transpersonal values—things like excellence, goodness, justice, truth, the alleviation of suffering, the salvation or enlightenment of others. Any leader serves his fellows, his community, his country, or company, but servant leaders ultimately serve their own notion of the highest or most sacred. The best of them serve that longing in the human soul that conjures up visions and possibilities. They have a

---

[2] See Jaqmes Carse, *Finite and Infinite Games*.

sense of vocation, of being "called" to serve and in answering to this they find their own deepest peace, their own destiny. This is *focused* creativity, going beyond +5.

Servant leaders make things happen that others have found impossible, they create new ways for human beings to relate to one another, new ways for companies to serve society, new ways for societies to *be*. The Buddha, Moses, and Jesus were such leaders. In our own times we have had the good fortune to be served by Gandhi, Martin Luther King, Mother Teresa, Nelson Mandela, and the Dalai Lama. But there is no need for such greatness in servant leadership. Any of us can be a servant leader if we act from the motive of higher service.

−6, Apathy: If Hamlet is the man of *anguish*, Macbeth is the man reduced to *apathy*. "Tomorrow and tomorrow and tomorrow/ Creeps in this petty pace from day to day,/ To the last syllable of recorded time/ And all our yesterdays have lighted fools/ The way to dusty death...[Life] is a tale/ Told by an idiot, full of sound and fury,/ Signifying nothing." Macbeth has seen all his dreams and schemes come to nothing and now he feels that he is nothing. In *apathy* we are overwhelmed with a sense of *anomie*, of having no role to play in life. Where the person of *anguish* suffers because he or she is no longer able to play life's game, the person of *apathy* can't see that there is any game to play. This is a very deep form of depression, −5.

+7, World-Soul: The servant leader at +6 is rooted in higher values, but their calling is to be of service in this world of daily affairs. At the next level up, +7, *world-soul*, a person sees himself, others, and nature as parts of the divine made manifest. Their consciousness has become one with the collective unconscious of our species (and sometimes that of other species, or the universe itself), and when they do speak or create works of art it is as though through these utterances they hear the voice of something beyond themselves. Mozart's music was literally dictated to him from this level. He said that he merely wrote down what he heard. So, too, does Shakespeare's genius for seeing and bringing to life the disparate points of view in a complex array of human characters. "All the world's a stage, and all men and women merely players," and Shakespeare saw them from the vantage point of a celestial playwright. Most of us will never reach this mystical level of motivation but we can gain intimations of it through the great works of the geniuses who dwell there, and this is why art, music, and literature are so necessary to the human soul.

−7, *Shame/Guilt*: *Shame* and *guilt* fill a person with an almost exactly opposite sense of being to that experienced by *world-soul*. When overcome by the motivations of −7, I feel wholly *apart* from any meaningful or deeper level of reality. Indeed, I feel out of joint with "existence," feel that I have no right to be here, or that my presence in some way makes the world a worse place. I experience myself as a wound or a scar on the face of existence, and may wish to destroy myself. I simply cannot face myself, or go on living with my guilt. Suicide rates are high among people driven from this motivation, often ritual ones. The Japanese tradition of *hara-kiri*, results from loss of face (*shame/guilt*), as did the practice of disgraced Roman generals falling on their swords. Judas killed himself out of unbearable shame. People acting from this level have sometimes betrayed their own deepest ideals, and their strategies may be ones of self-destruction—either directly through suicide or indirectly through drugs, alcoholism, or reckless behavior.

+8, *Enlightenment/Serenity*: We come at this point almost to a failure of words or images. As Lao Tzu wrote at the opening of The Tao te Ching, "The way that can be expressed in words is not the eternal way." That small handful of people in human history who have reached *enlightenment* and written about it can only allude, or speak in metaphor. They speak commonly of the total absorption or annihilation of self in "the Absolute."

It is possible to have experienced *enlightenment* and then to have returned to the world. The Buddha did so, as did those who have written about their experiences. But the return to the world is as an altered person, free of all negative motivations and partially identified with the experienced sacredness of reality. T.S. Eliot's *Four Quartets* expresses this thought, "Below, the boar hound and the boar, Pursue their pattern as before, But reconciled among the stars." Back in the world, these people live lives of grace. They are at peace with themselves and existence. Though they may pass as quite ordinary, the ordinary is for them exalted by an inner light.

−8, *Depersonalization*: A person who has reached *enlightenment* is all inner light without physical shell. A person who has undergone *depersonalization* is an empty shell with no core. Here, the sense of "I" has disappeared because the ego-self has disintegrated. There is no "person" left, only random utterances and uncoordinated behavior. This is the inner world of the hospitalized schizophrenic or the hopelessly burnt out alcoholic or drug addict. This is as close as we get to damnation while still alive. There is no further disintegration beyond it but death itself.

FINDING OURSELVES ON THE CHART:

Most of us, most of the time, act from motivations in the center of the motivational scale, that is between +4 and −4, and in any given relationship or situation, we can use our emotional intelligence (primarily self-awareness and emotional control) to improve things, or at least limit the damage. When I am aware that I am behaving in a destructive way, that awareness gives me the power to change my behavior, or at least to excuse myself from the situation until I am in a more positive state. But the use of a reflective exercise can greatly increase this ability to recognize the motivations at play in any real-life situation, and thus our ability to control our behavior within it.

This reflective exercise recognizes that, while the occasions may be rare, most of us at some time in our lives have experienced being affected by nearly every motivation on the chart, even the more extreme ones. By recalling past instances of this, and becoming aware during the exercise of a time when we were motivated by each of them, and what effect this had on our relationships or the situation, we can greatly increase our familiarity with the chart and our power to use it as a guide in the future. Thus during my own Quantum Management training programs, I ask participants to remember an instance in the past when they were moved by each of the eight negative motivations and then each of the eight positive motivations, to write that down, and recall the consequences of their having done so, also writing down each of these recollections. How did it affect a particular relationship? How had it made a situation worse? And then I ask them to go back to each of their negative experiences and relive it in their imaginations as they ask themselves what direction that relationship or situation would have taken had they instead been acting from the paired, positive motivation. People have found this exercise both painful and insightful, and most say going through it increased both their knowledge and control of themselves and their ability to be guided by the Scale of Motivations in future.

How We Move on the Chart

Once we see that we are acting from a lower motivation that has negative consequences, or we are inspired by a person or culture clearly acting from higher motivations than our own, we naturally want to know how to shift our own motivations. How can I get from thinking and acting out of −4, *fear* to at least −2, *anger*, which is *some* an improvement on my situation? If I am more ambitious, how can I move from −2, *anger* to +2, *cooperation*? Or how can I prevent myself from being dragged down from +1 *exploration* to −4, *fear*? In short, what are the dynamics of this scale of motivations and how does shift happen? This can be articulated in three basic principles.

Principle One: A negative person or culture cannot help another on the negative scale. Two people stuck at *anger*, −2, will just spark each other off and make each other more angry. Two *assertive* people at −1 will get locked into a power struggle. Similarly, using a negative motivation to make a change in a situation can *only* result in getting to some other negative motivation.

Principle Two: A person at −3, *craving*, is just canceled out by a person at +3, *power-within*. Equality of opposites is not enough to change the motivations of either person. To have the power to raise another up the scale, someone must make what chess players call a "knight's move." That is, it would take someone at +4, *relational mastery*, to raise a −3 to −2 or higher.

Principle Three: An individual at +4 can contain another who is coming from −3; but an individual who is only at +2 can be dragged down by someone who is at −3. Thus a culture or a group higher up on the scale can raise the game for those lower down. This is the point of having priests, good teachers, master artisans, and servant leaders in society. They inspire us upward with their example or vision. But it is also the case that another person, or our company culture, can drag us down. Motivations are intimately bound up with our emotional states, and our own and others' emotions can be contagious.

SEVEN STEPS TO USING THE CHART OF MOTIVATIONS

- Assess where you are now. What motivation is coloring your attitude or behavior in this situation or relationship?
- How is this motivation affecting your behavior or any decisions you have to make?
- What is the outcome as a result of your motivation?
- Ask what you would have liked the outcome to be?
- What motivation might better get you there?
- Work to make the motivational shift happen.
- Reap the behavioral, relationship, and outcome changes you would prefer to have.

PART III

The Quantum Leader

There is one thing upon which most people in the world's troubled Western democracies can agree: we have a crisis of leadership. And this is a crisis felt in both business and politics. Covid-19 brought to a head the fact that a large number of the men and women in corporate and national leadership positions are simply not meeting the challenges of the times. In part, this is a crisis of mindset, or philosophy, and thus competence, as I have been discussing throughout this book. Too many twenty-first century leaders are confronting today's challenges with seventeenth century models and "solutions". In part, it is a moral crisis, caused by a decline in leadership behavior and speech—the cheating, lies, personal opportunism, and sheer corruption that have so deeply eroded trust among those being led. In part, it is a cultural/economic crisis, the extreme self-interest and exaggerated individualism that have both led to and justified amoral (and often immoral), "me first", strategies among individuals, companies, and nations. And in part, it is simply a lack of vision, an inability on the part of leaders to "think big", to raise their sights above just getting by and getting on and to inspire the rest of us to strive for something better, inspire us to dream.

In these next few chapters, we will look at the challenges facing the quantum leader, focusing on company leaders, and the philosophy, character, principles, and thinking skills required to meet them.

CHAPTER 12

A Leader of Leaders

Different times need different leaders. In stable times, companies simply need a steady hand on deck, a leader who can manage the given and the expected with experience, expertise, and competence. But we are not living in stable times. A scientist describing the state of our world today would say that we are living "at the edge of chaos." This does not necessarily mean, as many of us fear, that we are living at the edge of an abyss, that we are standing at the edge of a cliff and about to fall off. Rather, the scientific meaning of "the edge of chaos" is the state of a system poised *between* order and chaos, and it describes a state of maximum instability, a state of crisis when both the challenges and the opportunities are at their greatest. Crisis is often the mother of opportunity. It makes us realize that "the usual" no longer works. There are not the familar goalposts to act as guides and people are called upon to create new ones for themselves. It is the same at the edge of chaos. The biggest challenge facing leaders in the twenty-first century is the uncertainty and rapid change of events and technologies. This is a time for creativity and reinvention, requiring both the leader and his/her organization to be creative.

The whole purpose of Quantum Management Theory is to describe the leadership thinking and organizational transformation required to maximize creativity and the adaptability it requires. We have seen that in the quantum world, any kind of outside interference or control destroys both. In material quantum systems, any outside interference

© The Author(s) 2022
D. Zohar, *Zero Distance*,
https://doi.org/10.1007/978-981-16-7849-3_12

such as observation or measurement causes the Schrodinger wave function to decohere, and all the multiple, superimposed potentialities offer just one reality. In living quantum systems, complex adaptive systems, outside control alienates the system's self-organizing relationships and destroys their holistic cocreativity. In companies, top-down management administered through layers of bureaucracy does the same thing, greatly diminishing both adaptive response to rapid, or unforeseen, change, and innovation. Companies burdened with bureaucracy are slow-moving dinosaurs, their heads too distant from the ground their feet must navigate.

Quantum Management principles call for hands-off leadership at the top and the removal of middle management, replacing them with a coordinated network of self-organizing teams empowered to make decisions "at the front-line." In the resulting quantum company, all employees become leaders and the CEO is now a *leader of leaders*. This demands both very different leadership qualities, and a new, quantum, leadership philosophy. It demands new leadership vision.

THE VISION OF THE QUANTUM LEADER

Quantum leaders practice the very essence of quantum thinking, thinking that takes us beyond the boundaries of all that was known or has existed before. They lead from a deep level of revolutionary vision. They change the system, invent a new paradigm, clear a space where something new can be. Zhang Ruimin is such a business leader in China, wanting to create a company where employees could develop their full potential and to create a kind of relationship with customers that had never existed before. Steve Jobs was such a leader, wanting to create a technology that would change people's lives. Elon Musk is such a leader, over and over again achieving what others had never thought of or had thought was impossible.

Quantum leaders achieve this not just from "doing" but, more fundamentally, from "being." They are servant leaders in the truest sense of that term. They serve possibility, the not yet born. Such leaders are essential to deep corporate transformation.

The unicorn has always been a special symbol in human culture. He is that most impossible creature of the human imagination, a beast conjured up by longing and the human capacity to dream, conjured up by passion and given space to be by those who dare to believe in the mere possibility that he might exist. Today, all new start-ups are called unicorns, and the leaders I have mentioned have fathered many. As we have seen, Haier China is a company of start-ups, a company of unicorns. The same is true of Tesla.

In quantum science, the whole of existence is a vast reserve of possibilities just waiting to be drawn up from the quantum vacuum's infinite sea of possibility. Some of these possibilities are plucked out by "observers," human beings just living our lives, asking our questions, making our experiments, and initiating projects. An awareness of their role as cocreators of existence can increase quantum leaders capacity to fulfill that role. They serve more than company or colleagues, more than markets or products, even more than vision and values as these are normally understood. They serve that longing that conjures up unicorns, and through their service they build successful, profitable companies that add some new dimension to both business and human well-being. Quantum leaders are servants of the quantum vacuum, of the very heart of our universe and its manifold potentiality.

Most entrepreneurs start a business because they look at the market and see that there is some opportunity to offer a new service or product. Others do so because they have a certain skill or talent they feel they can take to the market environment. But the motivation of the quantum entrepreneur is more spiritual, arising from a feeling of inner necessity, a sense of deep passion. They say, "This has to exist! This has to happen! I have to do it!".

At the very beginning of his treatise on the art of strategy, Sun Tzu says, "Command your people in a way that gives them a higher shared purpose."[1] Human beings are first and foremost creatures of meaning and purpose. This is what defines us as a species. We have a spiritual intelligence (SQ) that makes us seek meaning and purpose, and when we find it, it gives our lives and our work a sense of direction. We become highly motivated, highly productive. Employees who work for a visionary company find this sense of meaning and purpose because their leader's own purpose and passion permeates and inspires the company culture and is embedded in the very work challenges and opportunities they face each day on their jobs. They feel they are part of something big, something larger than themselves.

---

[1] Sun Tzu, *The Art of War*, Chap. 1, Line 15.

The Philosophy of the Quantum Leader

In his *Art of War*, the very first of the five principles that Sun Tzu outlines for successful leadership is, "Know your philosophy."[2] By this he means, know the values and principles that define your strategic mission, and embed them in the culture shared with those whom you lead. I argued much the same throughout Part I of this book when presenting the philosophical ideas and values that arise from a new paradigm, or world view, derived from the defining principles of quantum physics and the quantum universe it describes. I deeply believe that Quantum Management, and the decision to implement it through some adaptation of Haier's *RenDanHeyi* management model, commits leaders to a new leadership and management philosophy that is itself a philosophy of life. Here, I want to outline the basic principles of this new leadership philosophy:

- Quantum leaders know that everything is connected to everything, everything is part of everything, and thus that they and the company they lead are part of the universe itself. The best way for their company to be sustainable, evolutionary, and innovative is for the leader to follow the same principles that assure that for other quantum systems, and imbed them in the company operational structures.

- Quantum physics tells us we live in a participative universe and that, through our questions, decisions, and projects, we human beings co-create reality. We make the world we live in. Quantum leaders know they play a role in making the world, and thus that they have responsibility for the world. As company leaders, they meet this responsibility by building good companies that generate the wealth and create the conditions that will contribute to making the world a better place for their shareholders, employees, customers, and the community in which they operate. And they know all this includes a responsibility to protect the environment on which everything and everyone depends—including themselves and their companies. Quantum leaders give up power, but they never give up responsibility. They will always be responsible for overall mission guidance and execution, company vision, company morale, and the nature of company culture.

---

[2] Sun Tzu, ibid., Chap. 1, Lines 6 and 14.

- Quantum leaders know that quantum physics tells us every person plays a unique role in constructing the shared web of reality that we call our world, and that every employee of the company is an active player in making it what it is. They know there are no "little people," no "unimportant people" in their organization. Each employee is an equal partner in the company's shared enterprise, and an equal contributor to its success—a fellow leader. Recognizing this unique value of every employee, quantum leaders accord each of them dignity and respect, regardless of role or status.

- Quantum leaders know that the universe itself possesses infinite potential, and that human potential is infinite. They are committed to giving each employee the opportunity to achieve his or her own best potential, knowing this best realizes company potential. They also appreciate market potential and the infinite potential of customer needs, and are always looking for ways more fully to develop the company's own potential through new structural, product, and service innovations.

- Quantum leaders know that living systems are the most complex and creative systems in the universe. They appreciate the value and promise of life itself, and thus are committed to ensuring the best quality of life for employees through working conditions and rewards, and best improving the quality of life for customers through products and services. They do not expect employees to endure conditions they could not endure, nor customers to accept products and services they would find unacceptable. Quantum leaders always want to give value, to *add* value, to enrich the fabric of life itself.

- Quantum leaders know the universe itself develops its potential and innovates through the creation of ever new, borderless relationships, that the universe is an ecosystem. They are committed to building an internal ecosystem by nurturing and developing internal, collaborative, win/win relationships between employees and self-organizing teams within the company, and to building an external ecosystem by nurturing and developing cooperative, win/win relationships with customers, the community, and other companies. They are committed to the principle of Zero Distance.

THE CHARACTER OF THE QUANTUM LEADER

Business leaders are usually judged by their ability to deliver a healthy bottom line for shareholders, not by the quality of their personal character. Indeed, many are even admired for being "tough bastards" or unprincipled rogues. The culture of business-as-usual depends on greed, self-interest, and amoral decision-making. Adam Smith declared these to be founding assumptions of capitalism. An ability to wield and leverage power is what matters, and any moral flaws or consequences be damned. While it is all too obvious that moral flaws do have consequences for companies, corruption being a large contributing factor in today's leadership crisis, there are other reasons why the quality of a leader's personal character now trumps an ability to wield power.

We have seen that if companies are to become agile and resilient in the face of twenty-first-century challenges, leaders must surrender most of their accustomed power. In a quantum company, the leader's job is to motivate, inspire, be a role model for the company culture, and to serve the needs of employees who have now become leaders in their own right. Thus a quantum leader's character and integrity becomes a matter of great importance. Can they be trusted to have our backs? Do they walk the talk? Are they honest with us? Are they someone we can look up to? Thus for quantum leaders, it is not so much what they *do* that matters, but rather what they *are*. This requires a very different path to leadership development. Leadership development becomes *personal* development, character development.

- Perhaps the most important process required for personal development is increasing self-awareness, learning to know ourselves, who we are in different situations and with different people, getting to know our own feelings, what makes us happy and what we dread, how we respond to others and why, what we most aspire to and the fears or hesitations that hold us back, what motivates us and what we need to do to act from higher or more positive motivations, why some things make us angry and what better we can do to control that, why we find some things difficult, why we embarrass ourselves sometimes, why we need to control things, etc. Increasing self-awareness is a life-long process because the self is a process. Who we are changes and develops over time, and we need frequently to catch up with ourselves, to see where we are now and set the goals for what has to be accomplished next. Such self-examination and awareness cultivates the emotional intelligence we need to understand, empathize with, and lead others. Each of us is unique, but each of us also has an awful lot in common.

- Another important dimension of character is vulnerability, and the authenticity it creates. Business leaders are expected to be strong, to have all the answers, to be the one everyone can lean on or turn to, who can make the right things happen, who never say "I don't know" or "I need help with this." They were never such all-powerful superheroes, but they had to pretend. That made those who worked with them or for them have to pretend, too. It creates a false company culture that everyone here always knows what they're doing, never makes mistakes, never needs help. It creates the fear and the risk-aversion that dominates so many company cultures, the cover-ups and the blame-games, and in fact increased incompetence. Quantum leaders have the humility, the integrity, and the wisdom to own up that they, too, are vulnerable, they, too, make mistakes, they, too, need the help of others, their input, their different or greater expertise, their different way of looking at things. This sets an example and creates a culture of mutual reliance, a culture of safety. It also leads to an authenticity that builds trust.
- Today, character is also a factor of competence. In the Zero Distance quantum world, no company or organization is an island, and narrow expertise in just one area of life or work is no longer sufficient for any effective person. For a business leader, such insular narrowness is simply a recipe for incompetence. Thus *breath* and *depth* of character is essential for quantum leaders, a trajectory of constant personal growth. Just as it takes a lifetime to know oneself, it takes a lifetime to become oneself. Each of us has infinite potential, but potential must be nurtured and developed if it is to be realized. Quantum leaders are committed to a lifetime of self-cultivation, a lifetime of learning and exploration. They are always expanding their horizons, adding to their skills, exposing themselves to new ideas, new people, new situations. They are cultured, aware of the big ideas in the arts and sciences. They know today's world is fast, uncertain, and complex and the knowledge and experience they will need may come from anywhere. The character they grow will come from the effort they make to expand that. They know that to make the world, they must make themselves.

Quantum leaders are also committed to becoming better people. Moral self-cultivation has long been a fundamental principle of Chinese thought. The followers of Confucius believed all human beings are born with an innate knowledge of the good but that we must devote our lives to nurturing and developing this. The same has been the goal of all the world's great spiritual traditions, and is the point of most spiritual rituals and practices. The quantum leader's commitment to moral self-cultivation makes his/her leadership a spiritual practice.

THE QUANTUM LEADER AS A CRISIS LEADER

During the early months of the Covid-19 crisis, several people commented in the *New York Times* and elsewhere that America needed a "crisis leader," and there were various descriptions of the qualities such a leader must have. The best of these, I thought, was written by General Stanley McCrystal, former commander of the American Army's Joint Special Operations Task Force in Iraq, and his officer colleague Chris Fussell, who made the further observation that the need for crisis leadership is here to stay, an ongoing necessity for all twenty-first-century organizations. They believe the twenty-first-century leader must, in essence, be a crisis leader. The qualities they say are required in a crisis leader offer a good recap and summary of the qualities necessary in a quantum leader. Thus I want to end by quoting them:

- "Leaders must be visible with their plans, honest with their words and adaptable with their actions—all while maintaining compassion for the situation and the impact it is having on their team.
- Be seen to be there as a leader, show calm in the midst of chaos;
- Be honest with your team, even if this feels uncomfortable;
- Give up more authority than feels natural. Fighting through complexity requires quick and informed action at the edge...Organizations will need teammates making independent decisions close to the points of action, not waiting for directions. It's tempting in times of crisis to grab the reins and yank back, but this will be more disruptive than it is helpful. Be connected, listen and adapt based on what your front line is telling you;
- Be more compassionate than you think you need;
- Use digital communication to stay in touch with your people in the field. The Joint Forces command where both of us served, needed to

do this exact thing. We pivoted from being a centrally located, thousands strong enterprise to a network of small teams spread around the world.
- Connect, learn, listen, and inspire a team."[3]

We will see more of General McCrystal's leadership philosophy and practices and how these altered critical American Army operational procedures in Chapter 19.

We saw in Chapter 5 that the Taoists believed that Man is the bridge between heaven and Earth. Reflecting this, quantum philosophy sees our purpose as human beings is to embed the cosmic principles of the universe in the projects we build here on earth. By building quantum companies managed according to those principles, quantum leaders are fulfilling that purpose. After giving a speech at INSEAD in November 2019, Zhang Ruimin was asked what advice he would give to young people today. He said, "The greatest thing that I believe a young person can do with his or her life today is found a company."

---

[3] Stanley McCrystal and Chris Fussell, "Fight Coronavirus Like We Fought Al Qaeda," *New York Times*, 24 March 2020.

CHAPTER 13

Twelve Principles of Quantum Leadership

We have seen that becoming a quantum leader requires becoming a good person. It requires being a person of integrity whom others can trust. But even more than that, it requires being a person whose own example can inspire others, someone whose life and being can show others the way, someone who in his or her life has walked the quantum path of self-cultivation and ever-renewed self-creation, who can rise to challenges, aspire to higher things, and bring out the best in others, turn others into leaders. Typically, a Western guide or self-help book on such leadership would offer a formula, a set of steps to take or rules to follow, in the spirit of the Bible's Ten Commandments. But formulae and rules are contrary to the very spirit of the quantum paradigm and a quantum organization. Each quantum person is unique, just as each quantum company is unique, and thus a guide for quantum leadership should offer a set of general *principles* that each leader can follow in a self-organizing and adaptive way.

But *which* principles should guide a quantum leader? The Chinese word for "leader" is *"lingdao."* *"Ling"* means "to know," and "dao," of course, is the Tao, the Way. The Chinese believe it is the role of leaders to know the Way of the cosmos and Nature and to bring that into the world of human activities. Today, many complexity scientists agree with them. Men like complexity economist Brian Arthur and physicist Geoffrey West believe that human social systems like companies and cities function optimally as complex adaptive systems, i.e., living quantum systems.

© The Author(s) 2022
D. Zohar, *Zero Distance*,
https://doi.org/10.1007/978-981-16-7849-3_13

QUANTUM SYSTEMS	CAD'S	LEADERSHIP
Self-Organizing	Self-Organizing	Self-Awareness
Indeterminate	Bounded Instability	Spontaneity
Emergent Led	Evolutionary	Vision & Value
Holistic	Holistic	Holism
Contextual	In Dialogue With Environment Adaptive	Compassion
Potentiality	Evolutionary Mutations	Celebration of Diversity
Wave Function "Collapse"	Outside Control Destructive	Field Independent
Heisenberg Uncertainty Principle	Exploratory	Ask Why? Questions
Create New Realities	Recontextualize Environment	Reframe
Participatory Universe	Every Element of System Important	Humility
Negative & Positive Cosmic Forces	Order Our of Chaos	Positive Use Adversity
Driven Towards Complexity	Driven Towards Growth	Sense of Vocation

Fig. 13.1   Quantum systems, CAD's, and quantum leadership principles

That is also, of course, the argument of this book. Therefore quantum leaders should be guided by the same principles that define these systems. Thus, the twelve quantum leadership principles described just below are the conscious equivalents of the twelve defining qualities of quantum systems and complex adaptive systems. This correspondence is illustrated in Fig. 13.1.

The Twelve Leadership Principles Are

- **Self-Awareness**—Socrates said, "Know thyself." The principle of self-awareness is knowing who I am, what I believe in, what I value, and what motivates me. Knowing my strengths and weaknesses, both as a person and as a leader. Knowing how I affect others. How do others see me? Knowing my life's purpose and how that aligns with my purpose as a leader. Am I in touch with my inner compass and led by its sense of direction? Am I even aware that I *have* an inner compass, a deeper self beyond my ego and its daily concerns?

The principle of self-awareness relates to the fact that complex adaptive systems are self-organizing, and that quantum systems spontaneously reorganize as their environments change.

- **Vision & Value Led**—Acting from principles, deep beliefs, and living accordingly. Reflecting on our values and remaining true to them. Aspiring to make a difference, to make "the world a better place." Idealistic. Longing for "the not yet born." Positively motivated. Inspired and inspirational. Having a vision for ourselves or our companies is *not* just having a "goal" or a "target." It is about assigning a meaning to our lives or to our company, having a purpose, knowing what our lives or our companies are *about.*

The principle of being vision and value led relates to the fact that complex adaptive systems are driven by the "purpose" of both sustaining themselves and experiencing evolutionary growth. They are emergent, creative. Quantum relationships are emergent, furthering the natural direction of the universe toward creating ever more complexity, order, and information.

- **Spontaneity**—To be an authentic person or to lead an agile company, a person must have the capacity for spontaneous response. The principle of spontaneity calls upon us to live in and be responsive to the moment. Being able to see what this moment or this situation calls for and being flexible enough to adapt my decisions and actions accordingly. Not looking to the past for solutions or understanding, but responding to *this* situation or person *now*. Dropping the "baggage" of assumptions and conditioned thinking, the baggage of past "wisdom" and success, the baggage of past grievances or failures, the baggage of theory and ideology. Seeing the world through the eyes of a child. *Spontaneity is not the same as acting on whim or impulse.* These involve no thinking at all. By contrast, spontaneity is a feature of adaptive thinking.

Principle of spontaneity correlates with bounded instability of complex adaptive systems. These systems exist only at the edge of chaos, in a zone of radical instability, and thus maintain the flexibility necessary to respond and adapt spontaneously and creatively to changes in their environment. Quantum indeterminism allows the same flexibility for the evolution of quantum systems.

- **Holistic**—This principle means an ability to see larger patterns, relationships, and connections between things. Being sensitive to the relations at play in a situation, and building good quality relationships. Sense of belonging to the whole, of seeing yourself and your company as systems and as part of a larger system. Knowing that everything is connected to everything and that you are connected to everything and to everyone. Realizing there is no such thing as separation, and acting accordingly. Knowing that everything you do, every decision you make, has consequences—for yourself and for others. Seeing that every question has at least two sides, and that there is an underlying wholeness within the differences. Ability to see the infinite within the finite, and able to see deeper currents or patterns within events and situations.

The principle of holism relates to the fact that complex adaptive systems are holistic. Every part is related to and dependent upon every other part. There are no internal boundaries, no recognizably separate parts. The same is true of quantum systems.

- **Field-Independent**—This principle means having an ability to stand against the crowd and follow our own convictions. To have the strength and the courage to do what we think is right even if "everyone" is telling us it is wrong. To have the resilience to be unpopular, to not bend if we are mocked or excluded. To stay true to our principles in the face of temptation or criticism. And yet always to be self-critical, to be on guard against our own hubris and the traps and tricks of our own thinking. This protects us from fanaticism and gives us a reality check.

  Field independence relates to the fact that the creativity of complex adaptive systems is destroyed by outside control. These systems, if controlled from outside, lose their self-organization and revert to being simple Newtonian systems. Field independence also correlates with fact that measurement or observation "collapses" the quantum wave function.

- **Humility:** The wise leader is always alert to the ignorance in his own mind and the wickedness in his own heart. On this earth, there is no such thing as a Perfect Man, and thus no such thing as a perfect leader. The humility of the quantum leader reminds him/her constantly of this. Confucius realized this when he said: "I question myself three times a day." Humility requires a sense of being a player in a larger drama and of our true place in the world. Growing beyond arrogance and self-assertion. Realizing that others know things, too, and that no one person can ever know it all. Knowing when we are out of our depth and being willing to seek help or advice. Knowing that even I can make mistakes or be wrong. Being willing to acknowledge and respect the expertise of others. Being willing to trust others. Not always having to be the best, not always having to be the boss.

The principle of humility relates to property of complex adaptive systems that every element of the system is important and necessary, and each element depends on all. It also relates to fact that the quantum universe is a participatory universe.

- **Ability to Reframe**—Standing back from a situation or a problem and seeing the bigger picture; seeing problems and opportunities in a wider, or new, context; changing one's mindset. When we stand back from a problem, or from a decision that we have made, we gain the benefit of seeing our own behavior and thinking as though we were a neutral, third person, someone observing ourselves from a distance. We become our own coach or consultant. From this objective vantage point, we become aware of assumptions or habits that underpinned the thinking or the decision, and thus become better masters of both ourselves and of that situation or problem. We can then ask ourselves creative questions like, "How would this look differently to me if I surrendered that assumption? How would this situation be different if I acted this way instead of that? What if...?" Our minds begin to churn out new ideas, new questions, new *possibilities*. We begin to change the way we frame things, and then we find ourselves becoming new actors in new situations, now approaching things differently and able to make fresh, and quite possibly better, decisions. In a moment, I will outline a reflective process that helps us develop the skill of reframing.

  Principle of reframing corresponds to fact that complex adaptive systems recontextualize their environment, and quantum systems develop new, emergent properties through relationship.

- **Ask Fundamental "Why" Questions**—A need to understand things, to get to the bottom of them. Wanting to know how things work, why things happen, or why we are being asked to do something. Wanting to understand the logic behind events. Reluctant to take things for granted, instead questioning their reasons and foundations. Having a spirit of inquiry and a passion to learn. Being curious. Asking why myself and others behave as we do. Questioning my own and others' assumptions. Having the courage to rock the boat, even our own. Always wanting to go deeper into any question. Asking if things could be different or better. Valuing good questions over necessarily finite and short-term answers. Reflecting on life's "big questions."

Principle of asking fundamental questions corresponds to fact that complex adaptive systems are exploratory, and that quantum potentiality is transformed into reality by doing experiments and asking questions.

- **Celebration of Diversity**—Exposing ourselves to things, experiences, ideas, examples that are different. Seeking out and opening ourselves to others' points of view, to ideas and opinions that challenge or broaden our thinking. Recognizing that broadening our knowledge and experience is crucial to developing an appreciation for and understanding of others. Recognizing that truth is multifaceted, perhaps infinite, and thus in many circumstances there is no "one best way." Able to respect and even benefit from points of view that are different than our own. Going outside our own comfort zone to gradually extend its boundaries. Able to challenge our own assumptions and preferences. Appreciating others *for* their differences rather than *despite* them.

  Celebration of diversity corresponds with a complex adaptive system's reliance on evolutionary mutations for transformation. Mutations play a creative role in the newly emergent structure of these systems' future. Mutations, and the quality of mutability, play keys roles in the sustainability of life on earth. And quantum thinking allows us to hold two seemingly opposing beliefs or ideas and appreciate that, in many cases, both can be true. Quantum entities exist as both particles and waves at the same time, can be everywhere at the same time.

- **Positive Use of Adversity**—Sun Tzu's *Art of War* tells us, "Victory comes from finding opportunities in problems,"[1] and it is now almost common knowledge that the Chinese word for "crisis" contains the two elements, "danger" and "opportunity." Positive use of adversity is the ability to learn from mistakes, grow and learn from setbacks and suffering, and to turn problems into opportunities. Becoming stronger and wiser from having been tested. Able to carry on even though we have a tragic recognition that not all

---

[1] Sun Tsu, Chapter 3, No. 5.

problems have solutions. Able to look at our own weaknesses and overcome them. Resilient. Stubborn!

Principle of Positive Use of Adversity correlates with complex adaptive systems' ability to bring order out of chaos. They have "negative entropy," bringing new order and form into situations where, before, there was none. In quantum physics, the positive, creative force of the universe defeats the negative, destructive force of entropy.

- **Compassion**—Quality of "feeling-with" and deep empathy. Able to experience what others may be feeling or going through, and concerned about their plight. Having a desire, where possible, to make their circumstances less burdensome or painful—for their sake. Knowing that we are all one, and thus I *am* them. We are not just our brother's keeper; we *are* our brother. Feeling this common human bond and thus some understanding even of those who are our enemies or by whom we feel threatened, thus making forgiveness possible. Showing others respect and taking care of their dignity. Treating others as we would like to be treated.

  The principle of compassion resonates with the quality of complex adaptive systems BEING adaptive, in a co-creative dialogue with their environment. It also resonates with the contextual nature of quantum systems' being and identity.

- **A Sense of Vocation:** "Vocation" is derived from the Latin word *vocare*, "to be called." The first vocations were those of monks who dedicated their lives to serving God. Having a sense of vocation is to feel called upon to serve, to give something back, to leave the world a better place than you found it, or having a passion to bring something new into the world, a sense that this just *has to be*. And having found a way to act on this through our career or life's dedication. Thus having the feeling that our job or our life is our prayer, our contribution, or service. Feeling responsible to the world and for the world and taking that responsibility through our actions and commitments. Having a sense of vocation is much deeper than having an ambition or a goal. It is having a sense of purpose and direction in our lives, a sense of what we are here for, and of having found a path in life through which we can realize this. A sense of vocation is a definitive quality of the servant leader, and often of the entrepreneur. Let us ask ourselves: Do I feel I have a "calling," a life purpose? What is it? Am I able to live that purpose through my leadership? Or do I feel empty, dissatisfied, rudderless? Do I fill my life with ambitions, like getting rich or being successful? Am I just out for myself? Whom or what do I serve?

Having a sense of vocation resonates with the positive force in the universe driving the cosmos toward ever greater complexity, ever more order and information, and with the life force in complex adaptive systems that drives them both to sustain themselves and to evolve.

REFLECTIVE PRACTICE

We will see that reflective thinking is one of the skills of quantum thinking. To gain the most benefit from knowing these twelve principles of quantum leadership, it is best to use them as a guide to daily reflective practice. This is a practice I developed for my own use, and I have found it an effective way both better to understand myself and to put the day's activities and interactions into a wider perspective. Without question, any kind of reflection increases both self and situational awareness, but focusing such reflection on one or other of the twelve principles helps us better to live and lead with that principle.

Reflective practice is best done at the end of the day. It must be done in a quiet place where one can be comfortable and free from distraction. Personally, I go into my sitting room, turn off the lights, and sit by fire and candlelight. Once comfortable, it is important to bring our attention to the body, noticing how it feels. Where is my body tense or uncomfortable? Is there a "lump" in my stomach? Is my breathing fast or slow? Do I have a headache or a stiff neck? Am I clenching my fists or fidgeting? Our bodies act as the wastebins of the mind. All of the stressful events of the day get lodged in them, blocking their natural energy flow.

Once we've become aware where our bodies are feeling discomfort, we begin to ask, "What?" What happened today that might have upset me? Was it an incident at work? An exchange with someone at home? Am I stuck on a problem? Do I just feel too much has come at me today? Did someone or something frustrate me? If the answer to any of these questions increases the tension in my body, it needs further inquiry. So I begin to ask, "Why?".

Why did that exchange I had today upset me? Why do I get upset about something like that? What is it about me that made me vulnerable in that situation? Was the situation caused by something I said or did? Why did I say or do it? Could I have handled it differently? Could I have avoided it? Why didn't I? Do I get into exchanges like this because of some habit or leaning in my personality? Why am I like this? Could I change? Why? Why? Why? Each act of asking "Why?" gets us deeper into the situation and deeper into the way that we think and act about people and situations. It surfaces assumptions and habits and attitudes of which we had previously been aware. It also gives us a broader perspective on others and on their problems.

The reflective process of plunging deeper into some disturbing incident of the day is not endless. Inevitably, the act of repeatedly asking "Why?" will generate an insight that causes the body to let out a deep sigh of relief, and the tension it had been holding dissolves. This will have positive consequences for blood pressure, clarity of thought, and quality of sleep. It can be thought of both as a daily house cleaning of the mind, and an act of daily, increased self-awareness—and self-mastery.

We human beings are a species that asks questions, especially questions of meaning. If we think back to the lessons of Heisenberg's Uncertainty Principle, it is the questions we ask that give us the answers we get. The questions we ask tease out the potentialities of quantum reality and also the potentialities of our own minds and being. The questions we ask create the world we live in. And, most definitely, they create the person that each of us is. By examining ourselves with a series of probing Why? questions at the end of each day, we mine the hidden lessons and potentialities of the day and perform regular, small acts of self-creation. Becoming a better self makes each of us a better leader.

In the quantum organization, where *all* employees are leaders, these same twelve principles must underpin the organizational culture, thus encouraging all to live them.

CHAPTER 14

Thinking Principles for the Quantum Leader

Just as different times call for different leaders, different times also call for different leadership skills. Quantum physicist David Bohm famously said, "All the problems of the world are problems of thought. If we want to change the world, we must change the way we think." This reminds us that the most important leadership skills that must match the times are the leader's thinking skills and habits. For our new Quantum Age, those must be thinking skills and habits that spark constant innovation, maximize human potential, can thrive on uncertainty and rapid change, and that can recognize and benefit from the interconnectivity of events, people, and human needs.

Everything I have written in this book so far has been about the radical shift in mindset required to structure and lead organizations adapted to thrive in the twenty-first century, but here below are some specific thinking habits to guide leaders.

Intuition/Creative Insight

By intuition I am not referring to the quick, gut-level instinct that many of us experience as an unreflective sense of knowing what is best to do, or what is the best decision to make. Such gut-level instinct can be a very effective way to make spur-of-the-moment decisions or choices where quick action is needed, or when there seems no available, logical stream of thought for making a choice. But as Daniel Khaneman pointed out in

© The Author(s) 2022
D. Zohar, *Zero Distance*,
https://doi.org/10.1007/978-981-16-7849-3_14

his *Fast and Slow Thinking*, gut instinct can often be wrong, or mistaken. It is really a kind of "thinking without thinking," and can err, where "thinking something through carefully" would lead to a very different choice or decision.

When I write here about intuition as a source of creative insight, I am referring to the long, slow, ruminative process that can result in a sudden breakthrough, or creative insight that offers an entirely new way of understanding or seeing something. This, too, comes with a sudden "aha!" sense of surprise, a sudden flash of understanding or vision that seems "to come out of nowhere," but is accompanied by a sense of certainty far deeper and more sweeping than any certainty arrived at by logical, step-by-step thought. Indeed, that kind of logical teasing out of the "reasoning" that backs up the sudden flash of creative insight may then take hours, weeks, or years fully to work out. It may be the program for an entire lifetime's work fully to work out what came to us in that moment of insight.

This is a slower kind of intuition that came to Newton and Einstein in physics, to Mozart and Beethoven in music, to great painters like Van Gogh and Picasso, and in their cases we call it "genius." But perhaps less sweeping instances of it lay behind the breakthrough work of innovators like Steve Jobs, Mark Zuckerberg, and Elon Musk, great business thinkers and leaders like Frederick Taylor, Peter Drucker, Jack Welch, Jack Ma, and Zhang Ruimin. And smaller instances of it occur in daily life to gifted teachers, managers, designers, gardeners, parents, and of course, very commonly, to children. Indeed, I believe that this kind of intuitive creativity is available to us all as humans if only we know how to preserve and nurture it in ourselves. It is a very familiar skill of quantum leaders, and can be nurtured by certain qualities of mind. The quantum leadership principles that help us generate creative insights are:

- Celebration of Diversity: Many studies in neuroscience have shown that people who take in more data, who have a wider, richer range of knowledge and experiences on which the unconscious mind can ruminate and which it can see new relationships between, have more breakthrough, creative insights. Mervyn King, the former governor of the Bank of England, says about creative decision-making, "In the ordinary business of life, where we are constantly confronted with unique situations, we need a pluralism of approaches and models."[1] Thus constant feeding of our minds, cultivating ourselves by seeking new and unfamiliar experiences or reading widely outside our usual field of interests, provides "food for creative thought." King and his coauthor John Kay also point out that collaborative thinking in groups can further enrich the range of data and experience on which we can draw. "Successful decision making under uncertainty," they say, "is a collaborative process....We make better decisions in groups, because in a radically uncertain world the group holds more information than any one individual."[2]

- Openness (Receptivity): If creative insights are to arise from the unconscious mind, we must still the "monkey mind" of busy daily activity and its requirement of focused, left-brain attention. We need to sit quietly, without distraction, and simply open ourselves to whatever the deeper mind might be speaking to us. Engaging in a meditation practice can be very effective. For those who find it difficult simply to sit still and be receptive, taking our "mind off things" by doing something more active that occupies concentration but has nothing to do with daily tasks or the problem we are trying to solve—like playing a game of golf, going for a walk, preparing a meal, or listening to music—can free the more intuitive mind to surface. There are many reported instances of people getting their creative breakthroughs during deep, dreaming sleep.

- Spontaneity/Openess: When we are spontaneous, we are open to the moment and whatever it brings, not allowing our minds to dwell on other things. Our full attention is on the "now." Thus, while sitting quietly, we should, as best possible, simply be in a state of spontaneous awareness.

- Holism: Again, studies in neuroscience show that creative people have a greater tendency or capacity to see relationships between apparently unrelated thoughts or events, the *associations* between 'this' and 'that'. And it is the sudden insight that "this" is related to "that" that leads to the emergent "aha!" experience of new discovery. If, as a normal part of our daily understanding of situations and events, we practice looking for the relationships at play,

---

[1] John Kaye and Mervyn King, *Radical Uncertainty*, p. 412.
[2] Ibid., p. 416.

we strengthen the unconscious mind's ability to see ever more relationships.

- Asking Fundamental Questions: People who ask more questions train their attention to look for more answers. Behind every act of creative intuition, there is a mind that asks "Why?" or "How?" or "What?" Such people are constantly, often unconsciously, searching for more new and deeper understanding.
- Ability to Reframe: By its very definition, a creative insight gained through intuition is a radical reframing of previous understanding.

REFLECTIVE THINKING

In the previous chapter, I outlined a Reflective Practice that helps us better to live by the twelve principles of quantum leadership. We saw there that an ability to stand back from a situation or our own emotions and view them with a more cool detachment is critical to reflective thinking. Reflective thinking also helps us to understand what things mean, why they have happened, and thus what conclusions can be drawn from them. It helps us to understand why ourselves or others behave as we do, or make the decisions that we do, and thus opens an opportunity to engage in more beneficial behavior or to make better decisions. Reflective thinking also helps us to select the relevant data from a mass of information or a very complex situation. The quantum leadership principles that help us do reflective thinking are:

- Self-Awareness: Our own immediate involvement in a situation, or the concentration with which we have been focusing on a problem, can prevent us from standing back and reflecting on it. Strong emotion or strong commitment to a particular way of thinking about or doing something makes *us* part of the problem. Creative reflection becomes possible only when we stand back and become aware of our own involvement, of the assumptions, biases, or emotions that we have been harboring. Thinking about the role these have played is an important part of the reflective process.
- Asking Fundamental Questions: Using the distance gained by standing back, we can now ask why we or others displayed the emotions or commitments that we did. What was it about the situation that made us angry? Do we always get angry in such situations?

Why? Why do we behave as we do when we are angry and what contribution did that make to the situation? What does this say about us? Why were we or others so certain of some conviction? Are we too quick to rush to judgments or conclusions? Did we consider the wider context, the bigger picture? Did we look at all the arguments or possibilities critically? Why not? Look at the root of the problem. What really caused it? How might it be looked at differently?

- Humility: If we think we know best, and have all the answers, we will not have the receptivity and openness necessary for breakthrough insight. The capacity for self-criticism and an ability to recognize our own role in a negative situation is critical to sound reflection. We must have the humility to admit that we might have been wrong and then to ask "why?". And, of course, listening to others nourishes reflective thinking.
- Celebration of Diversity: Having a wide and varied range of knowledge and experience to draw on makes reflection much more creative.

CONTEXTUAL THINKING

In setting forth the key components of strategy in his *Art of War*, Sun Tzu advises "Know your position." He explains that this means the full context of the forthcoming battle—the climate, conditions on the ground, the motives and psychological state of your opponent, and the relationship of your position to the positions of the others.[3] Similarly, Mervyn King and John Kaye, writing about decision-making in the face of radical uncertainty, offer one piece of, primary, advice: "Always ask 'What's going on here?'" He points out that there is no one most rational decision to make in the face of radical uncertainty. Instead, he argues there are *many* ways to be rational, and which one to choose depends upon the overall context within which situation is set. Thus, always ask: What is going on here, in *this* context?

Quantum physics underpins the advice of Sun Tzu and Mervyn King by reminding us that we can never know or understand a thing or a situation unless we know its full context, that is, know what it is in relation to

[3] Sun Tzu, *The Art of War*, Chapter 1.

and thus what forces are at play in influencing it. The quantum leadership principle of most importance for contextual thinking is of course:

- Holism: This is realizing that everything is entangled with everything, that our company is not an island, and making ourselves aware of the network of relationships, and thus influences, of which our company is a part—the physical and climatic environment, political and economic conditions, public health, customers, partners, employee capacity, morale, and motivation, the competition, etc.— everything that comprises the dynamic system of which we are a part. *Contextual thinking is, effectively, systems thinking.* So when making any strategic decision, we must always ask, "What are all the factors and actors at play in the total system of which our company is a part? What is the influence each is having on company performance, and is there any pattern to our response?"

CRITICAL THINKING

This is having the capacity for independent thinking and judgment; the power to discriminate good arguments from poor ones, and to assess what is and is not relevant. Critical thinking is also the ability to surface our own assumptions and biases, or the assumptions and biases at play in a strategy or a line of thinking. And it is the ability to grow beyond or change these assumptions as necessary. The quantum leadership principles to follow to develop sound critical thinking are:

- Self-Awareness: Having an ability to recognize our own assumptions and biases, and an ability to see what role our own thinking or behavior might be playing in a bad situation or poor strategy.
- Field-Independence: We also must have the ability to stand outside the assumptions of our group or team and see how these might be having negative or undesired influence on behavior or strategy. We must be willing to question authority, our own and that of others.
- Ability to Reframe: Once we have recognized the assumptions and biases that have led to a poor strategy or situation, we must be willing to "think again," to look at the problem or situation from a new perspective.

ADAPTIVE THINKING

The one thing that all leaders can be certain of today is that the future is radically uncertain. We simply don't know what may come at us tomorrow. As Heather McGowan and Chris Shipley say in their *Adaptive Advantage*, "To thrive in the future of work, we must be agile and resilient, adept at both learning and unlearning, to continuously adapt to change."[4] The quantum leadership principles that most underscore adaptive thinking are:

- Spontaneity: Spontaneity is the very essence of agility. Being in, and responsive to, "now." We must recognize that what worked in the past may now be irrelevant, and not be too attached to plans we have made for the future. Act as *this moment* requires us to act.
- Celebration of Diversity: Again, the more knowledge and experience we have, the better equipped we are to deal with unexpected situations or events in an agile way. We must cultivate a love of learning and realize that learning is the ongoing work of a lifetime.
- The Positive use of Adversity: The greatest enemy of adaptive thinking and behavior is fear, a fear of losing what we have, a fear of letting go, a fear of the unknown. Such fears follow from a lack of trust in our own abilities and resilience, a lack of trust that life and situations have their own logic, and thus a tendency to cling to the familiar. They make us risk-averse, and any strategy in the face of uncertainty will necessarily involve risk. The positive use of adversity requires a "ready for anything" confidence and an openness to, ideally even a thrill in the face of, new challenges.
- Ability to Reframe: And, of course, the agility to adapt in the face of the unexpected requires an ability to change our perspective, to see events and situations in a new way, an ability constantly to reinvent our own mindset and thus to put in place new strategies.

---

[4] Heather E. McGowan and Chris Shipley, *The Adaptive Advantage*, p. 97.

Moral Maturity

Moral maturity is not something commonly thought of as a leadership skill or even as a leadership requirement, and yet it is something we recognize and prize in the great leaders who have possessed it and, I argue, is a must have for the quantum leader. This quality reflects the extent to which we are sensitive, thoughtful, responsible, and values-driven in our actions, decisions, and relationships, the extent to which we possess integrity. It reflects our ability to make and keep to commitments, and the depth of those commitments themselves. Also, it depends upon our ability to be open-minded and fair, to have a sense of the role we play as a leader and to fulfill it. Morally mature leaders are trustworthy, they inspire confidence and faith in those whom they lead, and their employees (or citizens) don't just admire or respect them, they love them. Thus they bring out the very best in others. I also believe that a morally mature quantum leader has a basic, guiding intuition that there is a moral order built into the universe itself and that this must be reflected in our behavior and decisions. Acquiring moral maturity requires life-long self-cultivation and is what we mean by building our "character." Thus, it depends upon practicing and living by all twelve of the principles of quantum leadership.

PART IV

The Quantum Organization

CHAPTER 15

What Makes a Quantum Organization?

It is in the very nature of "quantum" that no quantum organization would be defined by a set blueprint or formula. Each will adapt Quantum Management Theory to suit the needs and demands of the field of activity or industry in which it operates. Each will evolve its own organizational culture. We will see in the following four chapters how differently the Haier Group (a manufacturing industry) in China, and its American subsidiary GE Appliances, and Roche Pharmaceutical in India (operating in the healthcare sector) have shaped their quantum organizations, and the different company cultures to which this has given rise. But there are several characteristics that will be common to any such organization, and these derive from the defining principles of quantum thinking outlined in Chapter 2.

- *A quantum organization is holistic*: Quantum systems are holistic. The whole organizes the parts, and every part is related to and partially defined by its relationships to the other parts. In quantum physics, relationship helps to create *further facts and new realities. Events always happen in a context.*

In today's interdependent and globally interconnected business world, everything is related to everything. A quantum organization will see itself as a boundaryless, non-hierarchical *living* system in which every element of the system is defined through its relationship to all other elements.

© The Author(s) 2022
D. Zohar, *Zero Distance*,
https://doi.org/10.1007/978-981-16-7849-3_15

Thus it will have infrastructures and a culture that encourage and build relationships—between leaders and employees, between employees and their colleagues, between divisions and functional groups, and between the organization and its larger ecosystem—customers, the community, society as a whole, and the natural environment. Mechanistic, Taylorian models of the organization as divided into siloed divisions and functions, often set to compete against one another, cannot build these creative relationships. Nor can models of a corporate world consisting of companies acting as isolated islands, each ruthlessly pursuing its own self-interest. Cobbled together out of separate, uncoordinated parts and companies and yet impinged upon from every direction, these old models of conflict and confrontation must give way to new models of dynamic integration and cooperation. The integrity of individual concerns must be protected, while at the same time drawing all parts into a larger working whole.

- *A quantum organization will be agile, responsive, and adaptive*: Quantum and complex adaptive systems are indeterminate, or at least unpredictable. They are poised at the edge between order and chaos, between actuality and potentiality, and their indeterminacy makes them flexible, responsive to their environments, and primed to evolve in any direction.

Today's business world is complex, chaotic, and subject to continuous rapid change: technological, social, and geopolitical, changing customer and employee needs and expectations. Companies must be able to adapt and respond to all this—quickly! Mechanistic, Taylorian patterns of fixed, functional roles and rigidly organized, hierarchical structures for management and control, make these systems unwieldy and slow. Taylorian companies are heavy, lumbering dinosaurs in an age where light, winged birds command supremacy. The infrastructures of a quantum organization must be less like Meccano or Lego and more like plasticine, which can take any shape and be changed at will. Their products and/or services must be constantly innovative.

As I wrote earlier, a quantum organization should function more like a jazz jam session. It should have infrastructures and a culture that allow the free play of uncertainty and experimentation, where different questions can be asked, different goals, products, and functions considered.

Roles will be less fixed, employees encouraged to play "different instruments," to take risks and experiment with the "score." The quantum leader sees him/herself as holding the space where the background theme can emerge.

And finally, a quantum organization should not fear chaos. The ancient Chinese knew that yin/yang, the dark and the light, order balanced with chaos, is the nature and dynamic of the Tao, the Way of the Universe. Today's living quantum science (complexity theory) teaches us that new order arises *only* out of chaos. When my then 2-year-old daughter arrived home from playgroup one day to find that our house had been cleaned and all her toys neatly stacked away on shelves, she protested, "Too much space! We need some mess!" And she instantly set about making some. The mess made the house "home" for her, a place where she could play creatively. A home with too much order is like a society with too many rules or a company with too much bureaucracy. Too much order, too much tidiness, too much adherence to plans, is a form of imposed, outside control that dampens down the creativity of a system. As the ancient Greeks taught, "In the beginning was chaos, vast and dark....the void from which all forms arise, and to which they may return" (Hesiod, *Theogony*).

- *A quantum organization must be bottom-up, self-organizing, and emergent*: Quantum systems and complex adaptive systems are self-organizing and emergent. Each new whole constructed through relationship is always greater than the sum of its parts. Taking advantage of chaos and uncertainty, they are creative, always generating surprise, greater complexity, and new realities. These systems ensure their sustainability by constantly mining potentiality.

Companies today must be continuously innovative to ensure sustainability. We have seen that the *RenDanHeyi* management model ensures this, relying on bottom-up self-organization to do so. In the quantum organization, employees must be turned into responsible leaders in their own right, free to organize themselves and their work and to make decisions—not just self-organized, but also self-motivated, free to reinvent their jobs, their products, and their services in co-creative dialogue/interaction with customers and each other. Middle-management bureaucrats must be removed, and the CEO must surrender most or all of the power previously reserved to him/her. As we have seen, the quantum leader leads with a hands off, light-touch approach, serving his/her employees more as a mentor or coach and providing them with the resources *they* determine they need. This guarantees the emergence of an ever new, fit for purpose organization capable of constant adaptation and innovation.

- *A quantum organization will thrive on diversity*: Quantum and complexity science is both/and rather than either/or. Matter consists of particles *and* waves, and has the potentialities of each. Quantum systems explore many paths from A to B; living systems thrive and evolve through multiple mutations.

The quantum organization will abandon the old vision of one truth, one best way, perhaps one unambiguous product line, and instead take as its guiding principle: both/and, a plural way of accommodating the multiplicities and diversities of markets, customers, and employee potential. "My way" must give way to shared vision, shared opportunity, shared responsibility, and dialogue that recognize the validity of many paths from A to B and the infinite potential of both market opportunities and employee innovative skills. There will be infrastructures that mix levels of responsibility, teams that represent assorted educational, functional, and professional skills and backgrounds, thus assuring different styles of thinking for meeting challenges and solving problems, different products and different services suited to different users—all designed "to let a thousand flowers bloom." *And* there will be *both* some directive principles *and* the free-flowing lack of fixed structures, as appropriate to keep the ship on course while allowing the benefits of self-organization.

- *A quantum organization will be eco-friendly and eco-systemic*: Normal ecology concerns itself with protecting the natural environment. "Deep ecology" is more broadly concerned with life on earth as a *total human/environmental ecosystem*, a human meaning and value-centered dimension that is in symbiosis with a nonhuman but life-centered dimension. Quantum Management Theory adds the dimension of "alignment with the cosmic order."

A quantum organization both safeguards the environment and the natural order, and creates value for the human order—its shareholders and customers, its employees, and its community. Thus it is both eco-friendly and it makes itself the center of a human ecosystem. This ecosystem includes the community as well as internal, cooperative, often partnered relationships between teams and/or microenterprises within the organization and external ones with other companies. (See description of Haier ecosystem in next chapter.)

Like all mechanistic institutions, the Taylorian company assumes a natural dichotomy between the human world and the rest of creation. Newtonian organizations *use* their environment, they *exploit* nature's resources, just as they exploit their own employees and set themselves apart from the communities in which they are located—often polluting their air and waterways. For most of these companies, even the customer is "out there," "other." The quantum organization knows that it is *in* nature and *of* nature, *in* the community and *of* the community. It recognizes that companies are co-creative partners in the earth's ecosystem, both as dependents and as protectors. It replaces the coal and oil swilling machines of the Industrial Age, that have polluted the earth's environment and created a climate crisis that now threatens business as much as everyone and everything else, with green technology, and it finds ways to detoxify its waste. Quantum organizations devote research time and money to finding affordable solutions to community needs that impact the environment. They safeguard the natural order by making eco-friendly products for the market, and do so using eco-friendly manufacturing techniques.

- *A quantum organization is vision-centered and value-driven.* In Newtonian physics, which assumes a split between the observer and what he/she observes, the purposes, attitudes, and values of the observer are thought to play no role in *what* is observed. Newtonian science is "objective." But quantum science describes a "participative universe" in which the observer and the observed have a co-creative relationship. The question a scientist asks, the experiment that is done, determines what is observed. The quantum scientist's purposes, values, and assumptions thus frame the outcome of his/her experiments.

The old, business-as-usual model is focused on products, profit-maximization, and a transactional relationship with shareholders and customers. These companies decide what products to offer the market, and often manipulate public and market taste to make it want their products. They try to create situations of scarcity or discontent, and feed on modern society's illusion that personal and spiritual emptiness can be filled with *things*. Often the market fails, or ceases, to respond. The customers become bored or jaded, and the companies that have tried to satisfy them fail.

By contrast, the focus of a quantum organization is its sense of *purpose*, the opportunities, benefits, and services brought to the customer's overall lifestyle or needs, and a co-creative and mutually beneficial relationship with customers/users. Quantum organizations bring value to users—high-quality products and services, products and services that enhance the quality of users' lives. Such products and services make homes more efficient or user-friendly, may add beauty and balance to the home environment, improve users' health, and perhaps even add meaning to users' lives. Profit, and thus shareholder value, are still crucially important, but these are framed in terms of long-term sustainability rather than short-term benefit. And quantum organizations are ethical.

A food company putting junk food laden with fat, salt, and sugar onto the market when it knows full well these products are making buyers ill is not a quantum company. Pharmaceuticals that bury reports about dangerous or lethal drug side-effects, and oil companies that bribe "expert" scientists to write reports denying climate change are not quantum companies. Quantum companies know they can make healthy profits while giving their customers good food and safe medicine, while also adopting measures that protect the environment. They reject short-term profit maximization at any cost measures and instead build long-term customer loyalty and trust that also ensures their own long-term sustainability. In one of my earlier books, I described this ethical, long-term, high value approach as building "spiritual capital." Each of the companies I profile in the following chapters has adopted it in some measure.

CHAPTER 16

Haier: A Maker's Culture

Corporate Rebels has written, "No longer need we look *west* to Apple, Amazon or Google to learn about experiments and innovation in large corporations. Instead, we invite you to look *east:* and to Haier specifically. Maybe they will become your benchmark. For us, they are the most pioneering corporation of our times."

Haier, China's global domestic appliances giant, is the world's largest supplier of such appliances, and one of the world's largest IoT (Internet of Things) companies and, as the quote above indicates, perhaps the world's most pioneering company. Visited by 10,000 people every year, and the subject of scores of university case studies and magazine features, it was the first large, global company to implement the principles of Quantum Management Theory. Whole books have been written about Haier and its *RenDanHeyi* management model. Here, I can outline only a few of the company's main features.

Zhang Ruimin, the Chairman and CEO of Haier, is called the world's most radical CEO and is known as China's "philosopher CEO." His striking humility, scholarship, bearing, and grace of movement give him more the appearance of a Taoist sage than a business leader. Fitting for a man who says he aspires to leverage traditional Chinese wisdom and philosophy in his management model for today's IoT world. Zhang reads five books every week, and his speeches are always peppered with quotes from great philosophers, both Eastern and Western. Each of his company's internal communications offers a quotation from an ancient Chinese text like the *I Ching*, the *Tao Te Ching*, or the *Analects of Confucius* to illustrate his message. Though the head of one of the world's leading IoT companies, Zhang famously has no mobile phone or social media accounts, no social circle of friends, and avoids company parties and social activities. He finds such things a waste of time and says, "My time is better spent reading." He has his own very large library in his private office, which is decorated with Chinese traditional art and calligraphic wall hangings bearing quotations from Chan Buddhism and the *Tao Te Ching*.

Like so many boys of his generation, Zhang was forced to leave school in his mid-teens during the Cultural Revolution and sent to work in a rural factory. While there, he had what he told me was the formative experience of his life. "Many of fellow young workers and I," he recounts, "had ideas for how the factory could be run better and improve its production, but we were always told by our supervisor, 'You are not here to think. Just get to work and do as you are told.' I vowed then that one day I would found a company in which people would be allowed to think."

That was one of his motives for devoting his life to business leadership, but there was another. In a recent conversation I asked Mr. Zhang why a man with his intellect had chosen a business career. "You could," I said, "have been a very distinguished scholar, or even a very senior leader of the Party." (He is currently a member of the Communist Party Congress, and until recently was an Industrial Representative on the Party Central Committee.) His answer spoke directly to the passion for personal autonomy that drives his business philosophy.

"If I had become a professor, I would have had to become part of the academic system, and my thinking would have had to conform to academic fashion. And, of course, the Party has its own system, and as a Party leader I would be expected to follow that. But as a company leader, I could design my *own* system." And, indeed, as the CEO of Haier he has designed the radically new and pioneering *RenDanHeyi* business model that has won global admiration and acclaim. Recently, after having made several visits to Haier, Chinese Prime Minister Li Keqiang recommended the *RenDanHeyi* model as the business model for all Chinese companies should adopt, and many are doing so.

Zhang Ruimin joined Haier as CEO thirty years ago when the company was a small and struggling refrigerator company making very poor quality goods. One of his first acts as boss was to order the very dramatic "Smashing." In the presence of journalists, he ordered employees to line up 150 of the company's shoddy products and then smash them to pieces with a sledgehammer. "That is the end," he said, "of Haier's association with junk. From now on this company will offer our customers high quality products." But it was not yet the end of hard times.

In the mid-1990s, there was a month when Haier could not meet its payroll. Knowing that would mean his employees, who lived from paycheck to paycheck, could not buy their families' rice, Zhang went to a wealthy land owner in a village near company headquarters in Qingdao to borrow the $10,000 needed to pay his people. However, knowing well that Zhang did not smoke cigarettes or drink alcohol, the landlord decided to play a trick on him. He placed a large bottle of whiskey on the table at which they sat, and said, "I will lend you $1000 for each glass of whiskey that you drink." The young Haier executive who told me this story continued, "And Mr. Zhang drank the ten glasses of whiskey and was able to walk away with the $10,000. He did that for his people, and that is why we love him so much."

Zhang Ruimin's passion for personal autonomy became the central driving principle of all his reforms at Haier: a belief that every employee has unlimited potential and a desire to unleash that potential for the good both of the employee and the company. "In every big company," he says, "employees are treated like tools to be used by the company. Western companies are dedicated to maximizing share holders' value, not employees' value. I wanted to emancipate these people in accordance with Quantum Management Theory. That is why, from day one when I became leader of this company, I have never stopped thinking about providing opportunities and platforms where everybody can realize their potential. This is the essence of *RenDanHeyi:* putting the value of people at the center and fully realizing people's potential."

GIVING UP ALL POWER

In 2012, after several developmental pilot reforms along the way, Zhang finally introduced and began implementing the *RenDanHeyi* management model that has now made Haier both globally famous and a very large and successful global company with healthy profit and growth figures. In the years since, it has grown from being the world's largest white goods company to a diverse corporate group now involved as well in clothing, food, health care, biotechnology, sporting technology, agriculture, finance, and real estate, and the areas of diversification seem to be expanding exponentially. As I described in Chapter 3, that involved getting rid of all middle management and its associated hierarchy and bureaucracy and transforming Haier into a "company of companies," more accurately "a company of start-ups," that today comprises 4000 independent and self-organizing, multifunctional microenterprises (ME's), each designing and manufacturing its own products in a close, co-creative dialogue with its own users. Each microenterprise has its own CEO and comprises a team of usually four to twenty members. These are now grouped into cooperating Ecosystem Micro Communities (see below), making Haier a very quantum "systems within a system." All are supported by key company service platforms.

In keeping with Quantum Management Theory, and the Taoist philosophy that "The highest leadership isn't felt," Zhang Ruimin saw that to empower his employees he must give up all centralizing, top-down power himself. He ceded to each ME what he calls, "The Four Selves," the traditional powers of the CEO and top management: Self-Organization, Self-Motivation, Self-Direction (strategy and hiring), and Self-Remuneration. ME teams are not paid salaries by the company but instead generate their own revenue from sales and services to users and keep a very large share of all profit realized. Hence one key meaning of *RenDanHeyi*: "The value realized by the employee is aligned with the value realized by the user." If an ME is to succeed, and its members to earn their living, it must bring appreciated value to users. Each team then decides for itself how to distribute profit income among themselves.

People looking on at all this from the outside, of course, ask Zhang what is left to him with his job as CEO if he has given up all power. "My job," he answers, "is to serve." Seeing himself as a servant leader within the context of Quantum Management, Zhang says, "A leader should not seek to be an entrepreneur himself but instead see it as as his job to create entrepreneurs. My role as a leader is to create opportunities for my people, provide resources and support for their own entrepreneurial activities, vitalize and energize the ME's, and constantly to enlighten employees to use their own intellect to realize their own infinite potential." He sees management itself as a support function, not a supervisory function.

Because of his own very deep humility, Zhang himself would not mention the other things his leadership provides to his people. His humility, and a constant eagerness always to listen to others and care for others, is part of his character that is so loved and admired by his very devoted employees. That character, his extensive learning, wisdom, and reputation for constant inventiveness and experimentation have made him a hero in wider Chinese society. In 2019, Zhang was one of one hundred "Reform Pioneers" personally awarded a medal by President Xi Jinping for "laying the foundations of the new China after the Great Opening Up."

The resulting Haier "Makers Culture" (culture of entrepreneurial innovation), that features on the walls of its company museum the slogan, "At Haier, Everyone is a Leader, Everyone is a CEO" has indeed produced a highly motivated, innovative workforce, and very high employee morale. As the leader/CEO of one of the Smart Clothing microenterprises said to me, "Before *RenDanHeyi*, my wife always complained that I didn't come home from work until after 9:00 at night, but now she is very patient and proud about the hours I keep because she knows I am building my own company and working for the benefit of our own family. And I am making my *own* decisions, not acting on the decisions someone else has made." This man truly felt "emancipated." As Zhang Ruimin has said, "Being one's own CEO is being an autonomous person who can achieve self-fulfillment with dignity."

"THE USER IS THE REAL BOSS HERE"

"Traditional companies," Zhang points out, "serve their shareholders. At Haier, first we serve our people, but our people serve their users." This statement is key to what makes Haier different, the driving philosophy and methodology of its 4000 ME's, and even to how it has reinvented its financial statements and criterion of success. Zhang tells his people, "You must know your users better than you know yourselves," and in the Haier Museum, the slogan, "The User is the Boss," has pride of place. Emphasis is placed on "user experience," and every ME maintains direct contact with its own users through the internet, by telephone, and even occasional home visits, and these contacts are both co-creative and lifelong. This dedication to user service and interaction is part of the company's "Water Philosophy," drawn from the Taoist insight that "water is the most benevolent element. It doesn't ask for itself but only wants to do for others." Water also flows freely everywhere; it has no boundaries. One of Zhang Ruimin's own lectures about the company's Water Philosophy is titled, "Haier is the ocean." In my own quantum language, I would compare the company to the Quantum Vacuum, "a sea of potentiality."

Between them, ME's and their users conceive product iterations and even new product designs. "At Haier," the head of one ME told me, "our users are also our employees and our designers." This co-creative employee/user dialogue constantly generates new product ideas—like, in response to farmers' needs, a washing machine that can wash both vegetables and clothes, or another that is extra large to accommodate the cleaning of large and heavy robes worn by Muslim users, or smart kitchen appliances that can be controlled from the bedroom while a pregnant woman rests, also able to enjoy watching a smart ceiling TV while prone. More instances and advantages of the company's Zero Distance business model. The company has the largest data bank of user experience in the world, and Zhang Ruimin feels it is this constant feedback from and creative dialogue with users that gives Haier a tremendous advantage over large e-commerce sales platforms like Amazon, Alibaba, and Tencent which, he points out, have only transactional, anonymous relationships with their buyers. Haier's products and services, therefore, are not sold on the big e-commerce platforms.

The goal at Haier is not just to free its employees to use their potential, but also to offer this same opportunity to users. User experience data is collected by way of Haier's pioneering Cosmoplat IT platform. Working with more than 6000 software solutions and collecting user experience data from more than 40,000 companies, Cosmoplat has made a revolutionary move away from big data to the extensive use of small data. "We want to know *why* the user is using the product, and *how* they are using it, what kind of *experience* it is giving them," says the owner of the platform. "This allows us to make better design and manufacturing decisions. And we want to free our users from the tyranny of mass production." Because Cosmoplat enables interactive exchanges with the user, and can in turn respond to these with high-speed product alterations, Haier can now boast that it *has replaced mass production with mass customization.* "Our people no longer have to buy products and services that *we* choose to offer them. They can order from us and get what *they* want." I observed when hearing this that COSMOplat has created a new kind of "internet democracy." Haier has in fact given COSMOplat that name *Khaos*, the original Greek god from whom all other gods sprang. *Khaos* was known as "the egg of all things." We adopted this name, says Zhang

Ruimin, "because our aspiration is to become 'the egg of all things' in the industrial internet, and help all sorts of new species emerge."

Haier does not focus on one-time product transactions with customers, but rather on cultivating "engaged users" who are also buying services and enjoying experiences, and who then become "lifelong users." By multiplying value to these lifelong users through a constant iteration of its product offerings, and consistently multiplying its lifelong users, the company itself enjoys "value multiplication," and it achieves constant and reliable growth. Zhang Ruimin says, "The essence of *RenDanHeyi* is respect for human value and a mechanism to maximize human value," and all participants in the company's complex ecosystem gain from this multiplication of value. The value given to the user feeds back to the company, driving innovation and thus, in turn, adding value to the company. Thus fulfilment of the typically Chinese Haier win/win philosophy, where the winners are employees, users, stakeholders, and the company itself. And these win/win value-multiplication statements have replaced the traditional "profits after deductions" reports as a way of evaluating and communicating the company's success to shareholders.

Haier is called a "Makers' Culture," and most people take this as a reference to its creation of entrepreneurs who make "things" for the IoT market. But underlying this is the far more fundamental truth that, through the *RenDanHeyi* model, Haier makes *relationships,* the very stuff of which the universe itself is made. IoT is itself, of course, a relational technology, connecting smart devices to each other and to their users. But *RenDanHeyi* creates co-creative relationships between the CEO and all who work within or use the company's products and services, between the service platform leaders and the ME's they serve, between team members of each ME and that ME's users, and between the company itself and any citizen who might have a product improvement idea or even an idea that gives birth to a new ME. Everything is in relationship to everything, everything is aligned with everything. And, as we will see now, the model creates co-creative relations between the various ME's.

ECOSYSTEM BRANDS

Quoting, "The deepest cut doesn't sever," from the *Tao Te Ching*, Zhang Ruimin interprets this to mean "a holistic ('entangled') system consists of various entities that cannot be separated." This systems theory understanding from both ancient Chinese philosophy and today's quantum physics first inspired his idea of the microenterprise, and in 2019 it lay behind his new *RenDanHeyi* initiative, the launch of Haier's Ecosystem Brand.

Realizing that no user buys a product in isolation but rather as an addition to their overall life or home situation or lifestyle, Haier moved on from providing product and service packages to now selling "scenarios" and "user experiences," i.e., "total solutions." By doing so, it broadened both the structure and the meaning of *RenDanHeyi* by creating a new network of ecosystems to break down internal organizational boundaries and create new opportunities (Fig. 16.1).

If ME's were to stay small and agile, no single ME could meet the growing complexity of user needs. At the same time, if an ME sold just one product, say a refrigerator, it would at some point become outdated and no longer be wanted. This problem could be solved if several ME's were to band together and cooperate to provide a full spectrum of associated products and services, leading to the formation of new "Ecosystem Micro-Communities" (EMC's), and these EMC's are the latest iteration of the *RenDanheyi* Model. Groups of ME's self-organize and agree on a smart, dynamic contract among themselves to cooperate, support each other, and share the profit on providing one or another user scenario. One striking example of this is the Haier Internet of Food (IoF).

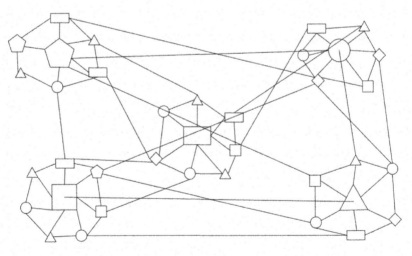

Fig. 16.1   Haier's loosely structured ecosystem network

Every household needs to consume food, but in doing so, it calls upon a whole range of products and services: appliances like the refrigerator and oven, of course, but also the purchase, storing, and preparation of food, and even perhaps a dietician for good advice. No one Haier ME, or even any collection of Haier ME's could supply all the goods and services needed, but other companies could. Temporary contracts were formed with these, mutual support assured, and profits shared, and all components of the scenario connected through IoT technology. If one ME sold an oven, another selling food would benefit, as would each if a user hired a dietician via the platform. If one ME in the EMC is struggling, all others step in to help, but critical to the dynamism and organic growth of the *RenDanHeyi* model, Haier ME's are allowed to fail, and some do.

Every aspect of our lives is an experience within a holistic scenario, and if a Haier ME cannot meet the full range of needs required by any one scenario by forming a contract with other Haier ME's, it is free, as in the examples just cited, to look outside the company to form contracts with other companies to do so. This has been the case with the sporting goods manufacturer Decathlon, for example, whose exercise equipment is included in the balcony scenario total solution and now sold as part of a collective "Ecosystem Brand." So far, these ecosystems have covered 40,000 enterprises in 15 industries. In 2019, Haier became the first and only IoT ecosystem brand recognized by the BrandZ Top 100 Most Valuable Global Brands list. In addition to the Internet of Food, there is an Internet of Clothing that integrates care, storage, and even stylistic advice, an Internet of Air that integrates the need for healthy air with conditions needed for sleep, and an Internet of Blood that literally brings the blood bank to the operating theatre surgery table. And all are designed to deliver "user experience." "Products that don't deliver an experience have no 'soul'," says Zhang Ruimin. All of these experiences/scenarios are on display at Haier's massive Smart Home Experience Center in Shanghai.

There are two types of EMC's, Experience EMC's, and Solution EMC's. Haier knows that user knowledge and user experience is a precious resource, often leading to new business ideas. The Experience EMC's keep in close touch with users, understanding their needs and "pain points" and hearing their desires. This feedback is then passed on to Solution EMC's who, of course, create solutions. They design, create, produce, and transport things that address the discovered needs. Zhang Ruimin now believes "products will be replaced by scenarios, and industries will be encompassed by ecosystems."

Placing the EMC concept within the context of Quantum Management, we see them allowing ME's to act as both "particles" and "waves." As particles, each ME performs its own functions of manufacturing, servicing, and delivering its specialities to its own users. As waves, each ME cooperates with others in an EMC to offer users scenarios and total experiences. And all EMC's act as both particles in providing the scenario in which they specialize, but as waves they are aligned with all other EMC's to share resources. In this way, again, Haier as a whole acts as a Zero Distance quantum system.

SERVICE TO THE COMMUNITY

Most companies boast some sort of CSR initiatives, but at Haier these are integral both to Zhang Ruimin's philosophy and to the company's operations. Haier positions itself to create value for society. Just as Quantum Management insists no company is an island, Zhang believes that companies must see themselves as "nodes of the community" and pursue more than their own self-interest. Haier does serve society directly every day just through its "value creation for all" company philosophy, but it also serves the community through extensive training programs and through its chain of Haier Community Stores. There is one of these in every one of China's 650,000 villages, and each serves as a community center providing after-school child care. The company acts as a service platform for any Chinese citizen who has an entrepreneurial idea that might in any way enhance the value or quality of a Haier product, suggest a new product, or even come forward with a good business model to found a new microenterprise. So *anyone* can be an employee or a designer for Haier. The company's Logistics Platform makes it possible for 90,000 individual owners of delivery trucks to earn money through working for it.

In the wake of the [19xx] tsunami that devasted many of China's coastal villages, Zhang Ruimin himself took a six month leave of absence from the company to join others in rebuilding homes. And during the Covid crisis, Haier put its vast transportation network to the service of delivering medical supplies to hospitals in the most badly hit districts as well as providing materials for face masks. Haier serves the planet through the generation, management, and usage of green energy, and it serves future generations through Project Hope, a program to educate poor children, and by supplying schools in China, Mongolia, and Latin America with tablets and software.

MAKING RENDANHEYI INTERNATIONAL

During recent years, Haier has acquired many companies abroad. It now has partner subsidiary companies in Japan, New Zealand, Italy, Germany, Russia, and America (see Chapter 18 on GE Appliances). At each of these, the *RenDanHeyi* business model is implemented, but they otherwise are afforded the same autonomy as Haier's own ME's and EMC's. Local CEO's are put in place and all employees are local to their own national region. There are no Chinese supervisors or bosses. "We know," says Zhang, "that each national region has its own traditions and strengths, for instance the well-known team spirit in Japan, and we believe that each of our international branches should play to this and develop it." He compares Haier's entire collection of international companies to a "mixed salad" made up from good local produce. "The various national locations provide the vegetables," he says, "and we provide *RenDanHeyi* as the salad dressing."

MORE LIKE A CITY THAN A COMPANY

Many recent business thinkers are suggesting that companies should be thought of as more like living organisms than machines, and indeed the complexity scientists at the Santa Fe Institute who study commonalities between biological systems and human social systems agree this is correct thinking. But in his book *Scale*, Geoffrey West points out that this is actually *bad news* for companies. Yes, West agrees, companies do function as complex adaptive systems, growing and evolving in dialogue with the market, but just like living organisms, at a point of reaching maturity, companies stop growing, and eventually die. This is because they grow "sublinearly"—they grow until they reach a certain size limitation which exhausts available energy, then they stagnate, cease having new ideas and innovation, grow old, and die.

West contrasts this finite life span of all living organisms and all large companies about which he writes with the constant growth, complexity, innovation, and apparent immortality of cities. Growing "superlinearly" (the larger they grow, the more energy there is available for each element), "cities become ever more diverse as they grow. Their spectrum of business and economic activity is incessantly expanding as new sectors develop and new opportunities present themselves... [They experience] open-ended growth, and expanding social networks – and a crucial component of their resilience, sustainability, and seeming immortality."[1] I believe that everything about the way that the Haier system functions makes it more like a

---

[1] Geoffry West, Scale, p. 409.

city than like other companies, and thus confers on it lasting sustainability and growth—"immortality." Let's look at why.

- West points out that the real essence of any city is its people, who provide its buzz, its soul, and its spirit. We have seen that Haier recognizes this fact and puts its people first—its own people who are employees, and the people who are its users.
- In cities, it is the complex connections and interactions of people that generate energy, information, and innovation. "cities are emergent complex adaptive social network systems resulting from continuous interactions among their inhabitants, enhanced and facilitated by the feedback mechanisms provided by urban life".[2] At Haier, there are constant interactions between the ME's and their users, internal collaborations between EMC's and their users and external collaborations between Haier EMC's and EMC's formed with other companies, and constant feedback mechanisms are provided by COSMOplat and its huge data bank of user experiences. And all these interactions and feedback mechanisms generate energy, information, and innovation.
- West points out that companies operate as highly constrained top-down organizations that maximize the efficiency of production to maximize profit. "To achieve greater efficiency in pursuit of greater market share and increased profits, companies stereotypically add more rules, regulations, protocols and procedures at ever finer levels of organization, resulting in increased bureaucracy...at the expense of innovation and R & D research".[3] Cities, by contrast, "operated in a much more distributed fashion, with power spread across multiple organizational structures...As such, they operate in an almost laissez-fair, free-wheeling ambience relative to companies, taking advantage of the innovative benefits of social interactions ...Cities are places of action and agents of change while companies usually project an image of stasis". We have seen that Haier rid itself of all top-down control and bureaucracy, achieves constant innovation through the multiple user interactions with its self-organizing ME's and EMC's, and pursues "value multiplication" instead of profit maximization. It is certainly a place of action and agent of change.

[2] Geoffry West, Scale, p. 253.
[3] Ibid., p. 408.

QUANTUM PRINCIPLE	RENDANHEYI PRACTICE
Indeterminacy/Spontaneity	Agile, Responsive Structure
Both Particles & Waves	Each M.E. Independent (Particle-Like)
	All M.E.s Cooperate & Collaborate (Wave-like)
Superposition of Multiple Potentialities	6000 M.E.s, Each A Potentiality
Universe Made of Relationships;	Employees Entangled With Users;
Everything Entangled With Everything	Haier Ecosystem; Ecosystem Brand
Heisenberg Uncertainty Principle:	User Feedback Vital; Questioning Culture;
Questions Evoke Reality	Self-Critical Culture
Observer/Observed Co-Creative	Employees/Users Co-Creative
Everything Contextual;	User Needs Determine Products/Services
Context Creates Identity	
Quantum Self is Dynamic Energy	Haier Employee Seen As Having Infinite Potential
Process With Infinite Potential	

Fig. 16.2 Summary of Haier's quantum features

- West also points out that while cities are resilient enough to survive all manner of disruptions and catastrophes, "a sizeable fluctuation in the market or some unexpected external perturbation or shock at the wrong time can be devastating to a company".[4] During the Covid-19 lockdown, nearly all large companies except the e-commerce ones suffered tremendous losses, and many failed. But Haier's flexible structure and its ability of its ME's to source local suppliers and to deliver to users, with whom it remained in constant contact, and the cooperation between ME's and EMC's to share resources, meant the company operated at 98.5% of its capacity during the crisis and returned to growth immediately after.

Saying that the key feature of any ecosystem is its ability to generate new "species," or new business models and players, Zhang Ruimin himself compares Haier to a tropical rain forest, "where every day some organisms are born and some die. The ultimate point is that the ecosystem is able to facilitate the generation of new species." Tropical rainforests, of course, are "cities" built by Nature (Fig. 16.2).

[4] Ibid., p. 395.

CHAPTER 17

Roche India: A Purpose-Driven Culture

In 2019, the *Mumbai Mirror* wrote, "Lara Bezerra has transformed leadership in the pharmaceutical industry forever."

Lara Bezerra's Golden Rule for company transformation is: "If you want to transform the company, you must transform the people first. If you want to become a Quantum Leader, you must first become a Quantum Self." The first question she asked new people arriving for a job interview was, "What is your purpose?", and her main criterion for hiring them was whether they could align that personal sense of purpose with a sense of purpose associated with working for Roche India. She has lived the wisdom of that necessity herself on her own journey toward becoming the Managing Director ("Chief Purpose Officer") at the company. Her employees know this, and they say that Lara's personal example of walking the talk inspires them to believe that they, too, can practice what she preaches.

Lara is a Brazilian national who has worked in the pharmaceutical industry for twenty-seven years. She was raised in São Paulo by her doctor father and her Japanese mother who, too, was a doctor, but also educated as a physicist. To this day Lara looks upon her mother as having been the mentor who shaped her life. When Lara was a young woman in her early 20s, her mother gave her two books for her birthday, a biography of Werner Heisenberg (aka The Uncertainty Principle) and a copy of my own first book, *The Quantum Self.* Both books, she has said, made a strong impression, and Lara felt that quantum physics touched her in some important way. Several years later, at a time of both personal and professional crisis that was making her question her purpose and role in life, a friend gave Lara a copy of the Indian classic, *The Bhagavad Gita*, for inspiration, and that became her leadership Bible. She was guided by its message and framed her own new sense of purpose: to become a business leader and help her employees become the kind of people she now wanted to be, and thus better to serve the needs of sick people. She took up a new position with Bayer in Hungary as General Manager responsible for the Pharma Division and Health Care in 2003.

After several more executive positions with Bayer, and now as Managing Director for Roche in Venezuela, she read the *Quantum Leader*, and has said this book helped her know better what kind of leader she would like to be and what kind of company she would like to build. She joined my Quantum Leader train-the-trainer program in Oxford in May 2016 and got inspired to develop more tools to cascade it down to her leadership team in Venezuela. She developed the tools that she would later implement in India. And so, when three years ago she was appointed Managing Director of Roche Pharmaceutical India, she was asked to develop a new strategy to challenge the status quo, focusing on increasing the engagement of the team and impact on patients. The strategy Lara and the leadership team had obtained approval for from Roche global senior leadership had included a pilot for "Quantum Leadership Transformation Program" at Roche in India. Within three months of her arrival in Mumbai in October 2017 to take up what she felt was the most exciting challenge of her career so far, she and her leadership team had worked out a new local vision, based on the global purpose for the company and themselves. In November 2018, 3 months after the rollout of the new strategy, business model, and culture, the team gave her the new title as Chief Purpose Officer.

I am now going to let Lara describe in her own words how that Roche experiment unfolded, and what it achieved:

The Roche India Experiment

"After reading *The Quantum Leader* and then participating in Professor Danah Zohar's train-the- trainer program for Quantum Leaders in Oxford, UK, I knew these were qualities I wanted to bring to my own leadership practice and, if given the opportunity, qualities I wanted to implement in an organization I was leading. I was still finishing out my contract as Managing Director of Roche Venezuela at the time, so there was only sufficient time left to implement the leadership training and the introduction of Quantum Management to the leadership team there. When I then transferred to my Managing Directorship at Roche India, and was given permission by the CEO of Roche Pharma Global to implement a new strategy, I was able to introduce the full concept and try to create the pharmaceutical industry's first Quantum Organization. My first ask after arriving in Mumbai was to outline my own priorities and sense of direction. These included:

- **A Clear Sense of Purpose**: We needed to ask, why does Roche India exist? Why do we want to work for this company? What impact can the company, and I as its leader, make to improve the human condition while at the same time growing a good business? I wanted to leverage the Roche global purpose of "Doing now what patients need next". The challenge was to bring the translation of this purpose to India. What this would mean to India? In a workshop, the leadership team decided that the vision for Roche Pharma India would be: "We inspire people to transform healthcare in India and care for every patient's life through sustainable, innovative solutions" – we should go beyond only commercializing our medicines. We have to be part of improving the health care in India, collaborating with other stakeholders."
- **Vision**: Knowing clearly where we want the business and ourselves to be after a designated period of time. How will we achieve making the impact we want to achieve in each of the communities and regions where we operate, and in the company's own performance? What are the first necessary steps we must take?
- **Strategy**: Adopting strategy that produces both short and long-term benefits was crucial. A balance needed to exist. Too much focus on short-term-results without consciousness of the long-term impact would affect the sustainability of the transformation.
- **Flexible Operating Model**: We must always be willing to review the operational set up as new ideas and unexpected developments demand new ways of working.
- **A Knowledgeable Core Team**: Develop a leadership team that is committed to the business, has a knowledge of the pharmaceutical industry, and a clear sense of what our transformation needs to achieve. A knowledgeable core team would be necessary to make the

right transition without losing momentum. Important that members of core team should not think they have all the answers, but rather possess growth mindsets, wanting to experiment to discover new ways to deliver more value to the customers.

- **Leadership Commitment:** In guiding the transformation, the most critical piece for implementing Quantum Management would be the alignment of the leadership team. Our company must work with its own dynamics and capabilities and adapt our implementation plans accordingly. The leadership team must be clear about our purpose and intention from the beginning, because thinking and behavior displayed by them will be reflected in the whole company. Our leadership team must be role models who play a significant role in our Quantum Management work.

Why Quantum Management?

Corporations and businesses will be crucial in the transformation needed for the future of our economies in the face of environmental and other uncontrollable challenges to come. By the end of January 2020, humanity had faced a challenge never seen before. The only solution to meet the COVID-19 threat was to change the way companies see success in the world. If any company followed the existing definition of success, maximizing profit and having more sales than competitors, it would fail.

Success in 2020 and onwards would have to be measured by the ability to work together and foster the right culture to build a better right environment to keep humanity healthy. I saw this need for the pharmaceutical industry before the Covid crisis, a need to redefine and renew its sense of purpose, and I felt that adopting the principles of Quantum Management would be the best way to achieve it.

When I learned that the quantum systems dynamics underpinning Quantum Management required leadership and employee commitment and positive motivation, as well as the company's purpose and values, as a part of a whole system approach that included societal and environmental impact, I felt this resonated with my own leadership values and past experience. And I deeply favored its emphasis on self-organization and less top-down control as a way of unleashing employee potential.

Quantum Management Implementation

We began by asking whether we are in the business of offering solutions/cures for specific diseases, or in the business of bringing better health and health care to the population? If our purpose is bringing better health and health care to the people, we would need others to work with us. We would need to include stakeholders, and even find ways to cooperate with competitors. And we would need to create a new and supportive company culture, embedded both in the mindset of every individual employee, and in the structure and processes of the whole organization.

Our company structure needed reinvention to allow for the self-organization that would give employees the decision making capacity and responsibility required to fulfill their own best potential, and at the same time enable them to bring the most personal and efficient service to our customers—the healthcare providers and patients. The leadership team and I discussed the possible removal of any middle management and bureaucratic impediments preventing this. During a workshop to develop the new strategy, the team had used many different models of companies with innovative business approach, presented by global transformation group. We were particularly impressed by the Haier *RenDanHeyi* model I had learned about from Danah. Accordingly, we decided to divide our sales force, which previously had served India as one market, into 9 independent, multi-functional regional teams, each one of which would serve a cluster of India's states. The logic of this was not just to create smaller teams, but was also an acknowledgement that both health needs and health care differ widely from one Indian state to the next.

To emphasize our new vision, we decided to change our titles accordingly. The Director of Financial Management became Director of Sustainable Solutions, the Director of Marketing became Director of Customer Value Strategy, each member of the sales force became a Value Specialist. The whole organization decided that my own title as Managing Director should be changed to Chief Purpose Officer. Each of these title changes indicated a change of approach and the nature of our new culture. For instance, the sales force would no longer approach a potential customer by saying, "Here is what I can sell you," but instead ask, "What can I do to help you give your patients better care?"

THE BEGINNING AND FIRST TRAINING

In February 2018, when I first shared the Quantum Management idea with my leadership team, everyone undertook the SQ and Quantum Leadership Self-Assessment test designed by Danah Zohar. We outlined the new strategy, operating model of the company, and the kind of new company culture we would need to build. I trained the Leadership team myself on the 12 SQ & Quantum Leadership Principles, Danah's Scale of Motivations, and Reframing, and we all did a purpose exercise.

The purpose of our work was to deliver our new vision for Roche India, which included impacting the healthcare in India in a positive way, collaborating with all stakeholders, and being ready to work for India and foster an environment where our team could excel. We knew this would require cascading down to every employee of the company the whole of the Quantum Management and Quantum Leadership training we had undergone ourselves. The entire organization then took the SQ & Quantum Leadership Self-Assessment test, received an understanding of the eight principles that define quantum physics and thus Quantum Management, were trained in Reframing practice, learned how to use the Scale of Motivations, and to apply Quantum Management principles to their own work responsibilities. For this entire project, all training courses and workshops were developed in house.

The outcome we wanted to achieve with Quantum Management was to make quantum leaders of every individual, inside the organization and outside as well (stakeholders). These new quantum leaders could then impact both internally and externally on the environment, thus transforming the culture and nature of work in the whole ecosystem. After our core leadership team had the task of transforming themselves into "teachers" to support the transformation of all other individuals in the company. As the team evolved towards adopting a Quantum Management style, new ways of working emerged, and the operating model began transforming itself.

Our HR Director (later People and Culture), Swati Yadav, had received the first QM training from me in February 2018. Some months later, she also participated directly in a training course with Danah and her team in Slovenia. She was an inspiration to many people inside the company and outside, training many of our own people and teaching many others about principles needed to use the tools that support implementation of the new strategy/operating model. Over time, members of Swati's team were able, using the principles of Quantum Management, to suggest even more HR tools that could support our company purpose.

Our Finance Director, Daniel Plüss, became the Scale of Motivations ambassador. From improvements in both his own personal life and work. Daniel saw the power of self-awareness and of "owning", and transforming. the emotions that drive our decisions. When he later moved on to head a new Roche department in Switzerland, he quietly brought many of the concepts and practices of Quantum Management to his team there."

This is the end of Lara Bezerra's own personal account.

Comments from Roche Employees Involved

On my very first visit to the Roche offices, my immediate first impression was, "These people are 'on' something!" People were smiling, chatting eagerly to each other, their eyes were bright, alert, and excited. They were dressed in casual, mostly Indian, clothing, and moved about almost like dancers in a synchronized rhythm. "We *are* 'on' something," one of them laughed when I related this impression. "We are 'on' love and purpose! We love each other and we love our jobs. We love working together. We are a family. And we have a sense of purpose that makes our lives and our jobs meaningful." She then pointed proudly to the string of "A Great Place to Work" banners strung around the ceiling. "We won that award!" she said.

During each of my visits to the Roche offices, people could not resist telling me how the transformation had changed them, not only professionally, but also as private people.

The Director of Marketing related how the Roche transformation had transformed his relationship with his 13-year-old son. "I had thought I should be a very traditional and strict Indian father, keeping my son just a little bit afraid of me," he said. "I thought this would make him want to obey me, and to live up to my high expectations. It was a very formal father/son relationship, and we were not emotionally close. But the training at work made me question this, and I shared my doubts with my son. "I was wrong to be so strict with you," I admitted. "'I love you very much and I thought that was the way to show it. But I don't want you to be afraid of me. I want you to love me, please. I want us to enjoy talking and doing things together.' Then, much to my son's surprise, I gave him a big hug. It took him some time before he could learn to relax with me, but now we get along so much better. And those grades I scolded him to get? His academic performance is so much better now, with no scolding from me!"

Another member of the leadership team told me that Lara's constant messaging about viewing others "with unconditional, positive regard" had finally even mellowed his behavior toward his in-laws. "We have to go so often to lunch with my wife's family," he said, "and most of her relatives irritate me. So I have normally been very rude to them, and of course this always upsets my wife. Our car journeys home after these events were never very pleasant. But last week, after a lunch with his mother's family, my son said to me on the journey home, 'Dad, what happened to you? You were patient and polite to everyone today. Is this Lara's influence?'" "Yes," I had to admit, "Lara has taught me I must even treat your grandmother with unconditional positive regard." The man chuckled with hearty self-congratulations after telling me this story.

Swati, the HR Director, told me she never used to think about things like purpose or meaning, especially not in connection with her work. "I used to go to work just to earn money for necessities," she said. "Anything that mattered to me happened away from work." But now, having gone through Lara's training herself, and then had the experience of training others, she said she now feels a real joy and sense of purpose about her work. "I feel that it means something. That I am making a difference." She was planning to take the Vipassana meditation course recommended by Lara, and in some of her spare time she had been attending Osho's wisdom teachings. "Lara has told us," she recounted, "that to become better leaders, we must become better human beings. I am now trying to become a better human being."

One of the sales reps, after telling me how much his job was now giving him a sense of real meaning and purpose, proudly told me how his new ability to make decisions on the spot, had allowed him to save a life the week before. "I was with a doctor at one of the veterans' hospitals," he told me. "One of his cancer patients needed one of our medications straight away. But there was a problem. The medication came in a box containing four sheets of tablets, and cost $400 per box. The doctor said that the hospital budget would only allow him to spend $100/month on any one medication. But it is a Roche rule that partial boxes of our medications cannot be sold separately. The doctor pleaded with me to help, and said that if the patient didn't get the medication within 24 hours, he would die." The sales rep then told me, "Because of my new power to make decisions without seeking permission from higher up, I made calls directly to the finance, quality and distributions teams and in 2 hours I could provide the treatment by handing the doctor just one sheet from the box. I told him I would let him purchase the medication like this every month from then on. This one occasion then opened a door for many other patients to benefit from this solution." Lara told me that if the sales rep had to "follow the usual channels," it would have taken six to eight weeks to get clearance from head office for that kind of exception. "The patient would have been dead long before then," she added.

And finally, the CFO, Daniel Pluss told me, "Going through this transformation has made me a better person, a better husband, a better father, and certainly a better and wiser leader. I owe 'quantum' and the experience of working with Lara everything that I may now do or become."

* * *

By the late summer of 2019, two years after Lara had taken up her position in Mumbai, lives and jobs had been transformed, lives had been saved, lasting collegiate relationships had been formed with hospital directors and doctors, an ecosystem had been built that even included MOU's with now cooperating competitors, three new cancer hospitals were being built, costs had been kept to sustainable levels, the employee engagement score had gone up from 46 to 82%, the attrition rate decreased from 35 to 11% (front line to 4%), there were many media reports of Roche having become a company which is truly there for the greater good and looking for sustainable healthcare solutions, Lara herself had been featured in several global business magazines, the Indian Government was asking to cooperate, several new positions had been filled with people who were purposely choosing Roche because of its culture and leadership, *and* overall profitable sales had increased by 5%; by 20% in the channel given most focus—the first growth experienced in five years. **But then..........**

.... *Lara Was Fired*

On a Monday morning, last week of November 2019, Lara was summoned to a hotel meeting room in Mumbai, and there confronted by her Regional Director and two of his associates. She was told that she would be released of her duties 4 days later, and asked to clear her desk and leave the Roche offices by Friday afternoon. Despite acknowledging a complex relationship with her Regional Head, the decision shocked her. There had been no prior warning or indication of such a drastic decision. This shock was shared by everyone back at her office. Staff quickly arranged a "Thank you and leaving party" for the Friday afternoon, and her departure was marked by confusion, group depression, and many tears. There was also furore and shock in the Indian media about this inexplicable firing of a leader who had brought a new perspective of purpose, and a new image to healthcare leadership, becoming something of a national hero. In the couple of months that followed, without a temporary replacement assigned to Lara's job, office morale declined sharply and many people left the company. Some members of the leadership team were laid off. Three others had been promoted to positions outside India previous to Lara's exit.

I was myself shocked and confused by Lara's sudden firing, and reached out to both Lara and people from her leadership team to discover some explanation. All confirmed that 85% of the problem had been a personality conflict between Lara and the new Regional Head. Two and a half years before, Roche Pharma India a new strategy, including the Quantum leadership transformation, had been approved by the Asia Pacific Regional Head and the Pharma CEO. Both were very supportive of this initiative, as it was aligned with the new strategy of Roche Pharma Global to initiate a global transformation to change the approach of the pharma business. Roche Pharma India was in the forefront of this transformation, with two other countries.

But in August 2018 (2 months after the implementation of the new strategy in India) a restructure was announced for Roche Pharma, where new regional structures were announced. Previously, the Managing Director of Roche India used to report to the Asia Pacific Head, who reported to the CEO of Pharma. In the new structure, 2 important changes impacted India. India has moved from the Asia Pacific region to a new region created with Russia, Baltic countries, Turkey, Pakistan, and Bangladesh. This new region had little knowledge of Indian history or culture, and its Regional Head had no prior knowledge of Lara's pioneering transformation program. Additionally, 2 layers of management were included between the CEO of Pharma and the General Managers of the countries, making it more difficult for the CEO to support local decisions of the countries. The CEO of Pharma and the regional head who had supported the new India strategy had left the company to lead other Pharmaceutical companies. Although there was still support from Basel and Roche Global, to Roche Pharma India project, decisions were taken on a regional level without much interference from more senior leaders.

The new Regional Head promoted to this position was an older man with a successful career at Roche of more than 30 years. This would be his last posting before retirement. His management style and Lara's were quite opposite, although they shared the goal of bringing success to India. He was a traditional, command-and-control manager, accustomed to having General Managers command their teams from the top. The team empowerment granted by Lara, her total trust in her leadership team, the new style of teams making presentations to senior global/regional leaders, the self-organized teams, all this came as a shock to his more traditional style of controlling results. Lara herself has admitted that she did not always handle well her tense meetings with him, during which he always expressed impatience and frustration with not seeing faster results, more data, and a lack of traditional strategies with more hierarchy in the states. Finally, on that Monday morning, he could take no more.

So, the conflict of personalities and leadership styles had been 85% of the problem. But I then wondered about that remaining 15% of reasons why the Roche India transformation had failed to meet expectations. Were there valuable lessons here for other leaders who might want to initiate such a program? Was there anything that Lara and her leadership themselves team might do differently today? Were mistakes made that were part of the learning curve involved with any such radical transformation, and might corrections have been made had the project been allowed to run its course? I spoke in confidence with people I knew from the company, and have collected together here as one narrative their "après le deluge" reflections in hope these may guide others. I draw particular attention to their fear of being "too Newtonian," because many business leaders have asked me whether building a quantum organization means you must throw away all Newtonian structures.

Former members of the leadership team commented: "We could have been more skilled at fully and clearly articulating our quantum vision. We were passionate, enthusiastic, and committed, and we were constantly reassured that our own very strong sense of purpose inspired all those who worked with us. But many of our employees were never really sure 'what this quantum is about' or how to use it in meeting the challenges of their own, newly independent, roles as decision-makers. During the training sessions, new, exciting, almost magical were presented, but perhaps staff were left too much to themselves to figure out how they might make practical use of it. We didn't sufficiently help them to design clear KPI's (key performance indicators) against which they could measure their own success or failure. So perhaps there was never a clear enough link drawn between the new quantum way of working and the results this was expected to produce, the results we needed *them* to produce."

I witnessed the resulting stress of this "not knowing what 'quantum' means" felt by one of the sales team during one of my own visits to Roche. The man came into Lara's office space saying that he couldn't secure a meeting with any relevant medical staff at one of the hospitals in his area of responsibility, and asked for her advice. "Just be 'quantum'," she told him. But, clearly frustrated by this, he burst out with, "'Quantum!', 'quantum!' I don't know what *is* this 'quantum'!"

Leadership team reflections continued with, "One general observation is that, when we are excited about implementing a very new process, there can be a tendency to be too dogmatic about things. For instance, we were perhaps too dogmatic about some elements of the motivation scale: don't be in fear, don't be in craving, etc. The fact is, we are all driven by these motivations more often than not, and the goal should not be to hide or deny this or but rather to recognize we are in this state of mind and then have the ability to reframe ourselves. We were perhaps too dogmatic in thinking that data is Newtonian, and therefore a distraction. Instead of monitoring things like sales data, we concentrated instead on counting numbers of patients treated with our medications, but while this was good in spirit, patient numbers can be very difficult to collect in India. Looking back, we realize in a more balanced way that not all data is bad. It is a matter of what you do with it after it is collected. How can this data be useful in reflecting better patient care? Also, we were dogmatic about being self-organized, which led some people to feel lost, yet uncomfortable to say so. In a nutshell we were in a constant fear of not living Quantum, and as a result neglected some essential elements of measurement, guidance, or guardrails from our toolbox.

Bringing it back to how we understood Quantum at the time, there was a feeling that whenever we measure things or guide the system, we will make the system collapse. However, the way we understand quantum systems now, they do employ very clear mechanisms/principles that define boundaries for the various moving parts functioning in a system, rather than letting them drift apart into complete chaos. Being self-organized and adaptive does not mean you do not gently guide the process, and defining these guardrails can be very important—in addition to providing the system with a signaling mechanism to show what works and what does not work. In a business context, this signaling would be some sort of metrics/KPIs of a qualitative and quantitative nature, providing transparency about whether things are moving in the right direction. We could then learn from these signals to adapt the system accordingly. We could have added some other measures to assess the success of the cultural transformation.

From an outcome perspective, we did not define the measures we would have needed:

(1) We had 7 strategic goals and should have defined qualitative and quantitative measures for each of them to know if we were moving toward these goals;

(2) We should have defined clear guardrails from a business performance perspective and should have held the organization accountable for delivering them—not in a top-down way but in a self-accountable way;

(3) We should have established a comprehensive set of reports, measures, feedback loops which could have served as the context for all the self-organized teams to adapt, based on the impact they were having;

(4) Whatever we removed, we should have reflected on how to replace it with something else—e.g., when removing the sales incentives, we should have replaced them with another system of recognition and incentives to reward successful performance; when we stopped having budgets in terms of sales and operating expenses, we should have replaced them, perhaps with guardrails/general system boundaries, and other ways of defining the outcomes we wanted to achieve and measure against.

If we think of a company like Roche, we operate in a circle of patients, sales, investment, profits—this circle needs to be sustainable or else we end in chaos. In the past we would look at the sales of last year and then model how much we can make this year, how much investment we need to do so, and hence patient impact and profits were a result. In the new setup, we started with the patient needs, then looked at which investments would be required to meet them. Sales and profits would come after, as measurable results. We understand better now that, if we use data and measurement in the right way, "these so called Newtonian approaches may lend themselves as important signals in a quantum system." In a further conversation with me, Lara added, "We should have made defining our governance strategy a first priority."

Roche had neglected one of the central principles of the *RenDan-Heyi* model: a self-organizing, quantum organization must be guided by a strong central operational system. This is not a rigid set of Newtonian rules, but a clear set of guiding principles that set priorities and goals and assess how they are met.

* * *

Still, despite these various problematic issues, every person from the Roche India leadership team with whom I spoke, and Lara herself, felt certain that their quantum leadership transformation was on the right track and, had it been given the five years that Lara had insisted from the beginning would be required for such a deep change to bear fruit, the whole project would have been an exemplary success. Unfortunately, Lara did not have the power or position of authority enjoyed by Zhang Ruimin to insist on this, and the combined impatience, lack of understanding, and lack of trust from her direct superiors caused the baby to be stillborn.

Yet, while Lara Bezerra herself suffered the loss of her job, and the transformation program at Roche India was abandoned, the seeds she planted during her truncated tenure with the company are now finding more fertile soil in new practices being adopted by Roche Global. Roche has been undergoing a transformation journey for over three years, guiding divisions in other countries to transform themselves in the kind of direction that Roche Pharma India had began in October 2017. The good work of Roche Pharma India during these years can be seen by the number of talents from India "exported" to other affiliates globally, including the three members of her Roche India leadership team who earlier had been promoted to more senior positions elsewhere in the company. They tell me that, in their new positions, "In our own quiet but determined way, we are spreading quantum, and we are seeing changes."

CHAPTER 18

GE Appliances: An American Catalyst

In June 2016, Haier purchased GE Appliances for several billion dollars. Headquartered in Louisville, Kentucky, GEA had previously been a division of General Electric's global conglomerate. It was not a failing company when taken over, but it had been stagnant, showing no growth in market share or profits, a moribund management style, and little product innovation. Employee numbers had been cut from their peak of 23,000 in 1971 to 9,500 by 1995. By 2015, with profits now falling, and management having to negotiate cost-cutting measures such as reducing starting factory wages to $12/hour, GE had had enough. It tried, unsuccessfully, for over a year to find a buyer for its domestic appliances division until Haier bought the business in 2016 as part of its own ongoing internationalization strategy. Haier also acquired the right to keep the GE brand for 40 years and outright ownership of GEA's existing appliance brands that included Hotpoint, Profile, and Monogram.

By end of 2017, only eighteen months after the Haier take-over, GEA was already showing double-digit profit growth, its best performance in ten years. As I write this in mid-2020, the company is now the fastest-growing domestic appliances business in America, and has achieved an overall growth of employee numbers, now upward of 14,000, market share, shareholder value, and profitability of over 6%. Much of this was achieved *during* the long months of the Covid-19 crisis when other companies were experiencing huge losses.

© The Author(s) 2022
D. Zohar, *Zero Distance*,
https://doi.org/10.1007/978-981-16-7849-3_18

Following the pattern of all Haier partnered subsidiaries, GEA began to implement the *RenDanHeyi* management model in 2017. This was at the same time that Kevin Nolan was appointed as the company's new CEO. Nolan is an engineer who had worked for GE the whole of his career. Before becoming CEO of GEA, he had risen to the level of Technical Director for GE. He is a man who has loved machines and being involved with machines since early childhood. When I first met him, in Qingdao just after his promotion to CEO, he said to me, "You can't do this job properly unless you love machines. I love machines!" He told me that his way of unwinding after a long day of executive work is to go home to his garage and "fiddle with my machines." Later I learned that he spends long hours of his weekends in the engineering and design laboratory of First Build, the company's incubation hub, "playing" with the machines and experimenting with new things to invent. During the years of his career so far, he has obtained thirty-nine personal patents for his inventions. When we met for a second time in St. Louis and he arranged we visit First Build together, he spent the required amount of time for introductions and pleasant chat before escaping into the engineering and design lab to see what his young inventors were up to that day. Through the glass window of the door I saw him listening to them with excitement and rubbing his hand on their machines, as a father might fondly caress the heads of his children.

Nolan has always loved challenges, but he admits that at first he was not ready for the challenge of implementing *RenDanHeyi* at GEA. Like many of the American company leaders who are among the 10,000 visitors to Haier in Qingdao every year, he wasn't sure it could ever work in an American company. "It started off rough," he reflected later. "I had never seen a business operate like Haier, and it was very new territory. But then it got better." And there was an incentive to try. GE had been trying to offload its Appliances division for some time, causing many people to leave the company and low morale among those who stayed. "We felt unwanted," said Nolan, "and now we had been bought by someone who really wanted us. We all knew we were going to have to do something different."

During the first year after its acquisition by Haier, and still led by a CEO who had managed the company for GE, GEA remained a pretty much a standard, integrated company run from the top. At its core was an efficiency-focused, function-by-product matrix run by a vice president of Product Management. Everyone but him, the CFO, and a few other vice presidents reported directly to the CEO, and all decisions were central-ized. As when owned by GE, most company products were moved to market through big retail chains like Home Depot, Sears, and Best Buy, and it was they who dealt with any customer service needs. An informa-tion firewall between GEA and these retail distributors denied GEA nearly all direct knowledge about the customers who were using the compa-ny's products. I met that original CEO at a lunch with Zhang Ruimin in Qingdao and commented to Zhang afterward, "He will never 'get it'." Zhang nodded knowingly, and within six months, Kevin Nolan had replaced him.

Nolan had spent those six months in Qingdao, learning everything he could about how *RenDanHeyi* worked at Haier, and for the first six months of his tenure as CEO he had the benefit of regular help and coaching from Haier's Foreign Acquisitions Manager by phone from Qingdao. "But ever since then," Nolan now says, "Haier has just left us to get on with it. They have great respect for national and cultural differ-ences and feel strongly that management is best left to local leaders who know their regions and their people. Aside from a once-a-month, casual catch-up call with Qingdo, we are left to adapt *RenDanHeyi* to our own needs and purposes. I have never known such light-touch management from central office, and I think our partnership is a great example of what can be achieved through the cooperation of American and Chinese companies."

Once Kevin Nolan was in charge of GEA, he began the process of ridding the company of much of its centralized bureaucracy and breaking it down into Haier-style, independent, and self-organizing microenter-prises serviced by central platforms. There are now fifteen of these, plus the First Build innovation hub inherited from the later GE days, making up the company so far, and direct contact with users through company IT channels has become a priority, as has taking control of GEA's own distri-bution and customer service operations. The company now maintains an extensive factory service system that is nearly unique in the appliances industry, and its answer centers deal with over 10 million customer calls each year. Where the original company had operated under a single brand, GEA has now become a "House of Brands," with each brand having different features that appeal to different user segments—a nascent version of Haier's own, more user-customized product "scenarios." Employee bonus compensation has also become much more democratic. During that first year after acquisition by Haier, only 170 top executives were receiving bonus payments; today nearly 3000 employees receive them. Not yet Haier's own, revolutionary pay-at-point-of-user scheme whereby microenterprise employees receive the bulk of their pay directly from their customers, but instead each bonus payment reflects a share of overall company profits, a share of microenterprise profits, plus individual KPI indicators.

GEA is now run by 3-person Executive Council that includes Kevin Nolan but, following key principle of *RenDanHeyi*, the power pyramid is inverted. As at Haier itself, the company's operating principle has become, "The Owner [of the product] is the Boss," The user is now at the top of the power pyramid, and the Executive Council at the bottom. This policy was laid out very clearly in "Creating the 5-Year Plan," a GEA internal communication circulated in August 2017:

> Transforming GEA to accelerate our growth starts with shifting the focus from inside-out to outside-in. We've traditionally had the approach of "management is the boss," where we make decisions based on management views, assessments, goals, etc. ..... Everything we do now, how we're structured, what we make, and so on, must be geared to delivering on the owners' needs/desires. The more focused and connected we are to the owners, the more value we will deliver and the more successful we will be.[1]

noindentBetween the owners and the Executive Council, and in direct contact with the owners, sit the microenterprises in the power pyramid. They make all decisions about product development and service and essentially determine all company strategies. GEA no longer has a Strategy Department, and Nolan says he leaves day-to-day running of the company to the microenterprises. "Usually," he says, "I don't even know what's happening until someone tells me." But the GEA microenterprises, while independent and self-organizing, are not complete companies, incorporating all functions in themselves as at Haier. Instead, things like sales, marketing, and distribution are left to shared service platforms.

GEA's First Build incubation hub is still the company's showpiece for breakthrough innovation, and is required to invent twelve new products each year. Its sole purpose is to discover unmet needs. Located on the

---

[1] Dennis Campbell et al., "GE Appliances: Implementing Haier's Made-in-China Management System," p. 11.

campus of the University of Kentucky, the massive and well-equipped First Build design and engineering lab is open to the community and often sees local high school students and students from the university working alongside GEA's own designers on the well-equipped facilities. It maintains a boundaryless, open-innovation policy, remains open during evenings and weekends, and buzzes with an air of constant excitement and invention. On the day of my own visit, two young men were demonstrating their just-completed, domestic-sized food smoking appliance by offering us all samples of still-warm, succulent smoked salmon. Inspired by this, I suggested, "You know, you really should follow this up with a domestic wood-burning pizza oven," but as the words left my mouth, another young designer took me by the elbow, led me across the room and, pointing to a nearly finished oven-style cabinet, said, "Take a look at this!" As someone who had built my own atom-smashing devices in my bedroom during my teenage years, I was loathed to leave First Build after my visit.

GEA and the Covid-19 Crisis

In an interview he gave in late September 2020, Kevin Nolan commented, "It was when the Covid-19 crisis hit us that *RenDanHeyi* really proved what it could do." Here's how GEA thrived and grew when most American manufacturing and retail companies were struggling or failing.

"When the Covid challenge became clear," says Nolan, "we realized that we were facing the most unpredictable and chaotic event of our lives. We stopped all work for three days and everyone just thought things through. We asked, 'How can we best respond to this? How do we operate now.'" As a result, GEA defined guiding principles instead of detailed plans: "Protect our people. Protect our business. And focus on supporting and meeting the needs of our customers and community." They articulated a crisis slogan to reassure and inspire both their own people and their customers: "When Covid keeps us apart, *RenDanHeyi* brings us together." And, perhaps most importantly, they adopted a positive attitude: to see the Covid crisis as an opportunity to grow the business.

"The crisis really brought out the entrepreneurial spirit," says Nolan. "Everyone pivoted immediately to meet users' new needs and to discover new business opportunities." Before long they noticed that during the lockdown restrictions, people were using their domestic appliances *more*.

Cooking more, doing laundry more frequently, and they saw they needed to step up production and really utilize the agility of their supply chains. Each microenterprise looked at its *own* users and its *own* supply chains. They helped users with their extra financial needs and made it a priority to get appliances and services to front-line workers by reaching out to them with a national campaign. They helped their independent outlets keep up with extra demand by providing online, brand training videos. Employees put in 157,000 volunteer man hours during the crisis, and even senior management, including lawyers, built machines. Instead of cutting back on production, GEA introduced new product lines during the crisis and launched direct consumer channels. No one was laid off or made redundant; instead, hundreds of new employees were hired. And the work they had done to make their factories safe during all this got GEA recognized as having the safest factories in America.

"Covid really proved the speed and the agility of *RenDanHeyi*," says Nolan. "The crisis moved us forward. It made us a better company. We will now be a lot more future proof." Summing up GEA's Covid experience, he adds, "Traditional organizations act as if the future can be predicted. They are living in a fantasy world. We have got to build our companies around the fact of constant, future crises like this. Covid won't be the last. We are no longer living in the world of plans and efficiencies."

Efficiency and bottom line goals are now replaced at GEA by an aspirational leading target: "To be the number one company in the American appliance industry – in terms of being seen as the most talked about and most exciting company." During the heady days of my own visit to the company, I felt they had already come a long way toward being that "most exciting company in America."

CHAPTER 19

Other Companies Featuring Quantum Management Principles

Because the wide, total framework for a new management paradigm that is offered by Quantum Management, embraces many, more narrowly focused new management ideas being offered by others, there are forward-looking companies that have, one at least knowingly, many unknowingly, implemented several features of Quantum Management itself and/or *RenDanHeyi*. These include new ideas like "the flat company," "the agile company," "the networked company," "the purpose-driven organization," "holocracy," and "humanocracy," as well as others that call for ridding companies of bureaucracy or empowering more self-organization. I think it may be useful to readers to look at a few of these. Perhaps implementing every feature of *RenDanHeyi* is not suitable for some companies, but these examples show there is much to be gained from adopting some of the key ones.

Volvo: Circles Within Circles

Volvo, when it was still a Swedish-owned company headquartered in Gothenburg, is the first instance I know of a large company that consciously set out to implement the principles of Quantum Management as I had so-far outlined them at the time. It did so in its engineering division with the goal of redesigning the company's car development process.

At the very end of the 1990s, Volvo management realized that the company's whole design model had a major problem. For years, Volvo had been turning out cars whose various models all looked very similar on the outside, but internally they were all different. Few components were universal, which kept production costs high, while the various models' similar outward appearance limited, customer appeal. Management finally realized that the ideal would be a range of distinctive looking models that nonetheless shared most of the same internal components. Achieving this would fall to design and engineering teams.

The original intention was to organize this reengineering process the way management has always organized things—with clearly directed, top-down control. Management would decide what teams were needed, would assign pre-chosen designers and engineers to those teams, and give them clear, already worked out instructions on what to do and how to do it. At the time, Volvo's learning model was, "Always go with what you know." Management knew how to do the thinking; the engineers knew how to follow their instructions; everybody could rely on predictable results.

But just before this reengineering project was to be initiated, the senior management team that would supervise it traveled to England to attend a training course at Ashridge Business School. Having recently published my first stab at Quantum Management Theory in *Rewiring the Corporate Brain*, I had been invited as one of the speakers on the course, and I outlined my early ideas about the logic and benefits of self-organizing teams and decentralized, bottom-up decision-making. The Volvo managers were intrigued, and when they returned to Gothenburg, they read my book, and others they could understand that outlined the main ideas of quantum physics. And they looked at other organizations that had abandoned a hierarchical, top-down model of control. Finally, acting more on intuition than certainty, they adopted a "quantum strategy" for setting up the necessary redesign process and, expressing their own trepidation about this, changed the project learning model to: "Leaving behind what we know; Jumping into the unknown; Surpise!" They handed over the whole project to the discretion of the engineers and designers.

Telling these employees only that the reengineering goal was to arrive at a range of distinctive models constructed of mainly universal components, management then left it to them to decide what teams would be needed, how the teams would operate, and who should be assigned to each team. In all, twelve multifunctional teams were organized, one for each of twelve crucial design features—chassis, seats, steering, etc., and engineers once siloed to work on just one of these now worked together as team colleagues. More specialized subteams were formed in each team, and some outside experts were invited to join. All twelve teams worked in the same very large design room each day so they could stay informed about what each other were doing, members of each team were encouraged spontaneously to join a different team or subteam when their skills might make this relevant, and all desks and computer terminals were put on wheels to facilitate this easy movement between teams. Once each week, representatives from each of the twelve teams met as a group to catch up and coordinate. Management who reviewed the work pattern designed by these teams, called their model, "Circles within circles" (Fig. 19.1). The whole thing was dynamic and self-organizing.

I spent some time with the engineers in their "work" room when I was invited to visit Gothenburg during the project. It looked and felt more like a Montessori classroom, with "toys" (bits and pieces of gadgets, Lego bricks, materials, and tools) spread around the periphery, and there was an atmosphere of children at play. Various individuals with whom

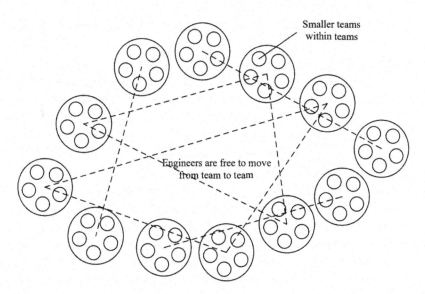

Fig. 19.1 Volvo circle of circles within circles

I spoke told me they had never enjoyed their jobs so much. And the whole experiment was a great success for Volvo. Before long, the new look Volvos offering customers a variety of models, all built using the same reliable components, were rolling off the assembly lines. Anna Nilsson-Ehle, vice president in charge of Change Management at the time, commented afterward, "We didn't know what we were going to get out of each team until we had the team. Their way of working surprised us and them. But it worked!".

Not complete *RenDanHeyi*, but the Volvo case foreshadowed many of its key features: the self-organization, the greatly enhanced self-motivation, the small, independent, multifunctional teams that also collaborated as a network, and Volvo's own decision to be led by customer needs.

VISA: THE CHAORDIC ORGANIZATION

Dee Hock used to be a vice president at a Seattle bank that licensed BankAmericard, one of the world's first credit cards. BankAmericard was successful at first, but an ensuing orgy of other credit cards issued by competing banks led to chaos. In response, Bank of America held a crisis meeting that resulted in a committee mandated to find a better model. Dee Hock was chosen to chair the committee, and both the method he conceived for arriving at a new model and many features of the model itself, were early implementations of Quantum Management principles—purposely so. Hock, personally, was fascinated by the "new science," quantum physics, chaos, and complexity theory, and particularly inspired by descriptions of the complex adaptive systems that explain why biological systems thrive. He wrote openly about how these ideas, and similar ones at play in the design of America's federal system of government, inspired his thinking as he developed his model for the new Visa credit card.

Hock rightly felt that the first step toward designing a new credit card system had to be having a clear vision of its purpose. "Unless we can define a purpose for this organization that we can believe in, we might as well go home....Far better than a precise plan is a clear sense of direction and compelling beliefs. And that lies within you," he told his committee colleagues. "The question is, how do you evoke it?"[1] The committee spent just over a year on this one issue, and any company that Hock touched throughout the duration of his executive career had to go through a similar, initial, and prolonged dialogue about its founding vision and purpose. As MIT's Peter Senge described it, Hock used that period of dialogue to "blow up the whole organization, dissolving power relationships, everything."

In conceiving Visa, Hock felt there had to be a healthy balance between competition and cooperation. This balance is stressed in both Quantum Management and *RenDanHeyi*. The Visa credit card would be issued globally by myriad local banks, each of which would want to serve its own customers with competitive terms and conditions. At the same time, the card had to be a global currency, with certain universal features available only through cooperation. Quantum Management would describe this as giving the card particle-like (local) and wave-like (universal) features. Dee Hock described it as "chaordic," poised between chaos (competition) and order (cooperation).

He conceived the organization behind it as a non-hierarchical, bottom-up power structure, an organization so "invisible" and flexible that no one could "tell who owns it, where it is headquartered, how it is governed, or where to buy shares." As M. Michael Waldrop further described it in *Fast Company* magazine,

> The organization must be adaptable and responsive to changing conditions, while preserving overall cohesion and unity of purpose... The governing structure must not be a chain of command, but rather a framework for dialogue, deliberation, and coordination among equals. Authority, in other words, comes from the bottom up, not the top down.[2]

In short, the "networked organization" Zhang Ruimin envisioned with *RenDanHeyi*.

---

[1] Quoted in M. Michael Waldrop, "The Trillion Dollar Vision of Dee Hock," *Fast Company*.

[2] Ibid.

Zappos: Moving Beyond Holocracy

Holocracy is a management model in which members of a team, or teams within a company, form distinct, independent, self-managing teams to accomplish company tasks and goals. The model was first introduced in 2007 by Brian Robertson, founder of Ternary Software, and has since been tried by several companies. It is pretty much a somewhat less hierarchical, hybrid of top-down design by management and self-organization by employees, that both fans and critics alike feel has some of the strengths and weaknesses of each. It has *some* elements of both Quantum Management and *RenDanHeyi*, but also differs in important ways. Holocracy was implemented by the American e-commerce company Zappos in 2015.

The essence of a holocracy is that employees are organized in "circles" which are multifunctional teams, and within the guidelines determined for each circle, their work is self-organizing. But the organization as a whole consists of network of circles-within-circles, and each circle that contains smaller circles has a greater power of decision-making than those smaller circles it contains. Ultimately there can be three or four circle sizes, and there is always a hierarchy of power that assigns more power to the larger of any enclosed collection of circles, and thus descending degrees of freedom to self-organize are allowed in each smaller circle. So while employees working in the smallest circles have *some* freedom to self-organize their assigned tasks, much of what they are asked to accomplish has already been decided by decisions taken by a larger circle that encompasses their own. There were some vestiges of this within the Volvo initiative described above.

But Zappos slowly became dissatisfied with the elements of hierarchy in the holographic model, realizing that it was limiting employee potential, and thus both product innovation and customer service by putting too much distance between those making decisions and the customers the company was serving. Zappos has always stressed that it is critical to know their customers, and that everything they do must "wow!" them. Toward those ends, the company has now moved much closer to using an adaptation of the *RenDanHeyi* management model.

Currently, Zappos' 1500 employees are still organized in circles that self-organize their work, but now the circles have equal authority and each functions as a small, independent company, "like a start-up," that deals

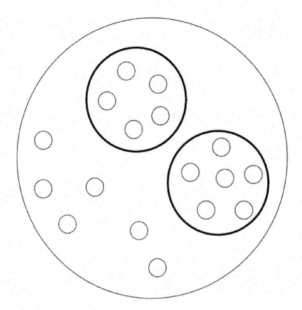

Fig. 19.2   Zappos holocracy

directly with customers and conceives new products or product adaptations in response to customer feedback. There are 400 circles overall, and each is multifunctional and made up of seven employees. These employees still each belong to three different circles for the purpose of coordinating work activities, and in all each employee might play a total of seven different roles in the various circles to which they belong. The whole company is a network of these coordinating circles (Fig. 19.2). At Haier's 2020 annual *RenDanHeyi* Management Forum, a senior Zappos executive was one of the speakers expressing how his company now looks to that model as its example.

As of 2020, a total of 62,975 enterprises, representing 29 countries, had registered as members of the global *RenDanHeyi* Alliance. 800, including 25 Fortune 500 companies, had registered for the *RenDanHeyi* training offered by Haier.

CHAPTER 20

US Army Special Operations Task Force: "*RenDanHeyi*" for the Military

During the first decade of this century, strategists affiliated with the United States Army began to investigate whether ideas from quantum physics and complexity science might have military applications. They knew the world was changing, the nature of combat situations and enemy tactics were changing, the make-up of the Army itself was changing as, now a volunteer force, many more of its officers, even those holding junior ranks, were well educated. The Army was scouting around for new ideas. But it was the experience of their Special Operations Task Force (the "Green Berets") while fighting Al Qaeda in Iraq that really focused the need for fresh thinking and led to a radical restructuring inspired by this new science.

I don't know whether the Army planners and strategists had heard the words "Quantum Management," and I very much doubt they were aware of Zhang Ruimin's thinking as he worked on designing the *RenDanHedyi* management model for Haier. Yet, for the same reasons, and inspired by the same science, the transformation that resulted in the Task Force's new "Team of Teams" military organizational model employs all the principles and recommendations of Quantum Management, and the command model used to implement is identical to the *RenDanHeyi* management model designed by Haier. In every way, the Special Operations Task Force's "Team of Teams" is an example of Quantum Management and *RenDanHeyi* adapted for the military.

© The Author(s) 2022
D. Zohar, *Zero Distance*,
https://doi.org/10.1007/978-981-16-7849-3_20

In 2003, General Stanley McCrystal took command of the Army's Joint Special Operations Task Force in Iraq. His mission was to defeat the Al Qaeda insurgent forces that had gained a significant hold in the country after the fall of Saddam Hussein. He expected this to be an easy task. His Task Force troops were "the best of the best." Though the Task Force itself was founded only in 1984, in response to the Iran hostage crisis, the Green Beret commandos who were its soldiers had long, previous experience in dealing with guerrilla insurgencies in Viet Nam, Africa, and elsewhere. The battalions dispatched to Iraq were disciplined, well-trained, well-organized, well-equipped, well-served with sophisticated communications technology, and thousands strong. By contrast, the Al Qaeda forces were small, dispersed, poorly trained, poorly equipped, and communication between their scattered guerrilla units was done mainly by sending messengers from one to another on foot. Their organization seemed a chaotic mess. Yet despite all this superiority and advantage, the Task Force soldiers found themselves struggling to defeat Al Qaeda's chaotic forces. Before long, General McCrystal began to realize it was precisely the advantages conferred by that "chaos and mess" that were giving Al Qaeda the edge (Fig. 20.2). He and his fellow officers learned that any hope of success would require forgetting most of their own military wisdom, and in its place, learning from their enemy. "We had to unlearn a great deal of what we thought we knew about war," McCrystal wrote later. "We had to tear down familiar organization structures and rebuild them along completely different lines."[1] He summarized the final result of this creative destruction in the following way,

> We restricted our force from the ground up on principles of extremely transparent information sharing (what we call "shared consciousness") and de-centralized decision-making authority ("empowered execution"). We dissolved the barriers – the walls and floors of our hierarchies - that had once made us efficient. We looked at the behaviors of our smallest units and found ways to extend them to an organization of thousands stretching over three continents. We became what is called "a team of teams": a large command that captured at scale the traits of agility that are normally limited to small teams.[2]

[1] Stanley McCrystal, *Team of Teams*, p. 20.

[2] Ibid., p. 20.

The story of why and how The Special Operations Task Force got to this is a military version of the similar story behind Haier's evolution of their *RenDanHeyi* model.

Traditional twentieth century military organization is built upon Taylor's Newtonian model that, we have seen, was designed for the radically different conditions and technologies of the Industrial Revolution. It relies on top-down, command-and-control leadership spread down in a bureaucratic way through descending levels of rank and function. Even though the small, special operations combat teams of the Task Force who confronted guerrillas were enabled to adapt and operate independently when "out in the jungle," they were still operating within all the bureaucratic constraints of the larger command superstructure. On their Iraq mission, the Task Force was also asked to operate in a different way than ever before. Its special commando units were traditionally dispatched individually to "put out fires" in limited trouble spots, now they were asked to fight a war as part of a thousands strong, massive force.

The Task Force that faced Al Qaeda was stratified, and fragmented into isolated operational silos, controlled by orders from above and ignorant of any battle plan they were part of. No one silo shared information with any others, no one silo had any understanding of overall strategic mission, and the highly specialized combat units simply did as they were told. Taylorian management, after all, mandated that communication between sectors and workers in a company should be kept to a minimum. The fear was that the sharing of different opinions between employees could diminish mission focus. And the parts in a machine have no need to understand the machine of which they are a part.

Still stricter communication barriers, and therefore misinformation and a lack of trust and mission coordination, existed between Task Force operatives and those belonging to partner organizations like the CIA, FBI, NSA (National Security Agency) and other, more traditional military units with whom the Task Force sometimes needed to coordinate. Even the off-duty activities and socializing of the various siloed units were fragmented, separating themselves into tribes "of their own kind" for accommodation, using different gym and leisure facilities, roping off their planning areas, only reluctantly sharing resources, and each displaying its own tribal arrogance. McCrystal says, "Our forces lived a proximate but largely parallel

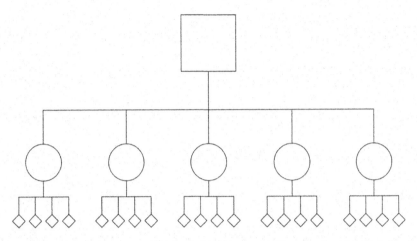

Fig. 20.1   US special operation task force hierarchical structure (Adapted from Team of Teams)

existence."[3] None had any meaningful sense of belonging to something larger than themselves.

The supreme value driving the entire secretive, centralized, rigid, and thus slow to respond behemoth that is the Taylorian organization is efficiency—getting the most out of the least investment of time, energy, and money. And having your organization function like a well-oiled machine is of course attractive to the traditional military mindset. But McCrystal soon realized it was the wrong match for Al Qaeda's small, dispersed, highly motivated, and very agile units, stitched together in a chaotic array (Figs. 20.1 and 20.2) and whose leaders were tech savvy children of the Internet generation who knew and mastered the power of boundaryless communication. "Adaptability," he concluded, "not efficiency, must become our central competency." That would require radical cultural and structural revolution that would take the Task Force time, and extended tuition from Army strategists who were learning that dealing with complex, rapidly changing, and unpredictable scenarios requires systems thinking. These strategists were learning that organizations handle complexity best when they are themselves functioning like

[3] Ibid., p. 122.

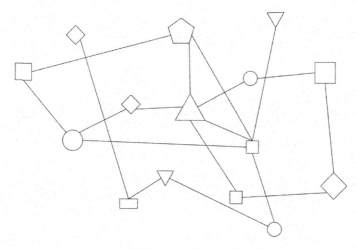

Fig. 20.2 AL Quaeda organization structure (Adapted from Team of Teams)

complex adaptive systems, and needed to communicate what becoming a complex adaptive system would mean in military terms.

The Special Operations Task Force had always seen the tactical advantage of small, agile teams that could adapt spontaneously to the immediate, local conditions of a crisis situation. They were its star units. But because these teams were traditionally embedded within the rigid, hierarchical, command-and-control structure of the larger force as a whole, their adaptive skills conferred no overall strategic advantage. Each team simply operated as an individual unit carrying out a specific exercise ordered by central command. Culturally, the Task Force leaders realized they had to change a team mentality that had stressed the individual qualities and achievements of each single operating team to a mentality that prized collective excellence and achievement of groups of teams working together. As General McCrystal expressed it, "We had to replace a 'They' culture with a 'We' culture."[4] Small team members needed to identify with and feel they were part of the larger, thousands strong and globally deployed Task Force as a whole, and its external ecosystem of partnering organizations.

---

[4] Ibid., p. 123.

Achieving this cultural shift required a newly structured, "BUD's" training program that set tasks at which individual small teams could succeed only if they worked out cooperative strategies involving others. As a sense of wider camaraderie and identity evolved, it became more natural for accommodation, social, and leisure activities now to blend members of different Task Force teams and their partnering organizations. The tribal barriers came down, and yet this had to be achieved without losing the great advantage of highly specialized teams that distinguished Task Force capability. As General McCrystal describes this challenge, "Our entire force needed to share a fundamental, holistic understanding of the operational environment and of our own organization, and we also needed to preserve each team's distinct skill sets."[5] He summed this up as a challenge to create the Task-Force wide, "shared consciousness" mentioned above. This would require a further cultural and structural shift.

It had already been discovered, as at Haier, that small teams comprising four to no more than twenty members could work best in a self-organizing way, and now it was realized that the Task Force must combine the specialized skills of these small teams with a much more holistic, general awareness of overall mission purpose, and thus how they could cooperate with other units possessing different specialized capabilities to achieve this. This required the existing culture of secrecy, suspicion, and tight information control to be replaced with a culture of openness, trust, transparency, and information sharing. To create the necessary, holistic, mission awareness and enable the spontaneous collaboration relying on this, everything had to be connected to everything, everyone needed to know what all others knew. Thus all the information barriers previously protecting the knowledge and operational capabilities of siloed ranks, functions, and organizations had to come down. The Task Force had to become as tech savvy as Al Qaeda and their successors and develop sophisticated, integrated, IT information distribution networks accessible by everyone. The whole organization had to recreate the "mess" that made their enemies so agile and adaptive.

Yet, all these deep cultural and structural changes could not deliver the self-organizing adaptability desired without an accompanying shift in leadership culture and structure. The much-loved and traditional, centralized, top-down, command-and-control leadership culture and all the

---

[5] Ibid., p. 153.

bureaucratic structure that enabled it had to be replaced with hands-off leadership from the top and a loosely structured, distribution of power and tactical decision-making to officers leading local teams who could freely adapt the way they used and shared that power as conditions required. Generals and their senior officer colleagues would now have to see their role as mission guidance, inspiring and motivating troops on the ground to do what was necessary to achieve overall mission strategic objectives, and providing them with required equipment and backup support. Generals accustomed to unquestioned obedience would have to become servant leaders, "quantum leaders."

Generals are perhaps more reluctant to surrender power than company CEOs. Long-standing military wisdom and tradition has conditioned them to believe their hands on the levers of power are necessary to mission accomplishment. Mess and chaos are anathema to traditional military culture, and centralized control the assumed secret of effective combat operations. How could hands-off, distributed power, and spontaneous self-organization ever get the well-coordinated, large-scale organizational effectiveness required for strategic success? To quell these doubts, their complexity science advisers used the example of beehives to introduce them to the quantum emergence characteristic of complex adaptive systems.

Because the brains of individual bees are too small to account for the very complex, cooperative behavior that underpins the structure and activities of beehives, it was always believed that the Queen Bee coordinated and controlled all activity in the hive by signalling orders to individual bees through a tightly structured system of top-down chemical signalling to worker bees. Beehives, in short, were thought of as small, traditional armies. But scientists studying their organizational behavior have more recently discovered that beehives actually operate as complex adaptive systems. There is no centralizing control from the top. The Queen Bee's actual role in the hive is simply to produce larvae that will grow into future worker bees, and the whole observed miracle of complex hive activity in fact *emerges from relationships* between many small, local, cooperative, and self-organizing activities by countless numbers of worker bees sharing chemical information. The resulting holistic unity of the beehive is greater than the sum of its parts.

The message from this to Task Force leaders was that that same emergent holism would result from the agile and adaptive self-organizing activities of a multitude of small teams spontaneously coordinating their capabilities in response to local situation requirements. In a later briefing paper recommending a US Airforce transformation similar to the one undertaken by the Army's Task Force, Lieutenant Colonel Eric M. Murphy explained, in military terms, the lesson of the beehive: "Force structures and the strategic environments they create are complex adaptive systems. That is, force structures are comprised of diverse, interdependent, adaptive elements inter-acting nonlinearly and exhibiting systemic behaviors including emergence, coevolution, and path dependence across multiple scales."[6]

The lesson was taken to heart and the Army's Special Operations Task Force was transformed to operate as a living quantum system. Figure 20.2 illustrates the structural map of the resulting "Team of Teams" organizational model that was adopted to achieve this. Note how similar it is to the Al Qaeda structural map shown in Fig. 20.1, and to the structural map of Haier's latest *RenDanHeyi* ecosystem-microenterprise model shown in Fig. 16.1, and its resulting Ecosystem Brand marketing strategy. Quantum Management principles have been implemented in a large military organization as they have been in large corporate organizations.

[6] Lieutenant Colonel Eric. M. Murphy, "Complex Adaptive Systems and the Development of Force Structures for the United States Airforce," Drew Paper 18, Air University Press, Airforce. Research Institute, Maxwell Airforce Base, Alabama: 2014.

PART V

The Quantum Society

CHAPTER 21

What Is a Quantum Society?

As a child growing up in the United States, I had understood myself almost wholly in terms of being "an American." This sense of being American can be, as many know, almost spiritual. It is associated with a vision of the good life, a vision of how one relates to one's fellow Americans and to the world at large, and a deep sense of the meaning and importance of one's life and actions so that these adequately reflect American values and bring credit to one's nation and family. Even my early teenage interest in science was awakened as much by a desire to serve America as by a fascination with atomic physics itself. But when I was in my late teens and early twenties, I lost all this. When I was nineteen, President John Kennedy was assassinated, and this was followed in deep succession by the assassinations of Martin Luther King, Bobby Kennedy, and America's deep involvement in the Viet Nam war. Some dark and irrational forces seemed bent on destroying all that was best in my society and what it stood for, and the whole edifice of my childhood beliefs came tumbling down.

For many years after finishing my university studies, I lived as an expatriate in foreign lands, feeling no desire to belong to any society. But when my young children were born, I began to imagine what kind of society I would like them to grow up in, what social values I would hope they could cherish. At that same time, people who had read my book *The Quantum Self* were writing to ask me what I thought a "quantum society" would be like. America was beginning its long slide into what

© The Author(s) 2022
D. Zohar, *Zero Distance*,
https://doi.org/10.1007/978-981-16-7849-3_21

ultimately became Trumpism, and I did not feel that the Britain I was living in at the time had all the qualities I would imagine in such a society. Relying instead on describing what kind of society I hoped and thought could arise if it were founded on the principles and values that underpin the quantum world view, I wrote my book *The Quantum Society*. That was many years ago, and my thinking about an ideal, "quantum," society has of course evolved. In the wake of Covid-19 social failures, both I and many others are asking, "What kind of society would we like to become?"

A COMPLEX ADAPTIVE SYSTEM GROUNDED IN THE WHOLE

To most people, the world of physics seems remote. Its abstract mathematical formulae and complex experimental results seem to bear no relation to the concerns of everyday life, to the passions that we feel, the kinds of decisions that we make, or to the nature of our society or our social institutions. Yet we human beings are physical creatures. The dynamics of both our bodies and our minds are guided by the same laws and forces that move the sun and the moon or that bind atoms together, and we are members of earth's living system. Quantum science tells us there is just one reality, and we and everything about us are part of that. Our societies are part of it, a part of the larger whole. Thus, ideally, our societies will mirror the same features and creative dynamics that distinguish everything else in our quantum universe.

In Part II of this book, we saw that we are "quantum selves," both particle-like and wave-like, individuals and yet defined through our relationships, manifold in our identities, our lives enfolded within everything and everyone, and everything and everyone enfolded within us. Our social lives should reflect those same balanced, mutually beneficial polarities, defining relationships, celebration of diversity, and holism. In Part IV, we saw the possibility of "quantum organizations" possessing these qualities, companies that are sustainable, innovative, and evolutionary when they are led and structured to function as living quantum systems, "complex adaptive systems"—and that the secret of our great cities' creative complexity is that they have naturally evolved as such systems.

We have seen that all complex adaptive systems are self-organizing, holistic, emergent (creative), exploratory, thrive on diversity, are poised at the edge of chaos (flexible and adaptive), and are in a co-creative dialogue with their environment. So it seems wisest that a quantum society should have the society-wide equivalents of those qualities and systems dynamics.

INDIVIDUALS, CITIZENS, AND MEMBERS OF THE NATURAL WORLD

One of the main challenges of our times is to link the inner world and value of the self with the outer world of society, and to see both within the larger context of the natural world. I believe this includes a spiritual challenge to link both individuals and societies with something larger than ourselves that will restore a lost sense of higher meaning to all our projects, both personal and social. This challenge is most urgent in the Western world, where exaggerated individualism has led to selfishness and lack of responsibility toward each other, and where the Newtonian assumption that human beings are separate from both the universe and nature has led to the exploitation of our fellow creatures and the earth's resources. At the same time, the traditional values of some Eastern societies can ignore or inadequately appreciate the importance or value of the individual. And since the Industrial Age, a careless, Newtonian disregard for Nature and the earth's environment has been shared by all developed and developing modern nations, regardless of whether they once had a more traditional sense of being fully part of and responsible for Nature and the wider universe.

We have seen that the sustainability and creativity of complex adaptive systems depend in part on each individual element of the system being healthy, and playing its unique role in the dynamics of the whole system. CADs are composed of important parts whose own nature and functions can then combine to create the complex web of relationships that make the emergent system larger than the sum of its parts. For that reason, both Quantum Management, and the *RenDanHeyi* model for implementing its principles in companies, stress the importance and infinite nature of individual human potential, and thus quantum companies embrace values and build structures that strive to maximize each employee's individual ability fully to realize his/her potential. I referred to this as the particle-like nature of the quantum organization.

Quantum societies, too, must possess a particle-like nature, values that stress the importance and value of individuals, and social and political structures that enable each individual to achieve his/her own best personal potential. Such societies take responsibility for the needs of, nurture the cultivation of, and provide opportunities for individuals, knowing this best serves the needs and cultivation of society as a whole. Quantum societies thus ensure each individual has quality health care, a high standard of education, access to public and cultural facilities, community environments that cultivate "body, mind, and spirit," support in times of need and old age, and the personal freedom to benefit from these, each in his/her own way.

But both quantum organizations and quantum societies also have a wave-like nature, the emergent, collective whole of which employees and individual citizens are a part. The collective, wave-like nature of a quantum society is the shared public space and public institutions, the shared, mutual responsibility to and for each other, and the shared meanings and values that are the cultural glue binding the society together, the sense that we all belong to each other as members of one family. These meanings and values differ in different cultures and societies, but in any quantum society, they will include mutual respect, mutual responsibility, compassion, a celebration of diversity, social harmony, and a shared sense that the society as a whole possesses a higher meaning and purpose due to its role in the shared purpose of human life itself, and humanity's role in Nature and the cosmos. This sense of its higher meaning and purpose is reflected back to members of the society through public symbols and aesthetics that themselves reflect beauty, balance, harmony, collective belonging, and the presence of Nature. The quantum society is an extended family, and its shared public spaces are an extended home.

And just as we quantum individuals find much of our personal identity through our wave-like relationships with others, our membership of a quantum society broadens that sense of identity through relationship with the social whole. It also broadens the meaning and purpose of our personal lives as we realize that our personal self-cultivation and transformation is the vehicle for social transformation and a cultivated society. In improving myself, I am improving the lives of all. Quantum physics teaches us that we make the world and are thus responsible for the world. The quantum individual makes society, takes responsibility for society, and discovers more of him/herself through being part of society.

As I write about the relationship between quantum individuals and the spontaneously self-organizing quantum societies of which we are a part, I have in mind the image of a free-form dance company—each member a soloist in his or her own right, but moving co-creatively in harmony with others. Each soloist stands out as an individual, and yet the dance they make together emerges as a new, further reality. The dance, the "work of art" or the "production," has a reality of its own over and above the separate and freely moving identities of the individual dancers; each dancer, while remaining distinctly him or herself, acquires a new, further identity—member of the company.

Yet, having said all this, we can see how very far those of us in most Western societies are from being either quantum selves or from living in a quantum society. In today's Western societies, we are all soloists without a production company, all *primidone's*. The freedom and rights of the individual that underpin the democratic ideal have become an exaggerated "me first": my right as a free individual to do whatever I like, regardless of any cost, harm, or consequences to others. We heard this daily on the media during the Covid crisis from Americans who declared that it was their "right as free Americans not to wear a mask." On a BBC broadcast about the need for us all to pull together, observe lockdown rules, and protect each other as a family, a prominent journalist protested, "England is *not* my family! My family is my family, and it is the government's responsibility to protect our right to live and go about our business as we want."

These people see themselves as isolated atoms bouncing about in an anonymous and amoral social space with no purpose or meaning of its own. As Britain's Mrs. Thatcher once famously stated, "There is no such thing as 'society.'" But basic physics and our own biological nature tell us this is delusional thinking. We live in a symbiotic world of Zero Distance in which everything is entangled with everything, everyone is *part of* and *within* everyone else. Every element of the cosmos and biosphere is an element in a larger system, dependent upon and responsible for the sustainability of that system. Society is a larger system of which we individuals are a part. It has an existence and an identity of its own. There is no "me" without "us," no "mine" without "ours," no "citizens" without society.

A COMMUNITY OF COMMUNITIES

Selfish individualism is not the only force fragmenting Western societies today. In most of today's Western democracies, social consciousness and the political loyalties which express it are dominated by populist "identity politics." Egged on by unprincipled politicians wishing to mask their own multiple failures to address the very real social and economic deprivations of working-class voters, social individuals have come to see themselves, not as fellow citizens, but as members of a racial, religious, minority ethnic, or special-interest identity group. Difference, not commonality or more inclusive kinship is emphasized, and every identity group different from mine is "other," a threatening other whose expectations of inclusion and equality would destroy "us" and everything "we" cherish about "our society." Today there are "African Americans," "Native Americans," "Hispanic Americans," "white Christian Americans," "Muslim and Jewish Americans," but no just plain "Americans." In Europe, there are "Citizens" and "Immigrants," in Brexit Britain, "Leavers" and "Remainers." All "tribes" threatened by other "tribes."

In their more positive form, ethnic "tribes" are known as "communities," and in more healthy, pluralist societies, communities enjoy a sense of dual identity. Like the individuals of which they are composed, each community has a "core," or particle aspect, and an "integrated," or wave aspect. Each is both a solo dancer and a member of the dance company, and is thus both self and others, others with whom it shares the public space and national life of the society. This is the ideal of a quantum society, which I describe as a "community of communities." Before populist fragmentation set in, the great American "melting pot" was such a community of communities, with Italian, Irish, Polish, etc. communities both celebrating the identity and customs of their countries of origin and at the same time celebrating a shared identity and national customs with all other Americans. This rich mix of dual-identity communities, and its celebration of diversity, was America's unique strength. Its overall national culture was a quantum-like superposition of individualist personal cultures and a more collective, ethnically integrated, community culture. It is a hope of returning to this that Americans today long for when they speak of their need for "national healing," but now any such healing must also bridge the chasm between the wealthy few and the deprived many.

DIALOGUE: THE CONVERSATION OF A QUANTUM SOCIETY

Complex quantum societies celebrate diversity and reap its benefits, but when people of different backgrounds, different needs, and who hold often quite different opinions live together, we must have ways to communicate our commonality and communality, our tolerance and mutual respect. We do so through shared symbols and shared public celebrations, but the most powerful and unique way that human beings communicate is through language, through the conversations we have with one another and the public conversations of our society. In today's Western societies that have been fragmented by populist divisions and plagued by the misinformation and sometimes utter abandonment of truth enabled by social media, the public conversation is angry, and dominated by opposition. But even in better times, the preferred Western mode of conversation has long been "debate."

Debate is by its very nature pugilistic, each side intentionally adopting opposing positions and then battling it out to see which can beat down the other's argument and "win." Debate is either/or discussion. If I am right, you have to be wrong; if I win, you have to lose. If my argument is stronger, yours has no validity, thus denying any possibility there can be two sides to a question, two ways to look at an issue. Such a speaking posture can only emphasize differences, and force people into positions of attack or defense. It invites black and white thinking and assumes that the more certain one's adopted argument, the more likely it is to be "winning." Debate thus discourages the critical thinking and humility required in a quantum society for people honestly to question their own and others' assumptions and finally breakthrough to a creative reframing that results in a wider, and often shared, perspective. It discourages shared exploration and mutual discovery.

Dialogue, by contrast, is an open-ended, open-minded form of conversation intended especially to facilitate shared exploration and mutual discovery. First conceived by Socrates as a method of teaching that was intended to make students question their assumptions and surface knowledge they didn't know they possessed, it was also used by the citizens of ancient Athens to get beyond conflicts and arrive at new solutions. Where debate is about *knowing* what is best, dialogue is about exploring all options and points of view and *finding* out what is best. In a debate, I have all the *answers*, and want to convince the other to accept them; in dialogue, I ask myself and others *questions*. Debate is a zero-sum game that only one of us can win; dialogue finds validity in many points of view and arrives at win/win outcomes from which everybody gains. Debate is about wielding *power*, my power to prove you wrong; dialogue is about listening and *respect*, my respect for the possible truth in what you say. Debate never produces new breakthroughs of understanding nor results in previously unforeseen solutions. The loser just accepts what the winner already knew. But dialogue is an *emergent* conversation in which breakthrough insights are larger than the sum of all original, individual opinions or ideas. Debate is "Newtonian" conversation, dialogue "quantum" conversation.

The either/or, one-best-way Western mindset has always found debate its natural mode of conversation, and this has always meant that society is characterized by opposition, confrontation, and dissent. In today's very fragmented democratic societies, this has morphed into an angry, almost warring, and fractured public conversation in which nobody listens to any point of view other than his/her own. Opposing political factions are paralyzed by ideological deadlock, and thus society's needs are not addressed by workable, agreed-upon solutions. Society is ineffective and lacking in harmony.

Quantum societies seek social harmony built upon tolerance, mutual respect, and the celebration of diversity. They seek win/win outcomes when different needs and interests must be satisfied. Their creative evolution requires the constant emergence of innovative ideas and solutions, and these arise from exploring multiple possibilities. Quantum societies need conversations that are quantum in nature, and dialogue is thus their natural mode of conversation.

CHAPTER 22

Governing a Quantum Society: Two Models

In a Quantum Society, the nation's top leadership circle, or government, should be a focus and source of inspiration, should reflect and reinforce the common vision and values that define that society, and direct a sense of national purpose. The very public figures who fill the posts of government should be men and women whose personal lives and personal behavioral and character examples reflect the fundamental values of the nation. They need to be exemplars and role models, "quantum leaders," as outlined in Chapter 11.

The government of a Quantum Society must have in place a strong, central "operational system" that sets certain national values, standards and goals, legislates a basic legal framework that defines, and protects the rights and responsibilities of citizens and future generations, and has the centralizing capacity to organize and coordinate all more local elements of the system in times of national emergency or when urgent national priorities must be set. But in keeping with the principles of Quantum Management, all such standards and laws should reflect a commitment on the part of government to leave as much freedom as possible for citizens to live their personal lives as they want and to self-organize in special-interest, community or local government groups as they wish. This is akin to the role the CEO plays in a quantum company. The head/heads of government, like the quantum CEO, *guide*, define, and set *principles* and *standards* by which national values are upheld and citizens protected, but

© The Author(s) 2022
D. Zohar, *Zero Distance*,
https://doi.org/10.1007/978-981-16-7849-3_22

they *do not control* the specific way that citizens or local groups live or self-govern within this shared framework.

Because China and America are now the two dominant superpowers, possessing the world's two largest economies, in our currently competitive global order, there is naturally fierce competition to decide which of their very different governing models should be the model of most popular choice. Each is bent on capturing the hearts and minds of developing countries, and even some of the more highly developed countries are taking a second look at their existing model. In asking whether the American democratic model or China's more centralized one-party model is the more "quantum," it is important to keep in mind that America is in many ways not typical of all liberal democracies, and China is far from typical of most authoritarian countries.

The individualism celebrated in America, and thus its social consequences, is far more radical than that cherished in many other democracies. The protection of individual rights like free speech and gun ownership, and unbridled freedom of the press, are also more extreme in America than in many other democracies. American mistrust of government, as well as the far less professional nature of its government and its dislike of elites and experts, are not shared by all other democracies, and the radically decentralized nature of American government is more extreme. And, of course, the world has always found American culture unique.

China's nature as a "civilizational state," over 3000 years old, and the many qualities and traditions developed during its long history that continue as advantages and characteristics of its modern governing style, make its, currently more authoritarian, rule radically atypical, and the consequences of it far more beneficial, than those shared by most other authoritarian states. A long tradition of great respect for learning and expertise that continues in modern China's placing high priority on quality education for all and expertise in government, and the resulting hugely professional nature and competence of its government, is of course atypical among far less developed, authoritarian states.

The massive anti-corruption campaign that President Xi Jinping launched in 2012 makes China's currently very low level of corruption in all public affairs atypical of most other authoritarian countries. Both a traditional Chinese respect for government, and the highly prized competent nature of its present government, make trust in, and voluntary cooperation with, government atypically high. Opinion surveys conducted in

China by Western polling organizations (Pew Research Center) indicate that 87% of the Chinese population feels a high trust in the government. This trust also follows from a sense that China's current leaders are principled men and women of high integrity who genuinely do their best to serve the needs and aspirations of the Chinese people, which is not the case in most other authoritarian countries. The benefits to the general population of China's one-party rule are, therefore, atypically positive.

I suggested that the defining values of any Quantum Society include mutual respect, mutual responsibility, compassion, a celebration of diversity, social harmony, concern for the common good, and a conviction that government works to ensure these are practiced. Both China and America espouse such values, but judged in terms of actual practice, and the extent to which they are embedded in real social attitudes and behavior, and effective social outcomes, there is wide divergence between how their two differing models have performed.

Democracy itself as a political model was inspired by Newtonian atomism. Just as atoms were thought to be the building blocks of the universe, so individuals were thought to be the building blocks of society. Thus, individual freedom and the rights of the individual were the focus of all other governing principles. But starting with the Hippie social movement in the 1960s, and then augmented in the early 1980s by a neoliberal "Reganomics" that passed tax laws and regulations favoring newly strident and harsh capitalist business practices, these individualist principles have evolved into a radical individualism indistinguishable from selfishness and a selfish disregard for others and for the common good. "I have the right as an American to do what is best for me (or my company)," and "My only duty is to myself," became defining social mantras for many Americans. The possession of adequate wealth for self-sufficiency became a symbol of moral virtue, leading to a conviction that those who do not have it are "lazy" or morally flawed, and thus not deserving of compassion or help.

Other problems and shifts in social attitudes during the past fifty years have resulted in further strains on America's democratic model. Long-standing, systemic racism now combined with an exaggerated admiration for wealth and material success led to "this justice for some, and a different justice for others," undermining democracy's fundamental principle of equal justice under the law for all. Self-interest, and the corruption to which it often leads, have given over-weighted power to lobbyists and special interest groups and motivated politicians to influence election outcomes by manipulating (gerrymandering) the boundaries that define electoral districts. Both have greatly diminished an honest connection between the way citizens vote and the policies actually implemented by government.

Growing political polarization motivated by identity politics and party self-interest has crippled the consensus politics on which democratic government depends. And extreme interpretations of the democratic rights of free speech and freedom of the press, combined with the power of uncensored and divisive cable news channels like Fox and social media like Facebook and Twitter, have led to the spread of toxic misinformation, conspiracy theories, acts of domestic terrorism, and undermined and further fragmented the reasoned public discourse required for democracy to work. Free access to the internet has also enabled a proliferation of pornography and sexism that has undermined women's rights and undermined the moral tone of society.

Thus America today is a racially, socially, and politically fragmented nation with an effectively broken political system. Its once famous "melting pot" that celebrated the diversity characterizing "a nation built by immigrants" has morphed into fear and hatred of immigration. Its self-interested capitalism and business practices motivated by a selfish, me-first mentality, and the political decisions bought to enable them, have sequestered 50% of the nation's wealth in the hands of 1% of its citizens. The low taxes paid by big corporations and the wealthy few have left a public budget inadequate to rebuild the nation's crumbling infrastructure or to maintain high standards and quality in its public educational system. Seventy million Americans live in conditions of poverty more commonly experienced in the Third World, its middle class is struggling on stagnated wages, and large numbers of Americans feel disenfranchised and betrayed by "the Establishment." The vast majority of Americans say they do not trust the government. All of this led to the populist uprising that resulted in Trumpism, and came to a head in America's inability to deal effectively with the Covid-19 pandemic. I fear it will take more than the election of Joe Biden to fix all this. A social revolution that resets American values and redefines the prevailing culture, embedded in new laws and political practices and a reform of political structures, would be required, and the distinctive political structures and culture of American democracy itself are weighed against this.

Many other democratic nations are facing the same problems and challenges, though most to a still lesser extent, and anti-democratic populism is a growing threat in most of them. Throughout Europe, working-class voters feel their needs and concerns are neglected by an "elitist Establishment." Britain's self-destructive Brexit was a consequence of this. As in America, the consequences of the Covid pandemic, and their common failure to prevent them, have brought social strains, systemic incompetence, and lack of effective leadership to a head in much of Europe. In nearly all Western democracies, trust in government is low.

Some of democracy's growing problems arise from what gives legitimacy to power in all such systems. The democratic model requires frequent, regular elections, forcing its leaders to adopt short-term thinking and strategies, often addressing temporary and less vital "issues of the day," that will please the voters, inhibiting the more long-term, whole-system thinking needed to govern nations successfully as complex adaptive systems. And a democratic decision-making process that requires consensus among many disparate power groups is necessarily slow, making it impossible for these systems to respond quickly to rapid change or crises with effective, adaptive strategies. Throughout today's democratic world, many intellectuals, and even political leaders, are questioning the efficacy of democracy itself. In a late November 2019 leader essay, the *Economist* magazine spoke of a "global democratic recession." Both leaders and citizens are asking whether big reforms could make democracy work better or whether other governing options should be considered instead. Some are even wondering whether the Chinese model might be the preferred option.

The origins of China's more authoritarian political model, and of its collectivist culture that remains strong even today, lie in the traditional Confucian conviction that society at large is modelled on the family. Members of families feel they belong to each other, and that they have responsibility to each other and to the family as a whole. It is common that family members put each other and the best interests of family ahead of personal interest. Thoughtfulness and mutual support are necessary for family harmony and security, and kinship bonds are strong. Siblings may quarrel, they inevitably will develop in different ways, have different personalities and passions, and go their separate ways as adults, but they are always there for each other in times of need and never lose their sense of family duty and loyalty. Individual needs and preferences matter in modern China, but they always take second place to collective duty and loyalty.

This same sense of all being members of one big family, and an accompanying sense that the nation is a communal home, is strongly visible today in the way Chinese people feel and behave toward each other, in their sense of collective responsibility for maintaining cleanliness and order in shared public spaces, and their collective pride in and loyalty to their country. When I remarked to one of my students about the complete absence on city streets of any litter, even cigarette ends, and asked if this was because strict fines were imposed, he replied, "No. Some small fines exist, but this is not why the streets are so clean. It is our values. We Chinese feel the public space belongs to everyone, and therefore each of us has a personal responsibility to keep it clean. If I drop litter on the street, people passing by will tell me off!" This collective tidiness is facilitated by the presence every few meters on city streets of ubiquitous litter baskets.

According to Confucian traditions and values, respect for parents and elders extends to respect for rulers. Just as families should respect the authority of parents, societies should respect the rule of those who govern, but in turn, those who do so are expected to be "good parents." Rulers have a duty to protect all citizens from danger, meet their needs, and provide them with opportunities ensuring the best quality lives possible. When they do not do so, sometimes even Confucian citizens rebel. Throughout China's long history, the people never chose the Emperor, but the Emperor was expected to rule with the *consent* of the people. Tradition has it that there was a consistent pattern of six "good Emperors," followed by a seventh "bad Emperor." In response to the bad Emperor's poor leadership, the people rebelled, and then a new dynasty would come to power. From an historical perspective, today's ruling Chinese Communist Party is the current ruling dynasty, and though the people do not elect its "emperors," they know that they, too, rule with the consent of the people. This is the historical basis of what Western observers wrongly see as the Party's "cynical pact" with the Chinese people: leave the governing to us, and we will keep you safe and ensure you have a good standard of living.

The Communist Party's one-party rule, and its censorship policies that impose limits on the media, forbid large street protests and demonstrations, and limit free public (but not at all, private) speech, also stem from long tradition and ancient values, and from historical national catastrophes. Daoism, and its philosophical conviction that we live in a holistic and harmonious universe, emphasized that the harmony of Heaven must be mirrored by harmony here on Earth. Thus harmony was the primary social value, it remained so during Confucian times, and maintaining social harmony and national unity is still viewed as the primary political responsibility of today's ruling Communist Party. But assuring social harmony has never been easy at any time during Chinese history. Despite their strong collectivist culture, the Chinese people have always been an independent and strong-minded, fractious lot, frequently given to intrigues, plots, and occasional coups. They are also a very excitable people, easily riled up by emotion. Three times in China's history, their tendency to fragment into different ruling factions so weakened the nation's unity that foreign invaders were able to move in and seize power, each invasion resulting in the massacre of millions of Chinese people. Fear of such weakening disunity is never far from the mind of China's current government, and if at times they err, they tend to do so on the side of caution and control.

Nonetheless, the Chinese Communist Party is not the monolithic organization that foreign observers believe, nor does it govern the country without consulting the people. The Party itself has over 90 million members, over 8% of the total population, and these members are drawn from every sector of society, every age group, and every one of the country's fifty-six ethnic groups. Within the Party, five recognized factions openly debate their different approaches to Party policy, and the leader of one of these opposing factions is second in power only to President Xi Jinping. Other, smaller political parties also exist in China and are allowed to hold annual party conferences, though they have little voice and no power in how the country is run.

The vast and extensive Party structure extends into every university and company, and its descending levels of authority reach right down to neighborhood cells that deal with the most local issues. It is the duty of every Party member to attend regular meetings of their local cell, and each has the responsibility to report any problems or issues raised by citizens in their local region to these meetings. Such problems or issues that cannot be dealt with at local level must then be reported to whichever higher level of Party authority can address them. In addition, regular national opinion surveys are done in which citizens are asked if they are satisfied with their lives and living conditions. All this is meant to give credit to the Party's claim that the Chinese people do enjoy "democracy-with-Chinese-characteristics." Of course, as was demonstrated in Wuhan during the very early stages of the Covid outbreak, local officials do not always have the competence to judge when a problem should be reported to higher authorities, or they may fear the disapproval of superiors if they do so. This is a problem of local government in all societies.

Such a vast Party machine responsible for organizing and responding to daily affairs at every level of society does require an equally vast bureaucracy, and this can make decisions and responsive actions painfully slow, often a source of frustration to individuals or groups waiting for them. And the various levels of authority empowered to make these decisions have a degree of self-organizing local autonomy, and some are not as efficient as others. But the almost miraculous speed and efficiency with which high-priority plans and decisions requiring concerted national effort can be achieved in China are due to central government's power to summon every level of the entire Party structure into coordinated action when required. It was America's lack of such centralizing power that partially accounted for its inability to cope with the Covid crisis more effectively. Few, if any, large democracies have this, and most would see it as a threat to the autonomy of local authority.

As I have said, Chinese culture has always highly valued learning and expertise. In Confucian times, all public officials, community leaders, and leading businessmen were expected to be "Confucian gentlemen," men distinguished by scholarship, expertise, and moral self-cultivation. Public officials who served the Emperor had to pass a very difficult exam proving a knowledge of the Classics. The modern Communist regime has only recently encouraged Chinese citizens to return to a knowledge of the Classics and traditional thought, but even Chairman Mao, who had simple rural origins, was a man of considerable learning. The moral self-cultivation of all citizens is encouraged by the ubiquitous public display of the country's twelve socialist values: four personal values of "patriotism," "dedication," "integrity," and "friendship"; four social values of "freedom," "equality," "justice," and "rule of law"; and four national values of "prosperity," "democracy," "civility," and "harmony." These are prominently posted in all public buildings, including public toilets, and in Shanghai I have seen them posted on every city lamppost in some neighborhoods.

Since Deng Xiaoping's chairmanship of the Party, all young people who hope to have a career in politics or public affairs must engage in a long leadership apprenticeship that combines learning and experience. After being invited to join the Party at age eighteen, a young person aspiring to high office must first become leader of their Party cell at their university or place of work. They then must progress to leadership of a neighborhood cell, followed by leadership of a city or rural district, mayor of a large city, governor of one of China's twenty-three provinces, membership of the Party Congress, and finally membership of the Party Central Committee. Only then can they aspire to membership of the powerful seven-member Politburo, and possibly the Presidency itself. Thus, every senior leader of the Chinese government has had experience, and gained a knowledge of the people, at every level of society. And even once in high office, every leader, even the President himself, must "go back to school" for a week or two each year to refresh their knowledge of current affairs, Party policy, and their own field of expertise. Several of China's recent presidents have been educated at Tsinghua University, and President Xi holds a Ph.D. from Tsinghua. This is how China assures great competency in high office.

Everyone in the world, including leaders of the world's democracies, has been impressed by China's miraculous and rapid development since Deng Xiaoping's "Great Opening Up" in 1979. In just forty-one years the country has progressed from being an extremely poor, rural nation to its present status as a great world power with the world's second, and soon to be, largest economy. By 2020, it had succeeded in its goal to raise one billion people out of poverty, and built a hyper-modern national infrastructure that would be the envy of any developed nation. Schools, universities, and hospitals were built, space science developed, and a tech industry that now leads in many sectors grew. China now leads the world in green energy development and artificial intelligence. In the short span of those forty-one years, China has progressed from the Age of Agriculture, through the Industrial Age, and now on to the Quantum Age.

The efficiency and speed with which this has been accomplished have of course been facilitated by one-party leadership that allows speedy implementation of huge, national planning with no need first to gain consensus between power blocks with differing views, and the ability to set ambitious long-term goals that do not require frequent voter consent. But in large part, all this progress has been due to wealth generated by China's new economic model, which in turn works so well because of Chinese values. Soon after assuming the presidency in 1989, Deng

Xiaoping put in place a hybrid economic system combining the wealth-generating advantages of capitalist free-market practices with socialist values that ensure this wealth benefits all of society. The Chinese call it "Socialism-with-Chinese-Characteristics."

China's economy comprises a combination of privately owned companies and state-owned ones. All profits from state-owned enterprises go directly back to the state budget to cover public costs and provide funds for social development. State ownership of a portion of shares in private enterprises provides further social funds. Both private and state-owned companies compete in the open, free market, though to date, due to their poor management and low employee motivation, state-owned companies have been far less profitable. Just recently, with this partly in mind, President Xi introduced a new "state capitalism" blending market mechanisms with government oversight. The goal of this is to better coordinate activities of the private and state sectors to achieve desired national targets, and the hope that state industries will learn better management practices from the private sector, while private industries will have their socialist values reinforced by practices in the state sector.

Owners of private companies do already contribute to social development through significant, voluntary charitable activities. A moderately wealthy friend of mine who owns a growing water treatment company is typical of his income bracket in paying for the establishment of a vocational high school in the rural village where he grew up. He also supported my research for two years. Leaders of larger private companies typically adopt a rural village, building a school, a health clinic, and upgrading its housing and infrastructure. Others fund cultural projects. Many of China's wealthy entrepreneurs spent their childhoods in poor rural villages and, having benefited from the country's public education opportunities to get where they are now, have a sense of wanting "to give back." One of the country's heroes is an early twentieth century, patriotic billionaire who owned a virtual empire of industries, and used many of his profits to build schools, orphanages, libraries, and hospitals, among other things.

Income from the state industries and shares in private companies, combined with this tradition of wealthy capitalists "giving back," has allowed the Chinese government to eradicate poverty, provide quality education and basic health care for all, and finance its ambitious infrastructure projects, while at the same time keeping taxes at a moderate level. Personal income tax is pegged at 19%, and standard corporate tax 25%, though this is reduced to 15% for industries like the tech sector that the government feels promote national development. Chinese entrepreneurs are allowed to get very rich—recently, five new billionaires have been created every week, and there is great income inequality in China, but instead of causing social resentment, this only seems to inspire ambition. People work very hard, but in turn everybody has the basic necessities of a decent life that can be lived with dignity, and everybody can aspire to realizing "the Chinese dream."

After forty-one years of massive growth and development, China today is a harmonious and well-ordered society at peace with itself and dazzling with palpable energy and innovation. People are friendly and polite to each other, even if total strangers, and especially so to foreign visitors like myself. There is no "otherness." Crime is low, the streets safe, and I feel very comfortable walking alone late at night in any big city neighborhood. High-rise life in crowded cities is compensated by easy access to green spaces and large, beautiful parks. As I observe people going about their business of daily life, I sense an air of general contentment, and small touches like special paths for the blind on all city pavements, featuring braille carvings to guide them around dangers, indicate government thoughtfulness about people's needs. As a frequent guest in China, weighed down by the constant bad news and reports of crises and disasters that feature in our Western media, I even derive a perverse relief from press censorship that mandates newspapers publish only happy, upbeat, and inspiring stories!

China is not, of course, a perfect country wholly without problems. All people, including university students and senior executives, work long hours, six days a week. Housing conditions and family rights for the millions of migrant workers who build China's expanding cities could be better, and working conditions in many factories could still improve. And, of course, there are the human rights issues relating to one of the country's ethnic minorities, that provide valuable anti-Chinese propaganda for Western interests, though these are less disturbing than civil rights deprivations suffered by African Americans due to centuries of systemic racism. Chinese intellectuals would like to see less censorship of the media and public debate. But no human society will ever be a perfect "quantum society." Throughout the whole of human history, all great powers have had their dark, or "shadow" side. As the Chinese would express this, "Where there is yang, there is also always yin." The measure of a society's strength, and the success of its political model, is whether the benefits to its citizens outweigh any problems they may suffer, and the extent of change necessary to address these problems.

I have suggested that for American democracy to repair its destructive divisions and to work for all its people, a social revolution and significant political restructuring would be required. And it remains an open question whether, in large and diverse, modern societies, any democratic system resting on frequent and universal, popular elections, and the need for multi-party consensus, can cope with the rapid change, uncertainty, complexity, large-scale challenges, and unlimited access to social media that typify life in the twenty-first century.

For China to address any current problems or discontent, no social revolution or major political restructuring would be required. Growing wealth will bring shorter working hours and better factory conditions where needed. Human rights issues would simply require the governing Communist Party to make better use of positive motivation when dealing with troublesome ethnic minorities and to loosen up a bit on censorship of the media and public speech. Its one-party, more authoritarian, political model is working very well for the vast majority of the Chinese people, and it has proven itself intelligent and efficient in coping with twenty-first-century challenges.

Whether the democratic model has failed America, or America has failed the democratic model, perhaps cannot be said. But judging by performance and delivery during these past forty years, the present state of American and Chinese societies, and likely ability to cope with future challenges and opportunities, my own experience and observations lead me to believe that the more professionally competent and efficient Chinese, one-party model, has produced something much closer to a quantum society than the American democratic model. But it remains an open question whether a model relying so greatly for its success on the distinctive character of Chinese culture and the Chinese people would work as well outside China itself. Quantum physics teaches us there is no "one best way," and perhaps any political model, if practiced in its ideal form, could deliver the benefits of a quantum society.

CHAPTER 23

A Quantum Global Order

When Apollo 11 landed on the moon in July 1969 and signalled back a view of earth from the moon's perspective, we saw earth for the first time in a way we had never imagined—a small, vulnerable planet suspended alone in what appeared to be the vacuum of empty space. It made our world, and us, feel small and vulnerable, but the vision of our living planet, bright in the reflected light of the sun and blanketed in its protective atmosphere, its landmasses and seas just visible, also made us realize how precious it is. As the years passed, our sense of earth's smallness and the interconnectivity and interdependence of our lives upon it was reinforced by new technologies and transport. When, in 2020, the apparent bite of a single bat in a city in China that no one outside China had ever heard of led to a global pandemic that threatened the lives and economic well-being of every person on earth, we were reminded still more forcefully that we live in a world of Zero Distance, and of the vulnerability of our entangled lives. We were also reminded that we had in place no global response to this global crisis, and what that cost us.

The response to Covid-19 was fragmented and acrimonious. There was a failure of transparency, cooperation, and trust. Individual nations showed themselves to be unprepared, and many then took hasty, unilateral action intended to benefit themselves without consulting even allies. The Trump government, with its strident "America first!" policies, performed most badly in terms of any meaningful international cooperation (and any effective domestic response), thus making the situation worse for

© The Author(s) 2022
D. Zohar, *Zero Distance*,
https://doi.org/10.1007/978-981-16-7849-3_23

everyone. And Western democratic governments could not rely on their citizens to take recommended collective action in the face of the crisis. The virus got out of control, and millions died.

I remarked at the very beginning of this book that the most serious problems facing all nations today are global problems requiring a cooperative global response. Many are existential problems that, if not addressed, will result in global disaster and perhaps human extinction. Consequences of the disastrous inaction and lack of cooperation in response to Covid are a harbinger of far worse consequences if similar inaction and failure to cooperate typify the global community's response to climate change, mass migration, nuclear war, etc. I believe these failures force us to realize there is, at the moment, no such thing as a "global community."

Our leaders speak all the time of a "global, or world order," but these words take their meaning from a paradigm that sees every nation as a separate, sovereign entity, one among a collection of separate nations, each isolated by its own boundaries, and relating through forces of conflict, confrontation, and competition, responsible only to their own interests. This is a Newtonian paradigm derived from Greek logic and monotheism, and in the Newtonian world that exists today, a "world order" refers to a large group of nations dominated by one great superpower that ultimately aspires to dominate the entire globe. Thus when President Biden promises to restore the "Western world order," he means a world dominated by American power and American values, and his real aspiration is that this *Western* world order becomes *the* world order, or at least a world order dominated by the American-led Western world. This, of course, would be unacceptable to Russia and China, and ultimately invite armed conflict, with China in particular. That is simply not a survivable possibility.

Just as China's one-party model for national governance offers an alternative to the democratic model, China's President Xi Jin Ping has offered an alternative model for global governance. For the past two or three years, nearly every one of his foreign policy speeches has promoted the vision of new global order that world be a cooperative, multipolar "community of shared futures." Many Western leaders have questioned his sincerity, suggesting Xi's vision is just a cynical cover for China intending its own global dominance. Some American journalists have suggested that China's ancient "All Under Heaven" philosophy is proof of this, rendering their own cynical interpretation of those words as meaning that China aspires to displace America as the world's greatest superpower, and rule all nations on earth. I cannot judge the sincerity of Xi's vision, but his words are a perfect headline for how I see a "quantum global order," and the true origin and meaning of China's "All Under Heaven" political philosophy lend credence to the possibility he might actually mean them.

"A Community of Shared Futures"

During the reign of China's first historically recorded dynasty, the Shang (1600–1046 BCE), the Zhou tribe who ruled one small state miraculously managed to defeat the combined armies of many larger states, and the King of Zhou found himself ruling over most of what was then China's entire geographical area. But there were constant uprisings and rebellions against him. The Zhou realized they were not strong enough to maintain their position by force, so the king conceived the entirely new *Tianxia* ("All Under Heaven") governing model. Instead of ruling by forceful domination, the Zhou would now position themselves as now among a vast network of cooperating states. All member states of this network would find it more in their own interest to cooperate with each other and the Zhou than to seek dominance for themselves. This multistate network occupied all of what was then the whole known world, so *Tianxia* was the first model for global governance. In quantum terms, this represents a paradigm shift from every nation or element seen as separate from every other nation or element, connected only by forces of opposition and control that are meant to manipulate the Other, to a paradigm of nations or elements connected through beneficial relationships that work together to grow something larger than the sum of their parts.[1]

Tianxia was the origin of China's long preference for win/win solutions, and of Xi Jin Ping's own multilateralism. It is also the earliest known precursor of what I call a quantum global order. The underlying building block of quantum reality, the quantum wave function, is a superposition of multiple possibilities. A dominant theme in the new quantum thinking and worldview is the celebration of multiplicity and diversity. We have also seen that one of the primary strengths of the *RenDan-Heyi* management model is its embodiment of multiplicity and diversity in organizational structures. A quantum organization, being a coordinated network of multiple micro-teams or microenterprises can explore many

---

[1] See Tingyang Zhao, *Redefining a Philosophy for World Governance*.

options or strategies simultaneously, thus giving it many "fingers into the future." Companies implementing a *RenDanHeyi* structure have an enormous innovative advantage. A quantum global order would mirror these; no longer the domination of "the greatest and the best," but a cooperative network enjoying the co-creative benefits of many centers of excellence.

If all nations or big power blocks in the world find it more advantageous to cooperate and strive to co-create a mutually beneficial future, then none will seek to be the dominant power. There would be no further need for conflict or war. As Xi Jin Ping expressed his call for a global "community of shared futures" in a November 2020 speech,

> As an old Chinese saying goes, 'Men of insight see the trend, while men of wisdom ride it.' Humanity lives in a global village where the interests and destinies of all countries are intertwined. People across the world have increasingly yearned for a better life. The trend toward peace, development, cooperation and mutual benefit is unstoppable. History has proven and will continue to prove that good-neighborliness will prevail over a beggar-thy-neighbor approach, mutually beneficial cooperation will replace zero-sum game, and multilateralism will beat unilateralism.[2]

Yes, China would gain from such multilateral cooperation, but so would everyone else.

The *Tianxia* governance model and philosophy underpins the development of China's ambitious, international Belt and Road infrastructure project, and something very similar is the model of governance used in founding the European Union. Both are precursors of a Quantum Global Order implemented by a *RenDanHeyi* management model. Just as in Haier's RenDanHeyii implementation of Quantum Management for companies, in both Belt and Road and the European Union, each participating nation retains its national sovereignty, governing itself in its own self-organizing way according to its own governing model, while cooperating with all others in the collective ecosystem. No nation needs to adopt a "one best size fits all."

---

[2] Xi Jin Ping, Speech for 20th summit of The Council of Heads of State of the Shanghai Cooperation Organization (SCO).

At Haier, the central operational system required to provide a shared sense of direction and necessary resources is provided by senior management and a network of service platforms. For Belt and Road, China is providing the impetus and international connecting links that join up all national infrastructure projects and, where needed, the financial resources required for each participating nation's national projects. And in the European Union, the Brussels bureaucracy and institutions like the European Central Bank, European Commission, and European Court of Justice provide the central operational system. For a Quantum Global Order to be successful, all nations or big power blocs would have to devise something like Brussels on a global scale. Global institutions like the World Bank, the International Monetary Fund, the World Health Organization, and UNESCO already exist to provide international service platforms, and others could be established as required. The main challenge standing in the way of a Quantum Global Order is whether Western nations, particularly America, can adopt the quantum paradigm and reinvent their "one best way for all," Newtonian mindset.

We nations of the world are at an existential crisis point. As Abraham Lincoln said on the fields of Gettysburg, "United we stand. Divided we fall." The reality of our fragile and interconnected twenty-first-century world is a quantum reality, a reality that Newtonian physics misunderstood and wrongly described. Newtonian atoms and Newtonian superpowers are misconceptions. They are dangerous, outdated delusions. Realizing we are "quantum societies" who can live together only in a "quantum global order" is not an aspirational ideal. It is a cosmological truth and a fact of Nature—an existential necessity.

PART VI

Conclusion

CHAPTER 24

The Quantum World View

This has been a book about the new quantum paradigm that is emerging to frame our lives, work, and leadership in the twenty-first century. We have seen that our scientists tell us that we live in a *quantum world*. Everything we see around us and everything that we human beings are is *quantum*. We are quantum people living in a quantum world, now powered and connected by quantum technology. Our bodies are quantum, our minds are quantum, and everything around us is quantum. The new quantum understanding of our universe tells us that the old, Newtonian way of thinking how we, and the world, work was based on an illusion, on an oversimplification, on a crude misunderstanding of the way things actually are.

Any such new paradigmatic understanding also ushers in a new "world view," a new overarching but largely unconscious understanding of how our own lives fit into the general scheme of things, what our lives *mean*, how we should behave, what we should aspire to, what we can hope for. Our world view is our general, background framework of what our lives, of what life itself, is *about*. It provides our lives with a theme and gives them coherence, uniting the personal, social, and spiritual dimensions of our experience. Though we may, from time to time when crises arise, stop to question certain aspects of what we believe about how our lives "hang together," few of us ever stand back and try to describe our general world view, or question it. It is just taken for granted that "this is the way things are," this is the world, or life, as we know it, "the only game in town."

© The Author(s) 2022   251
D. Zohar, *Zero Distance*,
https://doi.org/10.1007/978-981-16-7849-3_24

It is only at rare moments in history, through an accumulation of catastrophes and a sense of impending disaster that large numbers of people say to themselves, and then collectively, "this isn't working, this game of life is no longer playable, this script no longer makes sense," and we cry out for an entirely new edifice, a radical reconstruction of everything we think and believe and that we become ready for a new world view. And when such readiness is then accompanied by a new prophesy, a new teaching, or a new discovery that suggests some very different way of framing absolutely everything, an exhausted worldview then gives way to a new one. I argued at the very beginning of this book that we have reached such a turning point now as we feel our way through the twenty-first century.

It was at the end of the nineteenth century that the German philosopher Nietzsche pronounced, "God is dead." Nietzsche's meaning was that the whole framework that had guided the Western mind was now exhausted. Two decades later, as the entire world was engulfed in the first of the blood-drenched wars that defined the twentieth century as a century of catastrophic collapse and endings, William Butler Yeats added his own voice to Nietzsche's with the opening words of his poem *The Second Coming*, "Turning and turning in the widening gyre, The falcon cannot hear the falconer, Things fall apart, the centre cannot hold…" The Judeo-Christian world view that had held at least the Western world together for nearly 3000 years had largely given way by then to Newtonian science and its accompanying mechanistic world view, and as the twentieth century unfolded the social, political, and spiritual inadequacies of mechanism—its personal alienation and loneliness, its political fragmentation and constant wars, its inability to provide any place or meaning for human existence or framework for human morality, and its desecration of the natural world became all too apparent. These still haunt life in the early twenty-first century, but at the same time, as we have seen throughout this book, our new century is also seeing the emergence of something new and very different, the promise of a better way.

Everything I have written in these pages has described the new ways of living, working, and leading that arise from the discoveries of quantum physics, the achievements of quantum technology, and their accompanying philosophy. All along I have been outlining features of a quantum vision of the self, quantum social and business visions, and a new quantum world order. These in fact add up to a new quantum world view that changes the way we see ourselves, our relationships, our work, our way of living together and, indeed, the very meaning of our lives and of every-thing we do. Here, I would like to summarize and bring all that together as one coherent story that provides new, quantum answers to life's five oldest questions, and thus provides the foundations of a quantum world view. These five questions, asked in some way throughout the whole of human history are: Where do I come from? Who am I? Why am I here? What should I do? Where am I going when I die?

WHERE DO WE COME FROM?

Quantum physics tells us that our universe began about 14 billion years ago when an intensely compressed "singularity" suddenly exploded with a Big Bang. The first thing that was formed after the Big Bang was what scientists call "The Quantum Vacuum." The Quantum Vacuum is a very still "sea" (field) of energy. It is felt as a Force that is everywhere throughout the universe. It is not "up there," or "down there," it is everywhere, inside us and outside us. It is the Force that enables the universe to exist and work as it does. It is the energy Force underlying everything. If we were looking for a "God" within quantum physics, it would be The Quantum Vacuum. The Chinese call it the unseeable source of the Tao. In quantum physics, "God" is not a person, not a man or a woman. Rather, "God" is energy and the source of all energy. "God" is a Force acting throughout the universe, a Force acting inside you and me, and inside everything that exists. A Tao, or Way of the Universe.

The Quantum Vacuum is a field of energy, and our entire universe and everything in it is made of energy. You and I are made of energy. Every-thing that exists—the grass, the trees, our tables and chairs, you and I and all our social constructions, including our companies—are all *patterns of dynamic energy* "written" on (excitations of) the Quantum Vacuum. If the Vacuum is the universal "sea" of energy, then we are "waves" upon that sea. When we touch our bodies, they feel solid, but that is just an illusion. Our bodies are in fact a *pattern* of energy that temporarily collects atoms of matter and forms them into the shape of our pattern. But if we are more than seven years old, then there is not a single atom in our bodies today that was part of us when we're born. Because, within the period of seven years, every single atom in our bodies passes through the pattern of energy that we are and then passes out again, just as individual molecules of water are drawn into and expelled from the spiraling vortex we see as our bathroom washbasins empty. What remains as we grow older is our pattern, which is constantly collecting and emitting new atoms.

"The Quantum Vacuum" is badly named, in a sense. We think of a "vacuum" as something that is empty, like a vacuum flask. But the Quantum Vacuum is *full*. It is full of the *possibility* (the "potentiality") of everything that ever was, everything that is, and everything that ever will be. 14 billion years ago, when the Vacuum was formed, you and I were there within it as *possibilities*. Thus, however old we *think* we are, each of us is really 14 billion years old. And we have been here throughout the whole history of the evolving universe. We were here when space and time and gravity were formed, we were here when the first clouds of fiery gases were formed, when the fiery clouds of gases became stars, when the stars made the planets, and when at least some of the planets gave birth to life. So you and I contain the whole history of the universe within us. Our bodies are made of stardust, and our minds obey the same laws and forces that hold the universe together.

Our bodies and our minds also contain the whole history of life on earth, the whole history of biological evolution. The emotions and instincts of our primitive forebrain are identical to those of lower mammals like rats and hamsters. The cerebral hemispheres that make up our higher brain are those of the higher mammals. We contain the heart of the lion and the aggression of the wolf. 98% of our genes are identical to those of a chimpanzee. So only 2% of us is actually *human*. And yet we act and feel and think with it all, and we call it "human nature"! In fact, truly "human nature" is something we have yet to achieve, something we can aspire to and work toward.

WHO AM I?

In the quantum universe, everything is both "particle-like" and "wave-like." We, too, are both "particles," unique individuals, and "waves," patterns on the quantum sea of energy, overlapping with all the other waves. My wave-like self is the "me" that is made by all the people and things to which I relate. The individual, particle you has characteristics like your brown, or red, or blond hair, your brown or blue eyes. The particle "you" is a man or a woman, a short person or a tall person, and has the intelligence and the talents you have inherited with your genes. The wave you is who you are because you have the family, friends, and colleagues that you do, the you that has grown up in a particular community and country, that speaks the language that you do, that works in the environment that you do. If you had grown up in a different place and had different friends, the wave you would be a *different* you.

We *are* our relationships. In quantum physics, we learn that relationships make reality. Our relationships make you "you" and me "me."

In fact, in the quantum universe, everything and everyone is in relationship all the time. The wave aspect of who we are overlaps with the wave aspect of everything else. "I" am "you," and "you" are "me." In the quantum world, there is no such thing as separation. Separation is an illusion. We live in what quantum scientists call "an entangled" universe, where everything and everyone is connected to and affects everything and everyone else, a world of Zero Distance. If I snap my fingers, it is felt on the other side of the universe. If I tell a lie or do something bad, it puts bad energy out into the entire universe. If I smile, if I help someone, if I think kind thoughts, it puts good energy out into the universe.

In fact, quantum physics tells us that you and I *make* the world. There is a very important principle in quantum science called "Heisenberg's Uncertainty Principle." This principle tells us that the universe is a sea of infinite possibility, but that only some of these possibilities can become real, like the things we see in everyday life. *Which* possibilities become real things depends on *us*. When we ask a question, when we do an experiment or make a decision, it is as though we are dropping a bucket down into the sea of infinite possibility and pulling up a bucketful of reality. The questions we ask, give us the answers that we get. The more questions we ask, the more we will know. We can *never* ask too many questions. There are no such things as "silly questions." Questions make reality happen.

Our questions, our decisions, the things we build, the relationships that we make, the good or bad things that we do—all these things *make* the world. As the Rendanheyi management model expresses it, we make our own value. And that means, also, that we are *responsible* for the world. If the world is full of mistakes or the world is a mess, that is because *we* are making mistakes or *we* are a mess. If we want to make the world a better place, quantum physics tells us that we must make ourselves better people. If the world is to be kind, we must be kind. If the world is to be free from war, we must be free from anger or hatred. If the world is to have space for all kinds of people, we must have space in our hearts for all kinds of people.

And just as we make the world, we also make ourselves. Like the universe itself, the human brain and the human Self are also each a sea of infinite possibility. When we were born, we had trillions of neurons (brain cells) in our brains, but only a very few of them were connected up. It is the connections between the neurons (the "wiring") that gives our brains their many different abilities. At birth, we had just enough neural connections to allow our brain to control our most basic bodily survival functions—breathing, the beat of our heart, sucking, the ability to regulate our body temperature, etc. As we grow and learn and experience things, more neural connections are made. In the first year of our lives, we grew neural connections at a faster rate than any time since. But no matter how old we are, even if we live to be 110, we never lose our ability to grow more neural connections and to rewire our brain, our ability to make our brain "smarter." If we continue to explore, to learn, to have new experiences, to challenge ourselves, our brain will continue to grow.

Our Self, too, can develop many possible ego personalities and forms of expression during a lifetime. In quantum physics, the Self is a wave ("a wave function") that carries many possible ways to be expressed. Each relationship that we form, each experience that we have, each thing that we learn or job that we do has the possibility to create another "me," another take on life. "I am a multitude." But we needn't worry that we will scatter off in many directions or become schizophrenic! Because everything is connected to everything in the quantum world, our many sub-selves will have the capacity to add up to one, rich, many-faceted, fulfilled and happy person: our "Quantum Self." Our Quantum Self is like a choir with many voices, all singing in tune. The more voices that we add to our choir, the richer and more beautiful the music that we will make.

We also have the possibility to be both good and bad. The universe contains a "Good" Force ("coherence") that is always building better relationships and creating more information, and it also contains a "Bad" Force ("entropy") that is always destroying relationships and tearing apart things that have been built. Our Self also contains the possibilities of a "good me" and a "bad me." Every one of us can be kind, caring, and loving, but we can also be mean, jealous, selfish, and full of anger or hatred. We can help others, and we can also hurt others. It is *I* who choose what kind of person I will be. And in choosing who and what I will be, I choose what kind of a world I will make. We are responsible for ourselves, and we are responsible for the world.

WHY AM I HERE?

There is an ancient Jewish legend of "The Vessels." According to this, there was a world before our world, shaped as a sacred vessel because it contained the Divine Essence. This vessel collected light, but one day it became so full of light that it shattered. The fragments of the vessel, and its sparks of light, then rained down and were scattered among our world. One spark of this divine light is said to be lodged in each human being, and it is the sacred duty of humankind to gather up the sparks and restore the Unity of the original vessel, and thus the unity of the Divine Essence. The rabbis who speak of this legend say that the way we gather up the sparks is to make loving relationships. When our world is united in love, "God" will be healed, the One that it was at the beginning will be restored.

In physics, of course, most cosmologists believe that there was a universe before our universe, a Vacuum before our Quantum Vacuum. That first Vacuum contracted, as our universe will at some point contract, became condensed to a single point of light, then exploded to make the Big Bang that created us. And the fragments of the Big Bang are scattered throughout the universe. It is indeed correct to say that the universe has a purpose and that the direction of cosmic evolution is toward ever, greater complexity and ever, greater information. Both complexity and information are in essence made of relationships. So the essential drive of the universe is to make ever more relationships. And surely love is the purest of all forms of relationship.

To say that fragments of the Big Bang are scattered throughout the universe is to realize that there is such a fragment in each of us. As I said earlier, our bodies are made out of stardust, fragments of stars, fragments of light. The Self, "me," is a pattern of energy that waves within the Quantum Vacuum. Just as the sea is within each wave, the Vacuum is within each of us. And that is essentially what gives light to the human soul.

I visit Nepal quite frequently, and in Nepal they have a greeting, "Namaste." Every time you meet someone, you say, "Namaste" instead of "Hello" or "Nihao." I asked a Nepali friend what Namaste means, and he said it means, "I greet the god in you." I greet the god in you, I greet the divine spark in you, I greet the Vacuum within you. Imagine what the world would be like if we *really did* recognize and greet the god or the divine spark in each other. There would be no more "strangers," no more "others," no hatred, no wars, no "mine" vs "yours," or "me" vs "you." There would just be "us," all equal and all sacred fragments of light and each capable of bringing that light into the world.

When I speak about this in my lectures, people inevitably say, "But you can't love everyone. Some people are evil, some are monsters." But because each of us is a quantum person and thus has within us all possibilities, the possibilities of both good and bad, good and evil, I could be one of those monsters. So could you. There is a human being, a spark, within every monster, and a monster within every human being. None of us is in any position to judge another, to exclude another from our group or from the human race. We, too, might have done whatever they have done. At the very least, if we have the courage to face what is within us, we recognize that we have had the *thought*, or the *temptation*, to do something bad, or even evil. Then, perhaps, we can replace judgment with compassion, even with love, both for ourselves and for others.

Loving others, seeing the divine spark in even the worst of them, is of course the most powerful way of serving others. But we are also here to serve the universe itself, to serve the Force or the Tao that drives the universe to unfold and give birth to all the infinite possibility contained in the Quantum Vacuum. We have seen that each of us makes the world, each of us has the power to turn possibility into reality. In this sense, each of us is a servant of the Vacuum, "a thought in the mind of God," or "a movement in the evolving Tao." Like the leader in a quantum company, the Vacuum is a servant leader who energizes and vitalizes us, and we in turn, can use this to serve the Earth's community. As in the famous Taoist triad, each of us is a bridge between Heaven and Earth, between the Vacuum and those of its potentialities that we realize.

We are here to "think." Thinking involves seeing and giving meaning to things. It involves asking deep questions, imagining things that don't yet exist, seeing relationships between things and ideas that no one else has seen, seeing something in a flower or a situation that no one has noticed before. Thinking also means learning and dreaming and creating and aspiring to make your life matter. Each of us best serves the Vacuum, best serves the possibility latent in the universe, by doing the most and making the most of our lives that we can.

No two brains on this planet are the same. Even if I am an identical twin and my twin brother or sister has exactly the same genes as I, my brain will be unique. Our brain is "wired up" (neural connections made) by our individual relationships, thoughts, and experiences. So every one of us is not only a wave on the sea of the Quantum Vacuum, and thus a means through which the Vacuum can express itself on our level of reality, but each of us is a *unique* expression of it. Nobody but me can contribute to this world what only I can contribute. Nobody but me can turn the particular possibilities of the universe into a reality that I can. There are no "unimportant" people, no "invisible" people. Each of us is unique, and each of us is essential so that the future history of the universe can unfold. Only *I* can make the world that I can make. Only *you* can make yours.

What Should I Do?

So what can each of us do to make a better kind of world, to make the world a better place during our lives than we found it when we were born? We don't have to be Mother Teresa or Nelson Mandela to make a positive difference. Whoever we are, and whatever role we play in life, each of us has the power to bring love or happiness into at least someone's life, with a smile, a helpful act, an act of compassion or forgiveness, a small gift. All these simple things make the world a better place. If we have been chosen to become business leaders in life, we can build companies that empower our employees to realize *their* full potential.

We all know that our planet is in great danger because of rubbish and pollution. Perhaps you are a leader who has the power to make the oil companies stop drilling or the factories cease burning coal, but if not, you can still plant a tree, you can recycle your belongings and pass them on to others who have less. Perhaps I am a leader who can clean up all the rubbish that makes our cities and streets dirty, that poisons the ground and the water, but if not I can be still careful not to throw my own rubbish out of the car window or drop it on the street. Science now tells us that little things can make a big difference.

And remember, if the world is to be a better place, I have to be a better person. If there is to be more intelligence in the world, I have to make myself more intelligent. I have to realize what a rare gift it is that I read and explore and learn things. I must seize every opportunity to read and experience and expand my mind, I must do my bit to dispel ignorance and prejudice and pettiness. I must grow my character.

Many people say that because so many of us no longer believe in religion, we don't know how to be good, don't know what the rules are anymore. But we don't need a God who writes the rules on tablets of stone. We all know when we are being kind or cruel, generous or selfish, loving or hateful. The moral direction of the universe is within each one of us. The unfolding Quantum Vacuum is within each one of us, an inner "spark" or compass that naturally guides us in the right direction. This is what we call our conscience, or liangzhi, our intuition of the Tao and its Way. It is up to each one of us to have the character and the will to do what our conscience tells us to do. Building that character and summing that will is a ceaseless, lifelong project, a lifelong "spiritual practice".

WHERE AM I GOING?

Most of us realize by the time we are five years old that people die, and that one day, we, too, will die. And this knowledge of our finitude, the knowledge that our lives, and the lives of those we love, have a time limit, gives our existence a tragic dimension. For some, this can be a cause of terror or despair and lead to a feeling that life is ultimately without meaning. But if we fully understand the nature of the quantum universe of which we are a part, the very fact that our current life spans are limited can instead be source of focus, purpose, and meaning.

Every existing thing in our universe is a finite excitation, or manifestation, of a distinctive underlying wave function containing an infinite array of potentialities. The finite excitations exist (maintain their coherence) for only a limited time. They "come and go" in dialogue with their surrounding environments. But their underlying wave functions maintain their own coherence as larger patterns upon the background cosmic energy sea of Quantum Vacuum. These wave functions are eternal potentialities within the Vacuum, there, as we saw, from the formation of the Vacuum itself. In the case of human persons, I have referred to the temporary, manifested self as the "ego-self," and the eternal, wave function self as the Quantum Self.

In this life that I am living now, my underlying Quantum Self has taken on a particular ego-self energy pattern with one of its many possibilities. This finite pattern, fleshed out by the atoms of which my body is composed, is what I know as "me." When my body eventually dies, all that "dies" of my energy pattern is its temporary material form. Like a wave melting back into the sea, that "me" folds back into my underlying Quantum Self and into the Quantum Vacuum, and lives on as a carrier wave of potential, future "me's." Later, something in the environment will excite that underlying carrier wave to take on a new shape and emerge into the world as yet another "wave pattern" visible on the sea, another "me." This new ego-self may manifest as a man instead of a woman, "I" may be Chinese instead of English. I may even, as Hindus and Buddhists believe, take the shape of an animal or a tree in the next life. But my essential, underlying, eternal Quantum Self, will be present within my new body. As the Indian spiritual book, *The Bhagavad Gita*, says, "The Self is not born, the Self does not die. The Self is eternal."

In the quantum realm, there is no such thing as death. Only a series of new lives, cycles of existence, each born to live out its own story and destiny before returning to the sea of all existence. And, just as quantum physics teaches that both the past and the future are entangled with the present "now," these new "me's" will be entangled both with all the "me's" that I once was, and the many "me's" that I will become in my future material embodiments. The life I am living now both reaches back and affects the past, and it reaches forward, affecting the future. This is the quantum explanation of the ancient belief in *karma*. And because in our Zero Distance quantum universe each "I" that I am now is entangled with the "I's" of all others and with all other existing things, my own present existence is part of the unfolding reality of this world on earth and of the evolving universe itself. Like one of the "music makers" in the O'Shaughnessy's poem I quoted in Chapter 9, I play my role "in the [new quantum] age that is coming to birth." Each life of mine is a dream that is dying or one that is coming to birth. And the greater the dream that is my life, the greater the world that I make, the greater the company or organization that I lead.

In summary, the quantum world view expresses the connectedness of everything, and stresses dynamic relationship as the basis of all that is. It tells us that our world comes about as we make ourselves, through a mutually creative dialogue between mind and body, between ourselves and the material world, between our human organizations and the natural world. It gives us a view of ourselves as persons who are free and responsible, responsive to others and to our environment, essentially related and naturally committed, and at every moment creative. We have only to realize our potential, an opportunity promised to us as employees and citizens by any organizational structure that follows the principles of Quantum Management.

BIBLIOGRAPHY

Andersen, Kurt, *Evil Geniuses*, Ebury Press, London: 2020.

Arthur, W. Brian, *Complexity and the Economy*, Oxford University Press, Oxford: 2015.

Campbell, Dennis, Meyer, Marshall, Cao, Bonnie Yining, Lasu, Dawn H., "GE Appliances: Implementing Haier's Made-In-China Management System," Briefing Paper N9-119-099, Harvard Business School, April 2018.

Diamandis, Peter H., and Kotler, Steven, *The Future Is Faster Than You Think*, Simon and Schuster, New York: 2020.

Falk, Richard, *Explorations at the Edge of Time*, Temple University Press, Philadelphia: 1992.

Kalton, Michael C., and Mobus, George E., *Principles of Systems Science*, Springer, New York, Londonn, etc: 2015.

Kay, John, and King, Mervyn, *Radical Uncertainty*, The Bridge Street Press, London: 2020.

Kim, Jung-Yeup, *Zhang Zai's Philosophy of Qi*, Lexibton Books, New York, London, etc: 2015.

McCrystal, Stanley, and Fussell, Chris, "Fight Coronavirus Like We Fought Al Qaeda," *New York Times*, 24 March 2020.

McCrystal, Stanley, *Team of Teams*, Penguin Random House, London: 2015.

McGowan, Heather E., and Shipley, Chris, *The Adaptation Advantage*, Wiley, Hoboken: 2020.

Murphy, Eric M., Lieutenant Colonel, "Complex Adaptive Systems and the Development of Force Structures for the United States Airforce," Lt. Colonel Eric M. Murphy, Drew Paper 18, Air University Press, Airforce. Research Institute, Maxwell Airforce Base, Alabama: 2014.

© The Editor(s) (if applicable) and The Author(s) 2022
D. Zohar, *Zero Distance*,
https://doi.org/10.1007/978-981-16-7849-3

O'Shaughnessy, Arthur William Edgar, "Ode" in *The Oxford Book of Victorian Verse*, Clarendon Press: Oxford, 1925.

Prigogine, Ilya, and Stengers, Isabelle, *Order Out of Chaos*, Bantam, New York: 1984.

Scholem, Gershom G. (ed.), *Zohar: The Book of Splendor*, Schocken Books: 1963.

Sun Tsu, *The Art of War*, translated by Gary Gagliardi, Science of Strategy Institute/Clearbridge Publishing: Seattle, 1999.

Tilby, Angela, *Let There Be Light*, Darton, Longman, and Todd, London: 1989.

Tolle, Eckhart, *The Power of Now*, New World Library, New York: 1999.

Tu, Wei-Ming, *Confucian Thought*, State University of New York Press, Albany: 1990.

Waldrop, M. Michael, "The Trillion Dollar Vision of Dee Hock," *Fast Company*, October/November issue, 1996.

Watts, Alan, *The Watercourse Way*, Souvenir Press, London: 2011.

Watts, Alan, *The Way of Zen*, Vintage, New York:1989.

West, Geoffrey, *Scale*, Weidenfeld and Nicholson, London: 2017.

Wilhelm, Richard, translator, *The I Ching*, Routledge & Kegan Paul, London: 1965.

Wing, R. L., translator, *The Tao of Power*, Dolphin, Doubleday, New York: 1986. This is the translation of the *Tao te Ching* that I used, but section numbers given in various footnotes will be the same in any translation.

Xi, Jin Ping, Speech for 20th Summit of Council of Heads of State of Shanghai Cooperation Organization, Reported by CGTN: November 10, 2020.

Zhao, Tingyang, *Redefining a Philosophy for World Governance*, Palgrave Macmillan, New York: 2019.

Index

© The Editor(s) (if applicable) and The Author(s) 2022
D. Zohar, *Zero Distance*,
https://doi.org/10.1007/978-981-16-7849-3

Printed by Printforce, United Kingdom